ENGLISH COUNTIES AND PUBLIC BUILDING

1650–1830

ENGLISH COUNTIES AND PUBLIC BUILDING, 1650–1830

CHRISTOPHER CHALKLIN

THE HAMBLEDON PRESS

LONDON AND RIO GRANDE

Published by The Hambledon Press 1998

102 Gloucester Avenue, London NW1 8HX (UK)
P.O. Box 162, Rio Grande, Ohio 45674 (USA)

ISBN 1 85285 153 8

A description of this book is available from
the British Library and from the Library of Congress

Typeset by The Midlands Book Typesetting Company, Loughborough
Printed on acid-free paper and bound in Great
Britain by Cambridge University Press

Contents

Figures

Tables

Preface

This book is about building by county quarter sessions between 1650 and 1830, especially in its financial aspects. The justices were responsible for bridges, prisons and court houses throughout the period, and some benches provided pauper lunatic asylums and small judges' lodgings in the early nineteenth century. The growth of expenditure on these building types from the later eighteenth century was a significant part of a general rise in outlay on public construction. Between 1800 and 1830 county prisons, halls and asylums took about one-fifth of expenditure on all public buildings. Counties paid for nearly half of all bridge costs, although not responsible for the great London bridges. Because bridges are essential for trade and communication, prisons are needed as a protection by every society, and courthouses are used for administration and justice, the subject is important. Its study parallels the history of crime and punishment, transport, housing and other public building.

While the cost of housebuilding overshadowed expenditure on construction by counties and other institutional building, much more evidence survives for the latter. In the case of houses, apart from country mansions for the building of which estate records sometimes exist, the names of builders and building owners, the use of architects and surveyors, sources of short-term capital and the structure and layout are often (indeed almost always) unknown. As public building, including that of counties, was the work of groups or corporations, documents survive about precise costs as well as initial estimates and tenders, sources of finance, builders, surveyors and building plans and materials. Expenditure on smaller prisons, courthouses and most bridges was up to several thousand pounds in the eighteenth century, comparable to that on urban house projects, typically involving one of two or a small block of dwellings. The biggest public buildings, including those erected by counties, involved sums much exceeding those spent on normal housebuilding undertakings. Their cost was up to £40,000 or £50,000 by the end of the eighteenth century and similar to that of country houses. The justices' motives and their rates, loans and payments, building designs and use of surveyors,

contractors and craftsmen, are well illustrated in relation to many buildings and bridges, generally in more detail from the 1770s and 1780s.

Counties repaired and built many sizeable bridges; some of the largest and the innumerable small structures being funded by other means.
There were about 1200 shire bridges, mainly stone, in 1700. Sessions
work on them was steady during the hundred years between 1650 and
1750. As late as the early eighteenth century the inherited stock was
sufficient for growing trade. Further commercial expansion led to an
era of construction from about 1765, bridges becoming stronger and
wider and having more convenient approaches. Between the 1780s and
1830 the number of county bridges grew to about 3000.

All counties had a gaol and between one and five or six houses or
correction. The former held a majority of incarcarated debtors, felons
and those awaiting trial; the latter vagabonds and beggars. Building was
occasional between the later seventeenth century and the 1770s, when
outlay quickened. The rise in population, the greater use of imprisonment as a punishment, and the prison reform movements were among
the reasons for the erection of larger and more carefully designed prisons
from the mid 1780s.The rebuilding of shire halls was spasmodic until
the 1760s. Between 1770 and 1830 growing business and the desire for
more comfort led to the construction of courthouses by the majority of
counties. Some sessions provided judges' lodgings for use at assizes in
the early nineteenth century. Growing humanitarian feeling, more lunatics
in a growing population and the example of private institutions for those
who could pay led to about one-third of the counties building pauper
lunatic asylums between 1808 and 1830.

Most counties hold quarter sessions records beginning in the
seventeenth century. They include order and minute books, accounts,
contracts and plans all of which have been used in this book. A few
sources have been published. The records of some counties were more
varied and voluminous than others. The author spent several weeks on
average in each county record office reading the manuscripts that seemed
especially relevant.

This book is the first survey of English county building between the
seventeenth and early nineteenth centuries which is concerned with
money and costs; and the justices, builders and surveyors involved. It
was written largely when I was on the staff of Reading University, which
paid for part of my travelling expenses. Mrs Carol Mackay and her col-
leagues typed the original manuscript. My family helped in the collection of material from several record offices. My wife typed several final
chapter drafts. Martin Sheppard of the Hambledon Press suggested

improvements to Chapter 1, chapter titles and the revision of the footnotes. I am indebted to local archivists who wrote to me with lists with their documents, and the almost innumerable archive staff who produced documents. A grant was made towards publication by the Scouloudi Foundation, for which the author and the publisher are most grateful.

A Note on Building Prices

Between the 1750s and the 1820s the cost of building more than doubled. Normally only current prices are given in the text. The following index (average 1751–60 = 100) is an approximate indication of price changes.

1751–60	100	*1801–5*	224
1761–70	106	*1806–10*	260
1771–80	112	*1811–15*	270
1781–90	118	*1816–20*	250
1791–95	138	*1821–25*	234
1796–1800	166	*1826–30*	222

The index is based on surviving wage data, prices of imported soft-woods, and prices paid by Greenwich Hospital and the Office of Works for bricks.

Sources: C.H. Feinstein 'Capital Formation in Great Britain', in P. Mathias and M.M. Postanieds, *The Cambridge Economic History of Europe*, vii (Cambridge, 1987), p. 38; Lord Beveridge, *Prices and Wages in England.* (1939), pp 725–30; P. Deane and W.A. Cole, *British Economic Growth, 1688–1959* (Cambridge, 1964).

1

Public Building in England before 1830

There are many forms of building and construction. Houses are the most important type of building. Civilian public buildings and churches form distinct groups. Structures for military purposes include fortifications, barracks and naval dockyard buildings. Land drainage has been historically an important form of construction. There are also transport works such as improved roads, bridges, canals, railways, harbours and docks. All these types of building, except railways, were constructed in England in the seventeenth and eighteenth centuries. Houses are always being built: construction was particularly great in London throughout the period between 1650 and 1830, and in the whole country from the 1750s, because of population growth. By comparison there was a small but growing expenditure on public buildings such as almshouses, hospitals, prisons, court halls, markets, theatres and schools.

Coastal fortifications had been erected in the Tudor period, and on a major scale in the 1540s, costing about £200,000 in contemporary prices. They were built later, especially from the 1750s at Chatham, Portsmouth, Plymouth and Dover. Several million pounds were spent on barracks during the French Revolutionary and Napoleonic wars. The drainage of marshes and erection of embankments to stop the flooding of low-lying land was important in many parts of England. Road improvement spread in the eighteenth and early nineteenth centuries, while canal construction was especially prevalent in the 1760s, 1770s and 1790s. Throughout there was some harbour improvement. London's main docks were dug at the beginning of the nineteenth century. The naval dockyards at Chatham, Portsmouth and Plymouth and elsewhere were active from the seventeenth century.

County prisons and shire halls were two examples of a growing variety of new public buildings erected between the mid seventeenth century and 1830. Out of traditional buildings, bridges had, as always, to be maintained and built. As an introduction to the study of building by counties, this chapter surveys the rise and development of civilian public building and investment in transport during the period.

There had been modest though widespread non-residential building in provincial England from about 1550 in response to major social changes. Construction was greatest in London on account of its huge population, wealth from overseas and domestic trade, and its role as capital city with the court, law courts and parliament. Because of the magnificent legacy of medieval buildings almost no churches were erected. On the other hand, the growing number of poor resulting from rising population, and inadequate parish help, led pious or philanthropic merchants and gentry to found between 700 and 800 almshouses, often with just a few rooms. Several hundred grammar and elementary schools were created and at Oxford and Cambridge university buildings grew. Similar philanthropic zeal on the part of the well-to-do met the demand for classical education based on Latin needed by the gentry to act as magistrates, lawyers, clergy, teachers and doctors; at a lower level, the necessity of farmers and tradespeople to keep accounts, and the wish of more people to read religious works and popular almanacs and ballads was provided for. Growing trade in farm and manufactured goods encouraged landowners and corporations to build small market houses, often combined with town halls, for meetings, showing rising civic pride. The profits of London's overseas trade created Gresham's Royal Exchange (1566–71) and its copy the New Exchange in the Strand (1608). The London Inns of Court were extended on account of the growth of litigation that accompanied the rising prosperity of the gentry, and the consequent rising demand for legal training. The wish for entertainment and the popularity of the drama were symbolised in the building of theatres in Jacobean London. The typical almshouse, school or market building cost several hundred pounds, while many thousands were spent on the university college quadrangles and Inns of Court chambers.[1]

---

[1] K. Grady, *The Georgian Public Buildings of Leeds and the West Riding*, Publications of the Thoresby Society, 62 (1987), pp. 153–81; B. Bailey, *Almshouses* (London, 1988), pp. 75–120; W.K. Jordan, *The Charities of London, 1480–1660* (London, 1960), pp. 135–64, 237–48; idem, *The Charities of Rural England, 1480–1660* (London, 1961), pp. 123–26, 257–80, 322–38; idem, *Philanthropy in England, 1480–1660* (London, 1959), pp. 152–54, 280–81; J.A. Sharpe, *Early Modern England: A Social History, 1550–1760* (London, 1967), pp. 256–60; J. Summerson, *Architecture in Britain, 1530–1830* (Harmondsworth, 1957), pp. 100–106; K. Wrightson, *English Society, 1580–1680* (London, 1982), pp. 183–99; R. Tittler, 'The Building of Civic Halls in Dorset, 1560–1640', *Bulletin of the Institute of Historical Research*, 58 (1985), pp. 37–43; *Victoria History of the County of Oxford*, iii (London, 1954), pp. 45–46, 77, 255, 262, 279; R. Willis, ed. J.W. Clark, *The Architectural History of the University of Cambridge and of the Colleges of Cambridge and Eton* (Cambridge, 1886), i, p. 117, ii, pp. 248, 265, 270–71; W.R. Prest, *The Inns of Court under Elizabeth I and the Early Stuarts, 1590–1640* (London, 1972), pp. 18–19; W. Dugdale, *Origins, Juridicials, or Historical Memorials* (2nd edn, London, 1671), pp. 147, 189–90; A. Thaler, *Shakespeare to Sheridan* (Cambridge, Massachusetts, 1922), p. 204; see also histories of individual schools.

There was relatively little construction of transport facilities, probably because the growth of trade was insufficiently great, technical knowledge was sometimes lacking, and capital was short or expensive. A few more rivers were made navigable in the early seventeenth century, and the occasional harbour was built, sometimes for £10,000 or £20,000.[2] Although there was almost no civilian central government or parish expenditure on buildings, the growing administrative and judicial work of the counties included bridge repairs; the erection of several gaols; and the renting, buying or building, under acts of 1576, 1597 and 1610, of numerous and usually tiny houses of correction to punish or employ the swelling number of vagabonds, another result of population growth.[3] All this construction was the prelude to greater and more varied public works from the later seventeenth century.

London continued to lead the rest of England, both in regard to size and variety of public buildings. Construction was huge there between the later 1660s and after 1700, partly because of the accident of fire. It continued at a high level with old and new types of building during the eighteenth century. Various continental buildings provided London's examples. Its population became about one-tenth of that of England and Wales, as its role as the leading capital and commercial city grew. Yet perhaps the most marked feature of public building in this period was increased development outside London. Many new types of building appeared in the provinces, including workhouses, hospitals, theatres and assembly rooms. The population and wealth of their towns in aggregate were growing much faster than those of London, and road improvements spread ideas more quickly than earlier.

The Great Fire of London in 1666 led to the reconstruction of all the various public buildings, including four prisons for over £30,000: the Guildhall (£36,498), the Bridewell (£12,260), Sessions House (£5448), market buildings (£4137) and the Monument (£13,450). The Royal Exchange cost the City and the Mercers Company over £58,000. This expenditure was dwarfed by that on church rebuilding after the Fire of

[2] T.S. Willan, *The Inland Trade: Studies in English Internal Trade in the Sixteenth and Seventeenth Centuries* (Manchester, 1976), pp. 3–4; *The History of the King's Works*, iv, *1485–1660*, part 2, ed. H.M. Colvin, J. Summerson, M. Biddle, J.R. Hale and M. Merriman (London, 1982), pp. 736, 755, 769–77; J.R. Ward, *The Finance of Canal Building in Eighteenth-Century England* (London, 1974), p. 2; D. Swann, 'English Docks and Harbours, 1660–1830' (unpublished Ph.D. thesis, University of Leeds, 1959), p. 51; see also histories of individual ports, such as Dover.

[3] F.G. Emmison, *Guide to the Essex Record Office* (Chelmsford, 1969), pp. 13–14.

1666. The fifty-one City churches erected between 1670 and 1695 cost £263,786, and the majority of steeples were added for about £63,000. The most expensive churches, St Mary-le-Bow and St Bride, cost over £15,000, and the cheapest, St Matthew Friday Street, £2301. £440,591 was spent on St Paul's Cathedral, based on French and Italian examples, from 1674 to 1700, when the dome had still to be built; its final cost was said to be £736,800. These churches were all paid for by a tax on coals entering the port of London.[4]

A special group were the twelve large churches built in the London suburbs under the Fifty New Churches Act of 1711. Financing them in the same way, Parliament wanted to make up for the lack of churches in the now heavily populated parishes outside the City. As it was Tory and Anglican in sympathy, religious motives and the need to help and control the poor were both involved in the passing of the Act. The buildings, instead of providing the maximum amount of room, were adorned with towers and porticoes to show posterity 'the politeness of the age' (as the architect Vanbrugh hoped). They cost between £10,000 and over £40,000 each.[5]

Reflecting its wealth and prestige, the Mansion House was finished in 1753 for £42,639 by the City as a residence for the lord mayor, who had previously used the rooms of City companies.[6] In the last quarter of the seventeenth century there were two large charitable buildings of a special kind. The great Royal Hospital at Chelsea for army veterans begun in the 1680s had cost over £100,000 by 1700. This was exceptional in that much of the money came from the army poundage fund, consisting of a deduction of a shilling in the pound on soldiers' pay. A smaller amount came from donations. Even grander was the Royal Hospital for Seamen at Greenwich. An existing building became a hospital for seamen in 1694. Great additions were made between 1696 and 1728, paid for by royal and parliamentary grants, private gifts and levies on seamen's wages. By 1703 £89,364 had been spent and the total cost may have been as much as £200,000. The motives for building the hospitals were both philanthropic and patriotic, as concern for war veterans had been grow-

[4] T.F. Reddaway, *The Rebuilding of London after the Great Fire* (London, 1940), pp. 124, 193, 266–69; G. Cobb, *London City Churches* (1942; revised edn, London, 1977), pp. 34–35; R.J.B. Walker, *Old Westminster Bridge: The Bridge of Fools* (Newton Abbot, 1979), p. 225.

[5] H. Colvin, 'Introduction', *The Queen Anne Churches: A Catalogue of the Papers in Lambeth Palace Library of the Commission for Building Fifty New Churches in London and Westminster, 1711–1759*, ed. E.G.W. Bill (London, 1979), p. xi.

[6] S. Lewis, *A Topographical Dictionary of England*, iii (London, 1840), p. 119.

ing since the wars of the 1650s. The Invalides in Paris of 1670 was an example here.[7]

Major London buildings used for administrative and legal purposes were rebuilt for a variety of reasons. Although until the 1770s they were erected mainly in peacetime when the government had the money, wars (until 1713, 1739–48 and 1756–63) were the principal cause of the growth of financial and other staff which pressed on office room. The Customs House was rebuilt in 1718 after a fire. After a new Rolls House (£5923), Admiralty and Paymaster-General's Office buildings, a new Treasury was erected for just over £20,000 in 1733–35, the previous building being in a 'ruinous and dangerous' condition. The growing committee work of parliament and the needs of its officials led to piecemeal schemes for alteration and improvement to its buildings. A project for a Parliament House in the 1730s proved abortive, but alterations to the Houses of Parliament by the Office of Works included changes to the Court of Requests and the adjoining gallery in 1719–25 (£9516), and a new Clerk of Parliament's lodgings in 1754–56 (£5031). In the early and mid 1750s public expenditure on buildings was principally on the Horse Guards for the chiefs of staff, costing over £65,000. Between 1755 and 1770 a government building, 'the New Stone Building' on the east side of St Margaret's Lane, cost over £20,000. It was built piecemeal for various purposes, including the housing of records previously kept in ruinous rooms elsewhere and offices for a Board of Ordnance. The bad state of existing buildings (or occasionally their destruction by fire), their inconvenient siting and in particular the need for more offices and rooms together were responsible for the new London official buildings.[8]

Private enterprise in London contributed an exceptional variety of public buildings, among which a few dominated in size. Most alms-houses and schools cost no more than a few hundred pounds. Among the more substantial, the second St Paul's School building erected after 1669, consisting of a large schoolroom and a master's house at each end four stories high, cost about £6000. Lady Dacre's Emanuel Hospital in Westminster, founded in 1594, was rebuilt after 1695 in the form of an

[7] C.G.T. Dean, *The Royal Hospital Chelsea* (London, 1950), pp. 39, 48, 77; J. Cooke and J. Maule, *An Historical Account of the Royal Hospital for Seamen at Greenwich* (London, 1789), pp. 33–34, 43–56; A.J. L'Estrange, *The Palace and the Hospital; or Chronicles of Greenwich* (London, 1886), p. 88.

[8] *The History of the King's Works, v, 1660–1782*, ed. H.M. Colvin, J.M. Crook, K. Downes and J. Newman (London, 1976), pp. 405–30, 431–32, 436–39; J. Brewer, *The Sinews of Power: War, Money and the English State, 1688–1783* (London, 1989), pp. 65–67; P.D.G. Thomas, *The House of Commons in the Eighteenth Century* (Oxford, 1971), p. 3.

open court of mainly one-story almshouses, for £1776. By far the largest almshouse was the Foundling Hospital built in 1742–47. The site cost £7000 and the building of two principal wings for boys and girls £28,062.[9]

Special market buildings for particular goods included a brick corn exchange built in 1760 by a group of hoymen, corn factors and corn buyers with eighty shares. Theatres were built during the period, beginning with the Theatre Royal in Drury Lane in 1662–63 with a share capital of £2400, then rebuilt by Wren with Italian-type boxes after a fire in 1672 for between £3500 and £4400. Other new places of entertainment included Vanbrugh's Haymarket opera house in 1704–5, the Rotunda at Ranelagh of 1741 (based on the sale of thirty-six shares of £1000), and the Pantheon in Oxford Street (1769–72), with a great assembly room and sequence of vestibules and cardrooms, costing nearly £40,000, the majority of the capital coming from the sale of fifty shares. These buildings reflected the demand for plays, cards, dancing, music and conversation from the visiting gentry enjoying the London season, as well as well-to-do resident professional and merchant families.[10]

Charitable buildings to care for the ill became numerous. The Bethlehem Hospital (Bedlam) for lunatics was rebuilt in 1675–76 for £17,000 in donations and loans. St Thomas's and St Bartholomew's hospitals had been reestablished after the Reformation. Between 1693 and 1696 over £5000 was given to repair and improve St Thomas's, wards being built in 1717 and 1732. St Bartholomew's was rebuilt in 1730–69. Work on the first block between 1730 and 1732 was estimated at £8500; several thousand pounds was spent on the south wing between 1736 and 1740 and £14,363 on the west wing during 1743 to 1752.[11] Between 1719 and 1746 five new London general hospitals were founded. The Westminster began in an existing house in 1719–20, Guy's was finished in 1725 for £18,793, St George's was built in the 1730s, and the London

[9] M. McDonnell, *The Annals of St Paul's School* (Cambridge, 1959), pp. 239–40; M.F.J. McDonnell, *A History of St Paul's School* (London, 1909), p. 237; C.W. Scott-Giles and B.V. Slater, *The History of Emanuel School, 1594–1964* (London, 1977), p. 45; R.H. Nichols and F.A. Wray, *The History of the Foundling Hospital* (London, 1935), pp. 42–44.

[10] S.W. Dowling, *The Exchanges of London* (London, 1929), p. 303–4; Summerson, *Architecture in Britain*, p. 155; W. Wroth, *The London Pleasure Gardens* (London, 1896), p. 199; *Survey of London*, xxxi, *The Parish of St James Westminster*, part 2 (London, 1963), pp. 269–73, and xxxv, *The Theatre Royal, Drury Lane and the Royal Opera House, Covent Garden* (London, 1970), pp. 9–11; N. Pevsner, *A History of Building Types* (London, 1976), pp. 71–72.

[11] E.G. O'Donoghue, *The Story of Bethlehem Hospital, from its Foundation in 1247* (London, 1914), pp. xix, 213; B. Golding, *An Historical Account of St Thomas's Hospital, Southwark* (London, 1819), pp. 91–110; *The Royal Hospital of St Bartholomew, 1123–1973*, ed. V.C. Medvei and J.L. Thornton (London, 1974), pp. 282–89.

Hospital was completed for £18,500 in 1759. The Middlesex Infirmary was set up in 1745. Following a building contract of £2250 in 1755, several thousand pounds were spent on a west wing in the mid 1760s, and more on an east wing after 1775. Other new smaller hospitals followed in London. There was constant pressure for more hospital accommodation, but subscriptions and other sources of money, such as collections from concerts and plays and after sermons, were normally easy to get in the capital. The aims were partly philanthropic, partly the wish to make the poor fit for work again.[12] London's buildings for cultural entertainment and for the care of the sick set the provinces an example.

Although parishes did not build halls for vestry meetings, as the need was insufficient, rates were levied both for church and workhouse construction. In all England several hundred churches were erected, or largely or wholly rebuilt. There were about fifty new churches in provincial towns between 1700 and 1750, and about eighty in the next fifty years. Many town and country parishes altered, enlarged or rebuilt their churches by levying rates. Individuals led by local squires paid for rural churches, while in towns briefs and subscriptions were used, yet rates were the basic source for the extension or reconstruction of medieval churches, particularly in towns. The rebuilding of Penrith church in 1720–22 cost £2252 16s. 9d; apart from brief money (£344 1s. 5d.) and gifts, £1423 17s. 9d. was raised in four rates of two shillings in the pound in 1721–22. The usual cost of rebuilding a church by rate in the provinces was between £2000 and £5000.[13]

Indoor relief of the poor paid for by rates began with workhouses set up by the corporations of the poor founded in fifteen large towns, including London, between 1696 and 1711; the parishes in each centre were united to support its institution. The building at Hull in 1697 cost £498 9s. and that at Liverpool (1697–98) £7841 10s. 0d. The aim was to employ the poor at a profit and to reform the dissolute by religious education

[12] D. Owen, *English Philanthropy, 1660–1960* (Cambridge, Massachusetts, 1965), pp. 38–45, 50–52; Lewis, *Topographical Dictionary*, iii, pp. 156–57; E. Wilson, *The History of the Middlesex Hospital* (London, 1845), pp. 22–35; E.W. Morris, *A History of the London Hospital* (2nd edn, London, 1910), pp. 77–87; A.E. Clark-Kennedy, *The London: A Study in the Voluntary Hospital System*, i, *The First Hundred Years, 1740–1840* (London, 1962), p. 145; A. Highmore, *Pietas Londinensis: The History, Design and Present State of the Various Public Charities in and near London* (London, 1810), pp. 289, 294, 195.

[13] C.W. Chalklin, 'The Financing of Church Building in the Provincial Towns of Eighteenth-Century England', ed. P. Clark, *The Transformation of English Provincial Towns* (London, 1984), p. 284–306.

and labour discipline. The corporations showed the Society for Promoting Christian Knowledge, founded in 1698 as part of the moral reformation of the 1690s, that workhouses might improve the poor. Parish buildings were hired, bought and especially built from about 1715. By 1722 there were about fifty. The initiative came from wealthy parishioners and independent poor relief contractors, such as Matthew Marryott, and from the SPCK, which supported the Workhouse Test Act in 1723, encouraging their creation. The SPCK, through correspondence about policy with individual parishioners, was most influential in the 1720s and 1730s. By 1750 there were over 600 workhouses. They were normally in towns. Loans on the rates were essential to persuade reluctant parishioners to build for several hundred pounds. In the early eighteenth century magistrates wished to save on the costs of outdoor relief, to deter people from asking for help, and to employ the poor to make money for the parish.[14] Among early urban buildings 'upwards of £700' was spent in 1720 on the Maidstone three-story brick workhouse, presumably built like a sizeable dwelling. Most country buildings cost up to a few hundred pounds. The Morden, Surrey, workhouse erected in 1771, measuring forty-two by sixteen and a half feet, of two stories and attics, cost £260. Some workhouses in London and the leading provincial towns cost several thousand pounds.[15]

Corporations were unable to raise rates for buildings for their own needs. Occasionally, they paid for them out of their estates if they were wealthy. A guildhall and exchange was built in Newcastle in 1655–58 for nearly £10,000, and a four-story mansion house for £6000 in 1691. The rich Doncaster corporation built a mansion house costing £8000 in 1748. Some halls were erected as gifts to towns by local landowners or groups of residents, or MPs wishing to strengthen their political control and keep their seats. Local patriotism influenced corporations and rich residents as well as the desire for display and their own comfort. The upper story was often used for the council's meetings while the ground floor was open to the street for market trading. Woodstock had several possible benefactors for its town hall. About 1722 the duke of Wharton promised £600 for rebuilding. In 1757 the corporation demolished the

---

[14] J.R. Poynter, *Society and Pauperism: English Ideas on Poor Relief, 1795–1834* (London, 1969), pp. 15–16; T. Hitchcock, 'Paupers and Preachers: The SPCK and the Parochial Workhouse Movement', *Stilling the Grumbling Hive: The Response to Social and Economic Problems in England, 1689–1750*, ed. L. Davison et al. (Stroud, 1992), pp. 145–60; E. Hasted, *The History and Topographical Survey of the County of Kent*, iv (2nd edn, Canterbury, 1798), p. 316; A.F.J. Brown, *Essex at Work, 1700–1815* (Chelmsford, 1969), p. 148.

[15] Surrey Record Office, 2065/3/1; *House of Commons Sessions Papers of the Eighteenth Century, 31 George III, Poor Relief, 1775–1780, Second Report* (Wilmington, Delaware, 1975).

old town hall as the councillors 'flattered themselves' (according to a later comment) that their MPs would pay for a new hall. Finally, the principal landowner, the duke of Marlborough, provided a building designed by Sir William Chambers in 1766–67 for over £1100.[16]

The number and size of public buildings erected for commercial use grew. Among market houses the lord of the manor built one at Dursley, Gloucestershire, in 1738. Canterbury corporation spent over £1100 on a flesh shambles and herb market in 1758.[17] In a few towns there were special market buildings for textiles. A blanket hall was erected at Witney in 1721. The sale of West Riding cloths between manufacturers and merchants was handled at cloth halls during the seventeenth century. In the eighteenth century the new buildings were larger. A hall was erected at Wakefield in 1710. To stop it engrossing the wool trade, another was built at Leeds the following year, based on the contributions of £1000 by its merchants and tradesmen. The two-story building filled with stalls was arranged round a quadrangular court. An enlarged Leeds cloth hall was built in 1755, financed by the subscriptions of the clothiers. Subscribers also paid £5300 for a coloured cloth market at the same time. Local landowners built cloth halls at Halifax in 1708 and Huddersfield in 1766.[18]

After the example of London's Royal Exchange, several merchants' buildings were erected in the great ports. The largest was at Bristol in 1741–43 for nearly £50,000 (including the site). Liverpool had a combined exchange and town hall in 1749–50 for £30,000, while a three-story building with a newsroom above the exchange was erected at Hull in 1734.[19]

[16] Lewis, *Topographical Dictionary*, ii, p. 60; *Victoria History of the County of Oxford*, xii, ed. A. Crossley (Oxford, 1990), pp. 389–90; S. Middelbrook, *Newcastle upon Tyne: Its Growth and Achievement* (Wakefield, 1968), p. 77.

[17] Lewis, *Topographical Dictionary*, ii, p. 98; F.H. Panton, 'The Finances and Government of the City and County of Canterbury in the Eighteenth and Early Nineteenth Centuries', *Archaeologia Cantiana*, 109 (1992), p. 204.

[18] Lewis, *Topographical Dictionary*, iv, p. 567; H. Heaton, *The Yorkshire Woollen and Worsted Industries* (2nd edn, Oxford, 1965), pp. 360–9, 372, 379–82; H. Heaton, 'The Leeds White Cloth Hall', *Publications of the Thoresby Society* (1913), p. 22; Grady, *Georgian Public Buildings*, pp. 153, 157–58, 162–63.

[19] W. Ison, *The Georgian Buildings of Bristol* (London, 1952), pp. 98–99, 139–48; P. McGrath, *A History of the Society of Merchant Venturers of the City of Bristol from its Origin to the Present Day* (Bristol, 1975), p. 226; A.C. Wardle, 'Some Glimpses of Liverpool during the First Half of the Eighteenth Century', *Transactions of the Historic Society of Lancashire and Cheshire* (1945), 97, pp. 152–53; *Victoria History of the County of Yorkshire: East Riding*, i, *The City of Kingston upon Hull*, ed. K.J. Allison (London, 1969), p. 437; R. and W. Dean, *The Commercial Directory for 1818–1920* (Manchester, 1818), p. 236.

These commercial buildings reflected the growth of trade between 1650 and 1770. In particular, the output of West Riding cloth increased several times; and there was an enormous expansion of overseas and coastal trade through ports such as Bristol, Liverpool and Hull.

In the early eighteenth century cultural public buildings in the form of theatres and assembly rooms first appeared in provincial centres. Townspeople, sometimes but not always with the help of the neighbouring gentry, were trying to ape London by creating the buildings needed to house the cultural amenities which they hoped to establish locally on a permanent basis. Until the 1730s dramatic entertainment was in makeshift facilities at inns or barns. From the 1730s purpose-built theatres were erected, first in the bigger towns or resorts, such as Bath in 1750 (for £1000) or Bristol in 1764–66 (for about £5000). A smaller number of assembly rooms were built from the 1730s, costing about £2000 to £5000. They comprised usually a great room for dancing and the other principal entertainment of the evening, and two or three smaller rooms for card-playing or refreshments. Both theatres and assembly rooms were built by subscription.[20]

Subscribers were also responsible for more churches, often to buy pews. For substantial townspeople, owning or renting a pew in a church where the preaching was congenial was a fashionable habit. Outside London most of these churches were built in about a dozen towns which were expanding rapidly for commercial or industrial reasons. They were usually either chapels of ease in existing parishes or (less often) proprietary chapels outside the parochial system. For example, in Whitehaven, a fast-growing port in the early eighteenth century, churches were built in 1715 and 1753, adding to the first church of 1693 which replaced a tiny chapel. In the manufacturing town of Birmingham, where the population grew from about 6000 in 1700 to over 20,000 in 1750, churches were built in 1715, 1735 and 1747. Costs were under £1000 to £6000 or £7000. The trust deed for the building of St James, Whitehaven, in 1753 arranged for four classes of pews, selling for £50, £30, £20 and £10 'according to their largeness and commodiousness of their respective situation'. The contributors are listed. Apart from the local landowner, Lord Lowther, who paid £500, and one subscriber of £40, twenty-three people paid

[20] C.W. Chalklin, 'Capital Expenditure on Building for Cultural Purposes in Provincial England, 1730–1830', *Business History*, 22 (1980), p. 52; *Victoria History of the County of Yorkshire: City of York*, ed. P.M. Tillott (London, 1961), p. 53.

£50, nineteen £30, twenty-one £20, and thirty-three £10: or a total of £3190.[21]

These Anglican churches were far outnumbered by the many hundred little nonconformist chapels erected in the century, most costing no more than £100 or £200, paid for by the donations of members and collections at religious meetings. In the largest provincial towns, such as Birmingham and Liverpool, twenty or thirty chapels were erected, enlarged or rebuilt, on old or new sites, during the century.

Among educational buildings, fewer grammar schools were founded than in the century before 1650, as secondary standard teaching was increasingly supplied in academies teaching modern subjects in houses rented or owned by the masters. Many older schools were, however, improved or rebuilt. Nottingham corporation rebuilt the west front of the high school in 1688–89 for £63 5s. 9d; in 1708 renewals and additions which included classrooms cost about £250. Among the few sizeable schools, a three-story building with wings at Appleby Magna in Leicestershire cost £2800 in 1693–97.[22]

The new or rebuilt grammar schools were outnumbered by the new charity schools, to provide elementary education for the poor, built by subscription or the donation of one wealthy person. They were set up especially in the first quarter of the century: in 1704 there were fifty schools with about 5000 children, but in 1729 1419 schools with 22,303 pupils. Nearly all of them, particularly those in the country and the market towns, were tiny. They had a single room for one teacher, costing no more than £50, or at the most £100. At Marrick, near Richmond in Yorkshire, a legacy of £40 was left to build a school in about 1723 (not in fact erected), while at neighbouring Crackpot £30 was given to build a school in 1765. In the larger towns a few sizeable charity schools were erected, such as the Bluecoat School at Liverpool finished in 1726 and costing about £2000, with a central building and two wings forming three sides of a rectangle.[23]

University buildings at Oxford and Cambridge continued to be erected. At Oxford Wren's Sheldonian Theatre (1664–69), for awarding degrees, cost £12,000; the old Ashmolean Museum (1679–83), the oldest public

---

[21] Chalklin, 'Church Building', pp. 284–306.
[22] A.W. Thomas, *A History of Nottingham High School, 1513–1953* (Nottingham, 1958), pp. 80–81; M. Seaborne, *The English School: Its Architecture and Organization, 1370–1870* (1971) p. 74; see also other school histories.
[23] M.G. Jones, *The Charity School Movement* (Cambridge, 1938), p. 72; R. Fieldhouse and B. Jennings, *A History of Richmond and Swaledale* (Chichester, 1978), p. 368; *Gore's Liverpool Directory* (Liverpool, 1823), p. 144.

museum in England, over £4000; and the Radcliffe Camera, a library finished in 1748, £43,226, of which the site cost £9336. At Cambridge the Senate House was built between 1722 and 1730 when the Regent House became a library, the new building costing £16,386, of which £13,000 was actually spent on the structure. Most money went on college buildings such as libraries and chapels, and especially blocks and quadrangles of rooms for students and fellows. Worcester College, Oxford, was founded and built in the early eighteenth century. At least £18,000 was also spent on a new quadrangle at the Queen's College. The many works at Cambridge included the magnificent Trinity College Library, designed by Wren and built after 1676; the western building in King's College (1724–49), costing £11,539; and the chapel at Clare Hall in 1763–67 costing £7327.[24]

General hospitals for the poor began to be built in 1735. Sixteen existed by 1760 and twenty-one by 1775. The typical building cost several thousand pounds. Among infirmaries erected in the 1750s, £3700 was spent at Newcastle (1752), £2587 at Manchester (1753–55) and £6200 at Gloucester (1755–61). The Liverpool hospital, costing £2618 3s. 6d. in 1749, was eighty feet square, with three floors, attics and cellars, the first and second floors being mainly wards.[25]

According to David Owen, 'in some measure both the form and direction of giving were altered . . .' in the eighteenth century. While many almshouses were still built, such as twelve stone houses in Bishop Wearmouth after 1726 by a £400 legacy, the charity schools and hospitals were a new outlet for philanthropic impulses. Again,

> although Englishmen continued to give or leave considerable sums of money as individuals, they also discovered increasing merit in collective activity. Inspired, very likely, by the joint stock business ventures of their age, groups of Englishmen arranged to pool their effects in voluntary societies dedicated to mitigating particular evils or accomplishing special charitable aims.

Innumerable subscriptions were made to hospitals and charity schools because giving was now a habit among the urban middle class, now more

[24] *Victoria History of the County of Oxford*, iii, ed. H.E. Salter and M.D. Lobel (London, 1954), pp. 48–56, 140–43, 191, 233; S.G. Gillam, *The Building Accounts of the Radcliffe Camera*, Oxford Historical Society, new series 13 (1958), appendix 2; Willis and Clark, *University of Cambridge*, i, pp. 115–17, 563; ii, p. 546; iii, pp. 46–54.

[25] J. Woodward, *To Do the Sick No Harm: A Study of the British Voluntary Hospital System to 1875* (London, 1974), p. 36; Lewis, *Topographical Dictionary*, iii, p. 359; W. Brockbank, *Portrait of a Hospital, 1752–1948* (London, 1952), p. 17; B. Smith, *The Story of Gloucester's Infirmary* (Gloucester, 1967), p. 7; G. McGloughlin, *A Short History of the Liverpool Infirmary, 1749–1824* (Chichester, 1978), pp. 21–22.

numerous than in Elizabethan and Jacobean times. The reason was partly piety, the puritan spirit of the stewardship of wealth being important, and partly benevolence and (among some) the feeling of compassion for the distressed. Donations were also made from genuine religious conviction, as well as the wish to foster work among the poor. Providing for, training and healing the poor inspired the creation of workhouses, charity schools and hospitals respectively.[26]

From the mid seventeenth century expenditure on various forms of transport improvement grew. Increasing concern about the state of roads led to legislation between 1654 and 1691 enabling parishes to levy small rates to pay labourers for their work, instead of relying on unpaid statute duty. Expenditure on roads increased most noticeably with the coming of turnpike trusts, which charged traffic and borrowed on the security of the tolls. A series of turnpike acts began in the later 1690s. They were particularly plentiful in the later 1720s, and there was another burst of legislation in the 1750s and 1760s. The trusts set up before 1750 were mainly for roads leading to, and within one hundred miles of, London, and those around growing provincial towns and within expanding industrial areas. In the 1750s and 1760s there were schemes on main roads all over England. Surfaces were improved, foundations laid sometimes, drains and ditches dug often and roads widened.[27]

While a few bridges were built to replace fords and ferries, normally for a few hundred pounds, most works repaired, widened or rebuilt existing structures. Individuals, corporations, parishes, endowed trusts and later turnpike trusts were responsible as well as counties. Although the bridges were mostly medieval, they were often stone and soundly built, and just able to handle the growth of trade. Exceptionally, in the vicinity of London population growth led to the crossing of the Thames by several expensive bridges in the early eighteenth century. At Fulham in 1729 thirty subscribers replaced a ferry with a wooden bridge costing £23,975, and £8000 in compensation to the ferry owner. Quite on its own in terms of expenditure was Westminster Bridge, the first to be

[26] R. Surtees, *The History and Antiquities of the County Palatine of Durham* (London, 1816), i, p. 232; Owen, *English Philanthropy*, pp. 3, 13–14; M.E. Fissell, 'Charity Universal? Institutions and Moral Reform in Eighteenth-Century Bristol', in *Stilling the Grumbling Hive*, pp. 120–24, 129–30.

[27] E. Melling, *Kentish Sources*, i, *Some Roads and Bridges* (Maidstone, 1959), pp. 2, 4; E. Pawson, *Transport and Economy: The Turnpike Roads of Eighteenth-Century Britain* (London, 1977), chapter 6.

built in London itself after London Bridge itself. A lottery and annual parliamentary grants paid the charges of £389,500.[28]

River navigation extended from about 700 miles in 1650 to 1160 miles in the 1720s, with bursts of activity in 1662–65, 1697–1700 and 1719–21. The cost of making stretches of river passable varied between a few thousand pounds and £30,000 to £40,000, the average being probably about £10,000.[29]

Harbour construction expanded and dock building began. Individuals and trusts erected piers and quays at harbours for several thousand pounds. The first docks were built at Rotherhithe for £12,000 in 1700, Sea Mills near Bristol for about £9600 in 1712, and at Liverpool in 1709–15 and 1738–53 for £15,000 and £21,000 respectively.[30]

This varied range of public construction by the government, parishes, corporations, individuals and groups of subscribers dwarfed county work in quantity and scale. Shire halls were built by courts under pressure from judges holding the twice-yearly assizes, and justices attending quarter sessions, to replace decayed buildings and so as to have more and larger rooms. Eight were erected, re-erected, partly rebuilt or substantially repaired in the later seventeenth century, and eleven between 1700 and 1765, costing from £300 to about £4200. In a few counties sessions did not build halls, as they used premises belonging to corporations or landowners. Less than half the counties rebuilt their gaols between 1650 and 1770, and the majority one or more new bridewells; the former costing several thousand pounds and the tiny bridewells much less. Prisons stayed unplanned and dirty because numbers of inmates were low in most areas and interest in prison reform was slight and intermittent. Some, but not all, counties were active repairing and rebuilding bridges.[31] The more significant county contribution to public works was later.

The number and variety of public buildings continued to grow. Some were much larger than their predecessors before the 1760s and 1770s. Yet later prices exaggerate the increase in size, as building costs in part of the 1800s and 1810s were more than twice those of the 1780s. The

[28] Walker, *Old Westminster Bridge*, p. 24; S. Ireland, *Picturesque Views on the River Thames*, ii (London, 1972), pp. 73–147; see below, chapter 5.

[29] T.S. Willan, *River Navigation in England, 1600–1750* (London, 1936), p. 133; Ward, *Canal Building*, pp. 3–4, 10, 165.

[30] Swann, 'Docks and Harbours', pp. 6–7, 405, 410–11; D. Swann, 'The Pace and Progress of Port Investment in England, 1660–1830', *Yorkshire Bulletin of Economic and Social Research*, 12 (1960), pp. 33–34.

[31] See below, Chapters 5, 7, 8.

Excise Office had become decayed and too small to house a department which by the 1760s was responsible for much of the public revenue, the staff having risen from 1211 in 1690 to 3973 in 1763. A new building was erected for £39,339 between 1769 and 1776. Among new government structures, Somerset House has been described as 'the largest building operation carried out at public expense during the Georgian era'. Composing long, uniform blocks of building round a great central courtyard, it was the largest group of government offices anywhere before the Russian Admiralty of 1806–15. The dispersion of numerous departments throughout London had been uneconomic and inconvenient, and the existing palace was in poor condition. Somerset House's erection between 1775 and 1801 cost £462,323.[32]

There were some very large government buildings in London,[33] with one in Kent, in the early nineteenth century, inspired by the growth of trade, financial services, communications and prison reform. These included the Lazaretto (quarantine premises), at Chetney Hill, Kent, 1810–16, which cost at least £170,000; Millbank Penitentiary (a prison with 1200 cells), of 1812–22, at £500,000; the Royal Mint, 1805–15 (£288,656); the Custom House, 1813–29 (£435,000) (including rebuilding at £177,220); and the General Post Office, 1824–29 (£499,000, including the site bought from 1815, for £299,000).

Large sums were spent at Westminster on the Houses of Parliament and the law courts, work on the latter having begun in the 1780s. Between 1800 and 1814 the Westminster Improvements Commission bought and demolished many buildings to open up the Westminster precinct for over £250,000. In the same years more than £200,000 was spent by the Office of Works on rebuilding the Houses of Parliament and the Speaker's House. Among other works at Westminster in the 1820s the law courts were rebuilt for nearly £100,000 (1822–27). Much money was also spent on government offices at Whitehall: in 1824–26 about £80,000 was paid for the Privy Council Office and Board of Trade building with a facade on Whitehall of between 150 and 160 feet. The rebuilding of the British Museum began in 1823, though most of the work was done after 1830.[34]

[32] *History of the King's Works*, v, pp. 348, 363, 380; J. Harris, *Sir William Chambers* (London, 1970), p. 96; Pevsner, *Building Types*, p. 47; Brewer, *Sinews of Power*, pp. 65–67.

[33] *History of the King's Works*, vi, *1782–1851*, ed. J.M. Crook and M.H. Port (London, 1973), pp. 423, 433, 447–48, 454–55; H. Mayhew and J. Binny, *The Criminal Prisons of London* (London, 1868), pp. 235–36.

[34] *History of the King's Works*, vi, pp. 410–13, 511, 516–18, 551–59, 664–66.

Local government courthouses in London were rebuilt. The City sessions house in the 1770s cost £15,000 and the Guildhall was improved in the 1780s, altering buildings which were old, scattered and in need of a better appearance.[35] Prison construction was important in London in the 1770s and 1780s. While at the start the major influence was the growth of population and hence of crime, by the 1780s the prison reform movement and more prison sentences were important. The largest eighteenth-century prison, Newgate, erected in 1770–84 by the City of London, its purpose symbolised by two blocks of windowless wall, with three great courtyards for different types of prisoner, cost £100,000; partly because the Gordon Riots of 1780 destroyed the building when it was almost finished. Much of the money came from loans secured on the City's Orphans Fund, which received income allocated by statute, including £10,000 for the City's estates and a tax of sixpence per chaldron on imported coal sold in London; the final £30,000 came from three parliamentary grants in 1781–83. Despite the replacement of the dilapidated and overcrowded King's Bench Prison in 1754–58 with a building of 132 rooms by a parliamentary grant of £7570, rising debtors' numbers made it congested again, so it was enlarged by the Office of Works for £22,028 between 1774 and 1780. The Office also remodelled the ruinous Fleet Prison in the early 1770s at £13,442. In the 1780s two City debtors' prisons (compters) cost about £30,000, including £2357 paid from the Bridgehouse estate. They were surpassed by the New Debtors' Prison in Whitecross Street of 1812–14, its price of £125,810 being paid mostly by loans on the Orphans Fund. Thus the City's huge financial resources created two of the largest English prisons.[36]

The most varied and the biggest commercial buildings were in London. An Auction Mart was opened in 1810, a Commercial Hall in 1811 and a new Corn Exchange building in 1828, all paid for by shareholders. The duke of Bedford improved Covent Garden fruit, vegetable and flower market in 1828, and the City rebuilt Fleet Market, opened in 1829 as Faringdon Market, for £80,000, £200,000 more having been spent first to buy the houses on the extended site.[37]

Among cultural buildings theatres still appeared. The Surrey Theatre in suburban St George's Fields was erected in 1782 for £15,000, while

---

[35] City of London Record Office, Journal of Newgate Committee, 1767–85, p. 263; Lewis, *Topographical Dictionary*, iii, p. 119.

[36] C.W. Chalklin, 'The Reconstruction of London's Prisons, 1770–1799: An Aspect of the Growth of Georgian London', *London Journal*, 9 (1983), pp. 21–34; *Parliamentary Papers*, 1831, xv.

[37] Lewis, *Topographical Dictionary*, iii, pp. 115–16.

the largest eighteenth-century playhouse was the Drury Lane Theatre built in the 1790s at over £80,000. The largest theatres in the early nineteenth century were those at Drury Lane in 1809–11, costing over £150,000 paid by a joint-stock company with a capital of £300,000, and at Covent Garden for £187,888 by shareholders. Fires as well as the ever-growing popularity of the drama explain frequent building. Several build-ings were used for horse displays. The greater sobriety of the early nineteenth century led to the formation of gentlemen's clubs in London after 1815, in purpose-built structures, such as the Union Club, the Athenaeum and the United Services Club in the 1820s. The London Institution, formed in 1805, built a library, newsroom and lecture premises from its own funds and members' donations between 1815 and 1819. London's first university buildings were erected in the 1820s. The site of London University alone cost £90,000, the building contract £107,000. The estimate for the building of King's College was £140,000. Thus the desire for entertainment and learning greatly widened the types of cultural public building in London.[38]

Hospitals, churches, schools and a few almshouses continued to be built in London as population and needs grew. Small hospitals were founded from the 1770s. Among the most important later, the Charing Cross Hospital was erected in 1818, and St George's Hospital rebuilt for a little over £40,000 in 1827–34. They reflected the ever-increasing demand for treatment for the poor and the willingness of the wealthy to subscribe for its provision. The new St George's Hospital followed the board's decision that 'the accommodations of the present hospital are totally inadequate to the wants of the public'.[39]

Growing population, the increasing wealth of the middle classes and the example of London all encouraged provincial public building, particularly in towns. Everywhere church and chapel building increased between the 1770s and early 1790s. A few churches cost more than £10,000 in the later 1780s and 1790s, when building prices began to rise and urban growth peaked. Although heavy war taxation kept building down between about 1795 and 1810, the religious revival beginning in the 1790s finally helped to spur a sustained era of construction. While rates and voluntary local subscriptions were the basic sources of money, the great burst of building in the 1820s was made possible by the Church

---

[38] E.W. Brayley, *History and Descriptive Accounts of the Theatres of London* (London, 1826), pp. 67–69; *Survey of London*, xxxv, pp. 20–21, 78; Lewis, *Topographical Dictionary*, iii, p. 112; D. Watkin, *The Buildings of Britain: Regency* (London, 1982), p. 91.

[39] J. Blomfield, *St George's, 1733–1933* (London, 1933), pp. 40–41; J. Langdon-Davies, *Westminster Hospital* (London, 1952), p. 202.

Building Society and especially £1,500,000 provided by the Church Building Acts of 1818 and 1824, churches costing £10,000 or £20,000 in the major towns being particular recipients. This was the first parliamentary contribution to church building since the work of the Commission for Building Fifty New Churches set up in 1711. The aim was to provide more space in churches for working-class families, since existing buildings were full of pews rented or owned by more substantial townspeople. Church-going would improve them. 'Morals could only be inculcated by religious principles, and without them the nation could not prosper.' Impressing principles was not only good in itself, but would encourage self-discipline, hard work and respect for their betters.[40]

Parishes continued to provide more workhouses from the 1770s. By 1776 there were 1916, with 132 in Kent and 142 in Essex. Gilbert's act of 1782, authorising the setting up of a workhouse by a parish or a group of them, increased the number further. In 1802 there were 3765. Some workhouses in London and the leading provincial centres cost a few thousand pounds. The Liverpool building erected by the corporation in 1770–74 for about £8000 was enlarged in 1776, 1791 and 1796. The Manchester workhouse of the early 1790s, said to be large and spacious, cost more than £5000, helped by annuities and loans secured on the rates. By the early nineteenth century workhouses in rural parishes and country towns cost up to several thousand pounds. The one at Barnes in Surrey cost £1000 in 1813–16, paid for by the sale of annuities. £3000 was spent on the new Aylesbury workhouse in 1829, built to take more paupers.[41]

Accompanying the rapid growth of parish workhouses in the later eighteenth century, sizeable houses of industry were built to serve groups of parishes in some rural areas. Fourteen were erected in East Anglia between 1756 and 1785, the five in Norfolk costing over £40,000. With a central structure, sometimes adorned by a pediment, and with wings, they seemed like country houses. The largest house of industry was built in the Isle of Wight for the whole island under an act of 1770 to hold 750 paupers; with several ranges of buildings including substantial workshops, a chapel and pesthouse, it cost at least £20,000. Five small houses were also put up in Shropshire. These were exceptional. The

[40] M.H. Port, *Six Hundred New Churches* (London, 1961), p. 11.

[41] Poynter, *Society and Pauperism*, p. 189; W. Enfield, *History of Liverpool* (Liverpool, 1774), p. 57; G.B. Hindle, 'Provision for the Relief of the Poor in Manchester', *Remains Historical and Literary Connected with the Palatine Counties of Lancaster and Chester*, Chetham Society, 3rd series, 22 (Manchester, 1975), p. 36; J.E. Anderson, *A History of the Parish of Barnes* (Richmond, 1900), p. 14; R. Gibbs, *A History of Aylesbury* (Aylesbury, 1885), p. 61.

buildings were financed either by straight loans or tontines. The Loddon and Clavering incorporation borrowed £7000 in mortgages, the Forehoe incorporation £11,000 through a tontine.[42]

Turning to private enterprise, apart from Anglican churches built wholly or in part by subscription, hundreds of nonconformist chapels of varying sizes were built each decade. Chapels erected by Methodists, Congregationalists and Baptists sometimes cost between £1000 and £2000, with greater outlays in the larger towns. In Halifax an Independent chapel built in 1819 cost £6000 and a Wesleyan chapel of 1829 nearly £4000.[43] It is the number of these larger chapels, many of which still survive, which differentiate the 1810s and 1820s from the previous century.

Some commercial buildings were becoming larger and more specialised. A Sheffield market improvement scheme begun in 1786 by the duke of Norfolk, the greatest local landowner, included a one-story building with butchers' shambles, a market for dairy produce and shops for fruit and vegetables. Canterbury corporation spent £3881 3s. 0d. on a new cattle market and the demolition of a gate in 1802–3, by selling properties and raising loans. The market building erected at Chichester in 1807 'for the sale of all manner of flesh meat, fish, poultry, eggs, butter, herbs, roots and other vegetables, fruit, china, glass and earthenware, and such other things as are usually sold in public markets' cost the corporation £3362. The leading towns had much larger premises. St John's Market at Liverpool in 1820–22, which cost £35,000, was paid for by the corporation from its huge estate. A covered building, measuring 182 by 45 yards, its walls were lined by sixty-two shops. There were four ranges of stalls and standings divided up for the various goods.[44]

After London's example, eight or ten provincial corn exchanges were built between 1800 and 1830. The most substantial was at Leeds in 1825–28, costing £12,500 which was subscribed, with a colonnaded quadrangle in compartments for selling grain by sample; it also had warehouses and offices for corn factors and dealers, a hotel, tavern and large shops. The

[42] A. Digby, *Pauper Palaces* (London, 1978), pp. 34–39; Lewis, *Topographical Dictionary*, iii, p. 354.

[43] W. White, *Directory and Gazetteer of Leeds, Bradford and the Clothing Districts of the West Riding of Yorkshire* (Sheffield, 1853), p. 550.

[44] J. Blackman, 'The Food Supply of an Industrial Town: A Study of Sheffield's Markets, 1780–1900', *Business History*, 5 (1963), p. 86; Panton, 'Finances and Government', p. 205; F.W. Steer, *The Market House, Chichester*, Chichester Papers, 27 (Chichester, 1962), p. 5; E. Baines, *History Directory and Gazetteer of the County Palatine of Lancaster*, i (Liverpool, 1824), p. 196.

southern provincial corn exchanges were smaller, costing two or three thousand pounds.[45]

Yorkshire cloth halls reached a peak in the 1770s. The Leeds White Cloth Hall of 1755 was replaced by a larger building in 1775, comprising ninety-nine by seventy yards, round a quadrangle, the interior holding ten long rows of cloth stands, costing £4300. It was subscribed mostly by cloth merchants of Leeds and the other textile towns. Another hall was built at Halifax in 1778 for over £12,000, being three-storied and covering 10,000 square yards. In addition to the need to provide or increase local facilities, halls were sometimes built because of economic rivalry with other towns which had decided to erect buildings.[46]

Several commercial exchanges were built in the north in the early nineteenth century. Liverpool set the example, about £100,000 being spent on its exchange of 1806–7. It was built around a quadrangle which included piazzas for the merchants, brokers and underwriters. There was a news- and coffee-room, with an underwriters' room above, large counting houses and warehouses. The little Sunderland exchange cost £8000 in 1814, based on £50 shares.[47]

Philanthropy continued to be active, the evangelical revival helping it give it a new religious edge. The growing and prosperous middle classes provided the majority of donors, though the aristocracy and gentry were still generous. While almshouse building fell everywhere from the 1790s, many more provincial medical hospitals were begun. Among those erected were the Sunderland infirmary of 1822 for £3000, and the Sussex hospitals in 1825–26 for £7474. The donations for the Sussex hospitals of about £8000 came from more than 200 people, mainly living in west Sussex: from £600 by the duke of Richmond, who lived at neighbouring Goodwood, to £1 listed as 'a Sussex clergyman's mite'. There were also more dispensaries, some being in small buildings erected for the purpose, such as the new dispensary at Bolton in 1814 costing £1700.[48]

Many hundred charity schools were built under the inspiration of the Royal Lancasterian Association (1810) and the National Society for the Education of the Poor (1811). Many of the latter were just one big room and a small house for the teacher at £200 or £300. The National School

[45] K. Grady, 'The Provision of Markets in Leeds, 1822–29', *Publications of the Thoresby Society Miscellany*, 16, p. 170.

[46] Grady, *Georgian Public Buildings*, pp. 100–1, 157, 163.

[47] *The Stranger in Liverpool: or An Historical and Descriptive View of the Town of Liverpool and its Environs* (Liverpool, 1815), p. 74; Lewis, *Topographical Dictionary*, iv, p. 242.

[48] F.W. Steer, *The Royal West Sussex Hospital*, Chichester Papers, 15 (Chichester, 1960), p. 2; Lewis, *Topographical Dictionary*, i, p. 259, iv, p. 244.

at Wheathampstead in 1815 for one hundred pupils was thirty-six by fifteen feet and cost £183. Some new charity schools in bigger towns were much dearer. The Liverpool Welsh School erected before 1809 with a 'noble schoolroom' cost £1700, and over £700 was spent adding to the Bluecoat School before 1818.[49] As with the parliamentary churches, the aim was discipline and improved principles.

Secondary school and university buildings increased. Grammar schools were rebuilt and some new schools founded, as the demand for education from the expanding middle classes grew. At Ludlow, where the grammar school building was several centuries old, the corporation rebuilt and extended the headmaster's house in 1802 for £700 to make it a brick building of three bays. The back of the schools was rebuilt in 1828 at an estimate price of £650. Some new buildings were extensive. Mill Hill school, which opened in 1826 for 120 boys, was not intended to cost more than £15,000. It was architecturally imposing, with a portico and two well-balanced wings. Several classrooms, dormitories for the boys and accommodation for the masters made it also well-organised.[50] Teaching could thus be more varied and of higher quality.

Although there was almost no construction at Oxford, building throve at Cambridge, where matriculations rose from 150 in 1800 to 440 by 1830. Downing College was built between 1807 and 1820, the two main contracts totalling £28,360. A new quadrangle at Corpus Christi between 1823 and 1827, including the hall, cost much more than the three contracts, amounting to £45,438. The 'New Buildings' were built at King's College for £101,021. The cost and size of these university works rivalled those of London in the 1820s.[51]

Building for entertainment and culture grew, as in London. Many country towns built new theatres, as at Newbury in 1802 and at Woodbridge in 1814. Several appeared in small but rapidly-growing resorts such as Southend (1804) and Leamington (1813). A few large towns had sizeable playhouses. While the majority were similar in size to the 'elegant little theatre' built at Northampton in 1805 for £1500, Brighton

---

[49] Seaborne, *English School*, pp. 140–41; J. Murphy, 'The Rise of Public Elementary Education in Liverpool: Part One, 1784–1818', *Transactions of the Historic Society of Lancashire and Cheshire*, 116 (1964), p. 185; 'Part Two, 1819–35', 118 (1966), p. 106.

[50] D.J. Lloyd, *Country Grammar School: A History of Ludlow Grammar School through Eight Centuries against its Local Background* (Birmingham, 1977), pp. 93–94; N.G. Brett-James, *The History of Mill Hill School, 1807–1923* (Reigate, 1923), p. 60.

[51] Colvin, *British Architects*, pp. 895–96; Willis and Clark, *University of Cambridge*, i, pp. 304, 565, ii, p. 766.

had one of the largest in 1806 costing £12,000, with seating for 1400 people.[52]

Libraries, newsrooms and buildings for learning were also erected. Those in county towns and resorts were relatively small, of one or two large rooms and costing £1000 or £2000. A museum was built at Scarborough in 1828–29 for £1410. Gentry and townspeople were subscribers. Expenditure was greatest in the main provincial centres, Manchester and Liverpool, both of which had about 150,000 people in 1821, including an increasingly numerous and prosperous urban elite. In Manchester the Portico Library, with newsroom, committee room, reading room and library (1802–5), cost about £7000. A Literary and Philosophical Society had a hall and rooms by 1815 and a Natural History Society a museum in 1821. A Royal Institution was formed in 1823 to exhibit and lecture on art; by the end of 1830 its members, 'the principal merchants and tradesmen in the town and neighbourhood', had spent over £3225 on the site and £22,365 11s. 0d. on the building.[53]

The growth of expenditure on public buildings between 1770 and 1830 was accompanied by the expansion of transport works. Turnpike trusts continued to be created until the 1830s, though not at the same rate as in the 1750s and 1760s. Contemporary comment on the marked improvement of the roads, and the great advance in road engineering in the early nineteenth century, by men such as Telford and Macadam, imply that expenditure on new works and improvements as distinct from repair and maintenance was considerable. The size and number of bridge works much increased from the 1770s under the influence of better bridge engineering techniques and the ever-growing amount of road traffic, as well as higher county expenditure. Most of the major projects were paid for by toll levied by trustees or shareholders, set up by act of parliament, who borrowed to finance construction. In London, Westminster Bridge of 1739–50 was followed by Blackfriars Bridge in 1760–70, costing £160,000. In the 1810s and 1820s four other large bridges were erected there: Waterloo Bridge (1811–17) cost over £1,000,000 with its approaches; Southwark Bridge (1814–19) £800,000; Vauxhall Bridge (1813–16) over £300,000; and New London Bridge (1824–31) £506,000. Designed by Rennie, the first three of them were built by companies of shareholders, while the City mostly paid for New London Bridge. They dwarfed the new provincial bridges, which included most of those on the Thames and Severn, and were especially numerous in

[52] Chalklin, 'Cultural Purposes', pp. 58–59.
[53] Ibid, p. 60.

the 1770s. Among them were Maidenhead Bridge in 1772–77 at a contract price of £15,741 1s. 10d.; Sunderland Bridge (1795–96) for £33,400; and Grosvenor Bridge, Chester (1827–33) for £49,824.[54]

Canal construction (which included canal bridges) began in the 1760s and continued until the 1830s. Works were particularly concentrated in the 1760s and early 1770s and again in the early 1790s, after which few new canals were promoted. The average cost between 1750 and 1815 was about £140,000. Among the early canals, the Stroudwater navigation (1776–79) cost about £41,000, the Chesterfield canal (1771–77) £150,000 and the Trent and Mersey (1766–77) £300,000. Most of the money was spent on construction, with under 10 per cent on land purchase.[55]

Outlay on ports and harbours grew in the 1760s and 1770s and especially the 1790s. Some early nineteenth-century projects were on a much larger scale than those a hundred years earlier, such as a new pier at Whitehaven between 1823 and 1832 costing about £50,000. Dock expenditure also grew, that in London far exceeding provincial work. After 1800 joint-stock companies extended the Port of London in the River Thames. The West India Dock (1800–6) with its warehouses cost £1,200,000; the expensive London Docks (1800–18) £3,250,000; the smaller East India Docks (1803–5) £375,000; and Commercial Docks (1810–15) £390,000. St Katherine's Dock was authorised in 1825 with a capital of £2,352,752. Elsewhere the heaviest construction was in Liverpool. The corporation built three more docks between 1770 and 1800, including the King's Dock and Basin finished in 1788 for £35,000. The great Prince's Dock of 1816–21 cost £650,000. Hull built two docks and Grimsby and Bristol one each, all undertaken by joint-stock companies.[56]

County building increased from the 1770s. Thirteen court houses were erected between 1765 and 1800 for from about £1000 to £16,000, and sixteen between 1800 and 1830 for from £2500 to about £100,000. Their purpose was to handle more assize and sessions business in higher quality premises. Nearly all counties rebuilt gaols or houses of correction between 1770 and 1800 at prices up to £40,000, with one at £65,656, as prison sentences increased in number and the reform movement sought planned, specialised prisons. The same influences led to the building of

[54] J.W. Walker, *A History of Maidenhead* (London, 1909), p. 15; E.C. Ruddock, *Arch Bridges and their Builders, 1735–1835* (Cambridge, 1979), pp. 186–88, 234–43.

[55] Ward, *Canal Building*, pp. 28–38, 146–49, 165.

[56] Swann, 'Docks and Harbours', pp. 368, 425; idem, 'Port Investment', pp. 36–39; R.A.H. Page, 'The Dock Companies in London, 1796–1864' (unpublished M.A. thesis, University of Sheffield, 1959), p. 172; C.H. Feinstein, 'Capital Formation in Great Britain', *Cambridge Economic History of Europe*, vii, part 1 (Cambridge, 1978), p. 41.

over one hundred county gaols and bridewells between 1800 and 1830. While the Kent gaol (1810–19) cost about £200,000, many were built for a few thousand pounds. County building was extended under an act of 1808 which permitted the creation of pauper lunatic asylums. Fourteen were erected by 1831 for between about £15,000 and £124,440. Sessions also contributed greatly to the stock of improved bridges as they took responsibility for many more. Works costing several thousand pounds were numerous from the 1770s, the most expensive county bridge being Eden Bridge at Carlisle in 1812–16 at £70,000.[57]

This survey has shown the huge growth of public building between the seventeenth and early nineteenth centuries. It increased slightly between 1700 and the 1730s, and perhaps in the early 1750s. The rise was pronounced in the 1770s and about 1785–95, and again in the 1810s and 1820s. By the 1820s it was absorbing about £1,000,000 a year. The growth in the 1770s and later 1780s and early 1790s partly reflects the great urban expansion of these decades, visible in London and the leading provincial towns. The fall in house building between about 1794 and 1803 was paralleled by the decline in new churches, almshouses and hospitals in the later 1790s and the 1800s, as war taxation and high building costs discouraged voluntary giving. The 1820s were again years of urban growth. Churches, markets and public halls were a necessary part of town expansion. The timing of other types of building, such as theatres and some prisons, was probably in part encouraged by flourishing local building, especially housing. At the peak of the speculative housing boom in 1790–93 parish vestries also borrowed extensively to build large churches, the debts lasting long into the nineteenth century.[58]

The basic causes of the long-term expansion of public building are almost a reflection of the major developments in English society in the course of this long period. Thus the wars against the French at intervals from 1689 explain the growth of expenditure on London administrative buildings. The expansion of commerce and retail trade was the cause of market building. The growth of leisure and desire for entertainment explains the building of theatres and assembly rooms in provincial towns from the 1730s. The prison reform movement and growth of population were the reasons for the prison building of the 1770s and 1780s and

---

[57] See below, Chapters 5–11.

[58] St Chad, Shrewsbury, cost about £20,000 and the debt was not paid off until 1870, D.H.S. Cranage, *The Churches of Shropshire* (Wellington, 1908), p. 512.

the decades after 1800. The humanitarian movement and wish for social control were largely the causes of the building of charity schools, many churches and the (relatively few) pauper lunatic asylums in the early nineteenth century.

Beyond these basic causes were more general influences, such as the desire to emulate or follow the example of other towns or neighbourhoods or other large groups of people. The Liverpool Athenaeum was the 'avowed disciple' of the Newcastle Literary and Philosophical Society formed in 1793, apparently following a visit to Newcastle by Edward Rogers of Liverpool about 1795 and discussions with friends and fellow intellectuals on his return. Attempts by people in provincial towns to copy London by erecting buildings similar (though often smaller) to those in the capital were particularly important, though difficult to trace. Ideas came from the visits of gentry and merchants to London and membership of its societies, and the talks of itinerant lecturers in provincial towns. Large centres influenced smaller ones, with Manchester and Liverpool stimulating Leeds and Sheffield, and the latter other West Riding towns.[59] Civic and local pride also contributed to the erection of town halls and hospitals. In particular, the great growth of wealth in the hands of the more substantial townspeople enabled them to pay for a better urban environment and amenities, and for higher standards of accommodation and comfort in buildings used by them for public business and other activities. This not only involved street improvement, such as paving and the removal of nuisances, but the construction of more ample market buildings out of the way of traffic, of town and shire halls for assizes, and of churches with many more pews.

The construction of public buildings was usually a long process. First the responsible individual, society or corporation sometimes took several years to decide to build on account of the cost. If a structure was in use, repairing or improvement was an alternative. When the rebuilding of an old church was considered, the opinions of the minister, churchwardens and vestry might differ. The opinion of an architect or surveyor sometimes settled the question. Once the decision to build was made, plans and often estimates were obtained, usually in detail by the early nineteenth century. Construction often took two or three years. While before the

---

[59] C.P. Darcy, 'The Encouragement of the Fine Arts in Lancashire, 1760–1860', in *Remains Historical and Literary Connected with the Palatine Counties of Lancaster and Cheshire*, third series, 24, Chetham Society (Manchester, 1976), pp. 12–13; Grady, *Georgian Public Buildings*, pp. 100–4.

mid eighteenth century the architect sometimes also built, increasingly he just supervised, using a clerk of the works on the site if he lived elsewhere. The owner might change the scheme during construction and often had to borrow to pay for part or most of the cost. Contracts were either made with one or two undertakers to build for a fixed sum, or the principal craftsmen such as carpenters or bricklayers were paid for materials and work. Alternatively, the churchwardens bought materials and paid for work, in which case the craftsmen were paid on a measure basis as their job was done. For churches, which took between a third and a half of money spent on civilian public building, separate contracts with the various craftsmen for both work and all or most of the materials probably constituted the most frequent method.[60]

The great growth in transport investment began in the mid eighteenth century. Its main constituent was the expenditure on water communications, comprising canals, particularly between the 1760s and the 1790s, and docks after 1800. Altogether, by the 1820s transport expenditure in the form of roads and bridges, canals and rivers, docks and harbours (without vehicles and ships) cost at least £2,000,000 a year. Naturally the rise of trade was responsible for transport improvements, and the latter helped the further growth of trade. Among signs of its increase, services of the London road haulage industry to provincial towns grew ten fold between 1715 and 1840, and the tonnage of ships in coastal trade rose at least four fold between 1760 and 1830.[61]

---

[60] Chalklin, 'Church Building', pp. 299–304.

[61] D.H. Aldcroft and M. Freeman, *Transport in the Industrial Revolution* (Manchester, 1983), pp. 85, 147.

2

County Government

Throughout the period 1650–1830 the justices were both rulers of the county, with a wide range of administrative duties, and judges in innumerable cases of petty crime. They acted in three ways: as individual magistrates acting alone in their own neighbourhood; in groups of two or more justices; and collectively at quarter sessions. These last general sessions had to be held at least four times a year in the weeks following the feasts of Epiphany, Easter, the Translation of St Thomas the Martyr and St Michael the Archangel, all the justices being summoned. A general sessions both handled much of the civil administration of the county and was a court of criminal jurisdiction.

In many counties, not only smaller ones such as Hertfordshire and Leicestershire but also larger counties such as Essex and Gloucestershire, the court met first in a single town. There were often adjournments to other places for a particular matter, such as work on a local bridge. In other counties the court held the four annual sessions in different places. In Cheshire between 1679 and 1723 the meetings were at Middlewich or Northwich in the east alternately in January, at Chester at the west end in April, at Nantwich in the south in July and at Knutsford in the north east in October. In 1723 Middlewich ceased to be used; Nantwich and Northwich changed over in 1745. Finally, from 1760, meetings ceased to be held at either Nantwich or Northwich, while Chester in the west was used in January and April and Knutsford in July and October.[1] In several counties each sessions were held in two or more places by adjournment, with a separate group of justices meeting each time dealing with the business of the particular division of the county. Thus in Suffolk the sessions were adjourned from Beccles in the far north east to Woodbridge over thirty miles to the south west, then to Ipswich eight miles further on, and from there to Bury St Edmunds twenty-five miles to the north west.[2] This represented a

[1] *Victoria History of the County of Cheshire*, ii, ed. B.E. Harris (Oxford, 1979), p. 63.
[2] East Suffolk Record Office, 105/2/1–64.

practical division of the county for nearly all types of county business.

Presumably the use of several towns for meetings was done for the convenience of justices on account of travelling. A particular town might be chosen or abandoned according to the availability of a suitable hall for their meeting. Where a sessions was held in one place, there might be several adjournments during the following two or three months. The shire hall or local borough courthouse was usually the principal place of meeting, though some of the business at the main meeting and adjournments were often held at a local inn. The first meeting took two or three days or more in a larger county: two days was normal in Shropshire between 1625 and the late 1670s, two, three or four in the 1680s, and three in the late 1690s; two days was usual in the 1740s and 1750s. The West Riding took five days (Monday to Friday) in the latter part of the eighteenth century.[3] These meetings were partly formal public occasions as courts of justice (where the judicial process was used), involving the presence of juries and the various county officers for part or most of the time, with the public being admitted; and partly private meetings to deal with administrative matters.[4]

The numbers of justices attending quarter sessions naturally varied according to the size of the county: in the late seventeenth century and early and mid eighteenth century this might vary from as few as three or four to as many as fifteen or sixteen. In Nottinghamshire in the first half of the eighteenth century three or four was perhaps the most usual number, though sometimes there were only two, and occasionally there were five or six. In the larger county of Shropshire attendance was about seventeen in the 1670s, twelve in the 1690s, and sixteen in the 1700s.[5] Benches were often smaller between the 1730s and 1750s, but from the 1770s and 1780s more justices usually came to quarter sessions. This may reflect the growing numbers and enthusiasm of the justices and the amount of business that had to be handled. Attendance in two counties illustrates this pattern. In large but mainly rural Shropshire, where there was steady population growth in the later eighteenth and early nineteenth centuries, numbers at sessions about doubled between the 1720s and the 1830s. After over twenty in 1712–14 and in George I's early years, perhaps because the commission changed frequently, about fourteen magistrates on average were at quarter sessions in the 1720s and 1730s.

---

[3] *Victoria History of the County of Shropshire*, iii, ed. G.C. Baugh (Oxford, 1979), pp. 97, 119.

[4] S. and B. Webb, *English Local Government from the Revolution to the Municipal Corporations Act: The Parish and the County* (London, 1906), p. 441.

[5] Ibid., pp. 439–42; *VCH, Shropshire*, ed. Baugh, p. 95.

Then the average fell to nine by the 1750s, and between nine and fourteen in the 1760s and early 1770s. It was about fifteen until the 1790s when it began to rise, reaching eighteen in the 1800s and about thirty by the 1830s.[6] In Warwickshire, where the population rose steeply with the growth of Birmingham, about twelve magistrates attended courts in 1773, whereas by the 1830s the number was around thirty.[7] The majority of justices at meetings did not come regularly. A few regulars gave courts cohesion. In Gloucestershire three attended three or more times in 1750; the number of the regular group reached four by 1785–90 and eight by 1795–1800, reflecting the growth of the bench as a whole.[8] In shires with sessions at different towns the tendency for justices to attend just once or twice was marked. This pattern occurred at Cheshire sessions where they were held in four places until 1759 and then at two until the 1820s. Attendance varied from meeting to meeting, with often only two or three justices being at adjournments (Table 2.1). In 1784 Dorset ses-

Table 2.1

Number of Cheshire Quarter Sessions Attended by Individual Justices, 1665–1785

Year	One	Two	Three	Four
1665	10	3	6	2
1695	4	3	1	2
1725	9	4	3	0
1755	8	4	2	1
1785	6	12	1	1

sions had five justices in Epiphany at Blandford, eleven at Easter (Sherborne), eight at Midsummer (Shaftesbury) and twelve at Michaelmas (Bridport). Of six adjournments, three in the Antelope inn, Dorchester, attendances were two (four times), three and five. Some magistrates worked singly, or in a pair, but did not come to sessions. In 1701 a Shropshire justice, Richard Gough, commented about another magistrate: 'I cannot tell whether he knew where the bench was where the sessions were kept, for I never saw him there'. In the 1740s 41 per cent of Kent's

[6] Ibid., pp. 116–19.
[7] P. Styles, *The Development of County Administration in the Late Eighteenth and Early Nineteenth Centuries: Illustrated by the Records of the Warwickshire Court of Quarter Sessions, 1773–1837*, Dugdale Society Occasional Papers, 4 (1934), pp. 6–7.
[8] E. Moir, *Local Government in Gloucestershire, 1775–1800*, Bristol and Gloucestershire Archaeological Society Publications, 8 (1969), p. 45.

active justices were not at courts. This happened everywhere until the end of the period, despite attendances becoming greater.[9]

Quarter sessions gradually became more organised. Necessarily there was a clerk, or deputy clerk, who was an attorney, and a treasurer or treasurers; during the eighteenth century permanent surveyors were added. Many counties employed vagrancy contractors in the eighteenth century. There was a growing number of men paid for particular jobs. Landau's study of Kent justices (1679–1760) mentions the use of Samuel Eastchurch, an attorney, to defend sessions' decisions at assizes in the early 1740s; in 1747 he was made administrative officer to the gaol building committee. When he was appointed deputy clerk in 1753, he was obviously experienced at sessions work. As sessions became increasingly active by the 1790s on matters such as the poor law, the number of ad hoc employees grew. In the 1700s the West Kent clerk had at least one assistant and by the 1730s at least two taking notes of sessions orders, orders and verdicts. The chairman gave an opening charge and guided proceedings. A way of improving efficiency was the use of standing chairmen. They were able to develop a regular form of procedure and to apply their experience in dealing with business. Kent, the West Riding and one or two other sessions had this control long before 1700. For other benches at this time the choice of chairman was made at the previous meeting or from a rota. Other counties had standing chairmen in the later eighteenth century, including Oxfordshire from 1771. As the Webbs wrote: 'gradually . . . the importance of maintaining some continuity of procedure and the convenience of utilising the expertness given by constant practice induced the Justices, in one county after another, to drift silently into standing chairmanships'. These appointments helped to smooth the working of courts. Proceedings gradually became more formal. Before 1714 the Gloucestershire bench tried to stop new motions being introduced during other debates, which might also be disturbed by talking. It continued to be unmethodical and its business ill-arranged. Then the county used a timetable. The various regulations were sorted and printed in 1801 as the *Resolutions, Rules and Orders of the Court* concerning the order and times of business, behaviour and record-keeping. Courts tried to better formality in other ways, as this helped to add to their dignity and standing. In 1710 Norfolk sessions ordered counsel to appear in their legal gowns. In 1729, to promote 'the better regularity of proceedings', the West Kent Justices forbade attorneys, solici-

[9] *VCH, Cheshire*, ii, p. 62; Dorset RO, QS orders, 1783–97; *VCH, Shropshire*, iii, p. 75; N. Landau, *The Justices of the Peace, 1679–1760* (California, 1984), p. 262.

tors and justices' clerks from making motions to the court, as in theory only barristers might address the bench. Better buildings were erected, especially from the 1770s, and alterations were made from time to time. Finance was reordered by an act of 1739. A single shire levy was derived from parish poor rates to ease collection.[10]

As important as these change was the growing use of committees. They audited accounts and did other work long before the 1690s, when their use increased particularly. At the Michaelmas 1689 sessions for Gloucestershire two magistrates were asked to examine and report on the accounts for the repair of Keynsham bridge. During the eighteenth century and later two or three justices met for a particular task, such as the repair of a bridge or prison, or for a financial matter. Occasionally the whole bench might attend a committee if it wished. Committees handled the building of prisons and shirehalls, these being of particular importance from the 1770s. By the 1790s courts were appointing a standing committee of 'visiting justices' to manage the gaols. In the early nineteenth century other standing committees were gradually set up, such as those for bridges.[11]

Magistrates were appointed by the crown on the advice of the lord lieutenant, who noted public feeling and might take advice. In nearly every county the gentry constituted the majority of justices. This was inevitable as the work was unpaid and parliament opposed 'persons of mean estate'. At first the only qualification for office was that justices should be 'of the most sufficient knights, esquires and gentlemen of the law in the county', needing an estate of £20 a year; this was raised to £100 by the act of 12 George II c. 10. It did not exclude lawyers, well-to-do clergy, merchants and manufacturers.[12]

In the later eighteenth century clergy became a noticeable minority on benches, in some counties earlier and to a greater extent than in others. In Hertfordshire only 2 per cent of the justices were clergy in the seventeenth century, the proportion was a quarter in 1752–99 and greater in the next three decades. The Dorset bench had no clergy in the decade 1764–73 or again in the later 1720s and early 1730s. By the 1780s the clergy were numerous: of sixty-one justices attending in the three years

---

[10] Landau, *Justices of the Peace*, pp. 254–58; A. Fletcher, *Reform in the Provinces: The Government of Stuart England* (New Haven and London, 1986), p. 262; S. and B. Webb, *Parish and County*, p. 435; Moir, *Local Government*, pp. 99–101; see below p. 59.

[11] S. and B. Webb, *Parish and County*, pp. 529–33; LSE, Webb Collection, Gloucestershire 123; G.C.F. Forster, 'Government in Provincial England under the Later Stuarts', *Transactions of the Royal Historical Society*, 33 (1983), p. 38.

[12] Moir, *Local Government*, p. 40.

1821–23, twenty-six were clergy. Nottinghamshire began using them later: the first clergyman came to its bench in 1793 – and in the next seven years there were four energetic clerical justices. In contrast, clergy outnumbered the laity at the Leicestershire sessions in the 1790s. Between 1800 and 1824 the Northumberland bench had usually one clergyman or none, although its total size was relatively small. The larger Suffolk bench, with many clergy at this time, was more normal. The change reflected rising social status and prosperity among the clergy, especially cathedral prebends, rectors and pluralists. Tithes and glebe land became more valuable. While some clergy were children of professional families, perhaps in another county, a growing number of younger sons or relations of gentry were becoming parsons. Among active clergy on the Leicestershire bench in the 1790s Thomas Greaves, probably a Yorkshireman, was rector of Broughton Astley, where he owned the manor and part of the parish in right of his wife, the daughter of the previous rector, who had bought the estate in 1769. The father of Robert Burnaby (d. 1807) and Thomas Beaumont Burnaby (d. 1823) was the rector of Knighton and a prebend of Lincoln. Both held more than one living and Thomas was a landowner. Because of their education and moral vocation, many were active in local justice and administration. In Gloucestershire it was said about 1800 that '"the Magistracy" consists in many parts of the clergy. In this county [Gloucestershire] the business could not be done without them; "indeed they do nearly the whole"'.[13]

Justices linked with trade or manufacturing in some counties were usually men who had made fortunes and were withdrawing from managerial or directive work, or came from business families. In Lancashire, where the majority of justices were gentry, a few were mercantile men or came from a trading background, particularly in Liverpool or Manchester. Thomas Earle (1754–1822), of a Liverpool merchant family, was an active justice in the 1800s and 1810s. In his early life he had lived and worked as a merchant in Hanover Street, becoming mayor in 1787. He was a Volunteers commander during the French wars. He bought the Spekelands estate near Liverpool and built a mansion in 1804–5. Cotton manufacturers were not justices because they were thought to be unable to judge impartially in disputes between masters and men in

[13] G.E. Mingay, *The Gentry: The Rise and Fall of the Ruling Class* (London, 1976), p. 127; Moir, *Local Government*, pp. 40–42, 53; Dorset RO, QS orders, 1663–74, 1727–35, 1783–97, 1819–27; G. Welby, 'Rulers of the Countryside and the Justices of the Peace in Nottinghamshire, 1775–1800', *Transactions of the Thoroton Society of Nottinghamshire*, 78 (1974), p. 76; Leicestershire RO, QS 5/1/7–8; LSE, Webb Collection: Northumberland 211; Suffolk 230.

the industry. The membership of the Gloucestershire bench was influenced by the cloth industry around Stroud and the trading city of Bristol on its borders in the 1780s and 1790s, as Moir shows. Of the two clothiers attending most regularly, Sir G.O. Paul had handed the mill he had inherited to a cousin; and Nathaniel Winchcombe gave just one day in ten to supervising his mills. The Bristol merchants built mansions on the outskirts of their city or owned country estates, though remaining closely linked to the city as officials or merchants.[14] With the growing wealth of the outports and industrial areas between 1650 and the early nineteenth century, it is probable that justices connected with trade or manufacture became more numerous.

Senior lawyers, such as recorders, sergeants at law and barristers, were justices throughout the period in counties as near to London as Kent and as far from it as Shropshire. Normally they had studied at the Inns of Court and occasionally were doctors of law. Their legal knowledge was valuable to the courts. A few physicians attended everywhere.[15] Men linked with trade or the professions were most numerous in counties near London for the whole period. Parts were very populous and the absence of sufficient gentry led to their appointment to commissions. In north-west Kent around Deptford brewers were justices in 1751, while those in Blackheath hundred were tradesmen or professional people who were sometimes wealthy and lived in suburban villas but lacked estates. A little later Burke unfairly condemned similar men among the Middlesex justices as 'the scum of the earth – carpenters, brickmakers and shoemakers; some of whom were notoriously men of such infamous characters that they were unworthy of any employ whatsoever, and others so ignorant that they could scarcely write their own names'. In fact in the 1780s and 1790s several leading architects (James Paine, Sir Robert Taylor and Henry Holland) were justices and served on the building committees for the great Clerkenwell bridewell begun in 1788.[16]

Some of the gentry justices were on their benches for decades. A few landowning families supplied magistrates over two or three generations. The gentry varied from men owning extensive estates of many

[14] T.A. Earle, 'Earle of Allerton Tower', *Transactions of the Historic Society of Lancashire and Cheshire* 42 (1892), pp. 52–55; *Parliamentary Debates*, 26, p. 100; Moir, *Local Government*, pp. 50–52.

[15] *VCH, Shropshire*, iii, pp. 95, 119; Moir, *Local Government*, p. 53; PRO, E 362/3, 6, 8, 10.

[16] Landau, *Justices of the Peace*, pp. 316–17; S. and B. Webb, *Parish and County*, p. 325; C.W. Chalklin, 'The Reconstruction of London's Prisons, 1770–1799: An Aspect of the Growth of Georgian London', *London Journal*, 9 (1983), pp. 25–27, 30.

thousand acres in different parts of the county, or often in two or three adjoining counties, to those whose property was several farms in two or three adjoining parishes. For most of the period benches tended to include a higher proportion of the wealthier gentry than the poorer. Often the great county names had at least one or two representatives at sessions. Some were deputy lieutenants and borough or county MPs. In most counties outside the south east the typical gentry justices came from families founded in the sixteenth or seventeenth centuries. The Dorset bench between 1664 and 1673 included former royalists such as John Tregonwell (1625–80), who lived at Milton Abbey, seven miles north east of Dorchester. William Okeden (d. 1696) lived in a mansion on an estate at More Crichel near Blandford, which had passed to his family on a marriage with the heiress of the Uvedale family in 1598. Some of the Lancashire bench near the end of the eighteenth century belonged to families who had owned estates for several centuries, either through the male or female line. Wilson Bradyll of Conishead Priory, Ulverston, who attended the Lancaster sessions, was the heir of Thomas Bradyll (d. 1776) who had modernised their mansion. Although the Bradylls had been settled first near Whalley, Blackburn, on another estate, and a John Bradyll had bought and sold monastic land in the sixteenth century, a later Bradyll married the heiress of the wealthy Dodding family and had settled at Conishead. The ancestors of Sir Ashton Lever of Alkrington Hall (b. 1729 and a justice from 1766) had been clothiers in the seventeenth century, though his father, who had built the hall in 1735 and been high sheriff, was a gentleman. The Lever property extended over much of south-east Lancashire, including Manchester and its neighbourhood. There were often a varying number of justices whose fathers and grandfathers had been in trade or industry and had used the fortunes they had made to buy an estate. Such men were numerous in the south east, where wealthy Londoners bought land. While lesser gentry with property in two or three parishes always attended, except under George I and George II the larger landowners were normally regarded as having a right to be there. Sometimes they attended infrequently because their views would be respected even in their absence. In the decades after 1700 the gentry of the North Riding normally attended the sessions in their own district. Sir James Pennyman went to Guisborough meetings, writing to his fellow justices at another bench in 1721 to emphasise the importance of active high constables. In Nottinghamshire, where sessions business was handled in three divisions with a meeting in each one, several hundreds were reallocated in 1776 'during such time as George Smith resides there [East Stoke] and may choose to act for the Nottingham division of Quarter Sessions'. Peers were seldom prominent as justices even before 1714; after 1714 they hardly ever attended some sessions, such as those of Shropshire. Other benches sometimes had one or two aristocrats. Between 1800 and 1810 Bedfordshire sessions were joined occasionally by the duke of Bedford or his sons, the marquess of Bute and the heir to an earldom who later became lord lieutenant. The London brewer and Bedfordshire landowner Samuel Whitbread was regular. Most were well-established or new gentry or energetic clergy. One reason for the frequent absence of peers was probably residence in London or on an estate elsewhere, accounting for the absence of a strong local interest. Another factor was that it was unnecessary. They were always consulted on important issues because of their social standing. When the eastern division of Sussex built a new county hall at Lewes between 1808 and 1812 the building committee met weekly for over a year; the local landowner, the earl of Chichester, was contacted at every stage but attended rarely.[17]

Benches did not differ simply in the background and status of their members. As has been shown, their size changed, with a slight decline in many counties between about 1720 and 1760, and then a gradual rise, becoming sharp from the 1790s. The degree of enthusiasm also varied. The major landowners led most benches until the death of Queen Anne. This was helped by the remodelling of commissions in 1660 at the Restoration and following the Exclusion Crisis after 1681, as Tories constituted the majority of wealthy property owners. The conflict of Whigs and Tories under William III and Anne encouraged attendance at sessions by members of leading families interested in politics and elections as well as social order. Between 1715 and 1760 Whig governments kept Tories off the commissions; Whig landowners did not trouble often to

[17] J. Hutchins, *The History and Antiquities of the County of Dorset* (3rd edn, London, 1861–73), ii, pp. 130, 685, 720, 726, iii, pp. 8, 128, 468, 628–29, iv, pp. 63, 372, 414; Lancashire RO, QS 02/120–69; T.D. Whitaker, *A History of Richmondshire in the North Riding [Together with] the Wapentakes of Lonsdale, Ewecross and Amounderness in the Counties of York, Lancashire and Westmoreland* (London, 1823), ii, p. 398; D. Foster, 'The Changing Social Origins and Political Allegiances of Lancashire JPs, 1821–51' (unpublished Ph.D. thesis, University of Lancaster, 1971), p. 44; W.J. Smith, 'Sir Ashton Lever of Alkrington and his Museum, 1729–1788', *Transactions of the Lancashire and Cheshire Antiquarian Society* 72 (1965), pp. 61–73; J.S. Cockburn, 'The North Riding Justices, 1690–1750', *Yorkshire Archaeological Journal*, 41 (1963–66), p. 482; Welby, 'Rulers of the Countryside', p. 76; J. Godber, *History of Bedfordshire, 1066–1888* (Bedford, 1969), p. 422; R.F. Dell, 'The Building of the County Hall, Lewes, 1808–12', *Sussex Archaeological Collections*, 100 (1962), p. 5; *VCH, Shropshire*, iii, pp. 95, 117; Moir, *Local Government*, p. 45.

be at sessions because they did not have to compete with Tories and their enthusiasm for business waned. At least in some counties in the south east smaller landowners, often linked with trade or the professions, were the most frequent members, as in Buckinghamshire.[18]

From the 1760s the reappearance of Tories and the increased number of justices due to the growth of population swelled the benches. While many were lesser gentry, at least a few leading families reappeared. Some of them were more dedicated than those of the mid eighteenth century. This is noticeable from the 1770s. Paul Langford quotes the contemporary remark about the Buckinghamshire justice Thomas Hampden in 1779 who 'talk'd of Militia, Farming and Justice business all day long'. A few magistrates gave outstanding service to their county from zeal and sense of duty. Among them were T.B. Bayley in Lancashire (1744–1802), Sir G.O. Paul in Gloucestershire (1746–1820), and the Rev. J.T. Becher of Nottinghamshire, a social economist who handled the rebuilding of Southwell bridewell in 1806 and led the maintenance of order in the popular disturbances of 1811–12.[19] Several reasons may be suggested for the greater enthusiasm of some justices. More clerical magistrates on the bench helped to encourage greater zeal and understanding of various problems. Some of them took a keen interest in prison reform and the trial of criminals, as their education and background gave them a good understanding of the law. They wanted to bolster their local influence and personal ties with the gentry by acting on the bench. Rising rents followed higher corn prices and encouraged greater expenditure. The growing efficiency of national administration, with tighter control of expenditure from the 1780s, had a local counterpart. The gentry as a class felt growing fear of the lower orders following the French Revolution. The apparent threat to life and property led them to give particular attention to the punishment and reform of criminals. Finally, the growing refinement of manners and humanitarianism encouraged the creation of healthier prisons, the more careful control of alehouses and a measure of sympathy for lunatics.

Sessions had three major areas of responsibility. First, there was the problem of poverty, which included the supervision of the poor law run by overse-

[18] P.B. Munsche, *Gentlemen and Poachers: The English Game Laws, 1671–1831* (Cambridge, 1981), p. 84; P. Langford, *Public Life and the Propertied Englishmen, 1689–1798* (Oxford, 1991), pp. 392–401; Landau, *Justices of the Peace*, p. 262.

[19] Langford, *Public Life*, pp. 393–95, 403–6; for Bayley and Paul see below pp. 170, 172–73; F.O. Darrall, *Popular Disturbances and Public Order in Regency England* (London, 1934), p. 244; for the activity of some justices in suppressing disorder, see pp. 234–44.

ers of the parishes and local justices, and the passage of vagrants. Secondly, courts were responsible for the easing of the movement of traffic through the county by foot, horse and wheeled vehicle. They supervised the local maintenance of roads and many small bridges, themselves handling the repair of larger bridges. Thirdly, they had care of prisons and their inmates. Quarter sessions also dealt with a variety of regulatory business, usually involving the enforcement of statutes. Over the whole period the amount of business grew greatly. Activities increased between the Restoration and the beginning of the eighteenth century as a result of growing legislation. Work grew relatively little during the sixty or seventy years after 1700; though some new legislation needed implementing, certain laws inherited from the previous two centuries became gradually less used. From the 1770s business increased steadily. In Gloucestershire the total number of judicial cases in 1775–79 averaged 109 annually (thirty-nine per session in 1775); in 1795–99 the expansion of routine business led to 214 cases annually (sixty-two per session in 1795).[20]

Throughout the period the supervision of the various types of poor law was a major concern. The bulk of administrative work recorded in order books concerns poor law business. Parish officers were guided by local justices but, when there was uncertainty or dispute, quarter sessions decisions gave supervision and control to the working of the whole poor law. Parishioners' appeals against poor rate assessments and appeals by parishes about removal orders were heard frequently. There were 995 removal appeals in Cambridgeshire between 1660 (when the system began) and 1831. In the larger North Riding of Yorkshire 581 are recorded in the years 1700–49. The Suffolk sessions order books in the 1820s record chiefly poor rate and settlement appeals. Affiliation proceedings also kept sessions busy. The North Riding court had 330 recognizances binding putative fathers to attend between 1700 and 1749. In Lancashire bastardy orders in the 1770s and 1780s were always very numerous at the sessions in Wigan – on 10 April 1780 sentences covered ten pages of the order book. With the growth of illegitimacy in the later eighteenth century orders increased.[21]

Before the 1790s, quarter sessions did not try to formulate a policy on the poor; apart from handling appeals and bastardy orders, they left the

[20] Moir, *Local Government*, p. 110.
[21] Cockburn, 'North Riding Justices', pp. 505, 508; *Kentish Sources*, iv, *The Poor*, ed. E. Melling (Maidstone, 1964), p. 68. The Hertfordshire orders illustrate the growth in numbers (330 between 1752 and 1799): *Hertfordshire County Records: Sessions Books 1700 to 1752*, 7, ed. W. Le Hardy (Hertford, 1931); and *Sessions Books 1752 to 1799*, 8, ed. W. Le Hardy (Hertford, 1935).

overseers and vestries to follow custom and precedent. From the 1790s, they became more interventionist in the face of growing economic strains on the poor and the need to relieve the able-bodied. Particularly in the south, paternalist benches often interfered to increase allowances. In one emergency, the grave food shortage of 1795, they took what amounted to legislative action. Most counties south of the line from the Severn to the Wash followed Buckinghamshire, Berkshire and Hampshire in printing tables showing the weekly income to be ensured to each family, varying according to the price of wheat. In Buckinghamshire the court, taking into 'consideration the situation of the poor industrious labourers and their families', decided to abandon the 'roundsman' system and ordered the income of each family to be made up from the poor rates to a minimum of six shillings a week for a married couple, with additions for children. The control of policy on poor law matters by sessions is shown by the fact that most bills on poor law matters were handed round the justices for discussion.[22]

The passing of vagrants on their way to their parish of settlement was another way in which the poor were managed. From the beginning of the eighteenth century constables were paid according to fixed rates for transporting and lodging vagrants; or contractors were appointed at a fixed annual sum to convey all vagrants. Removing vagrants was a major county expense throughout the century, though the proportion of the county rates spent on conveying them declined in later decades, as expenditure grew on such items as gaols and bridges. Numbers rose with the growth of unemployment after the end of wars. Considering the earlier period, vagrancy was the chief burden on county finances in Shropshire, with its important London-Chester road, in the early and mid eighteenth century. In the North Riding about 600 vagrants were passed in the seven years 1708–14; between 1736 and 1749 there may have been less than 200 a year. Most were women, often alone, and children. The large number earlier may represent an influx of Scots; or tight administration to cure the original excess of vagrancy. A contractor was appointed in 1714 at £80 a year for the vagrants on the Great North Road. In the early nineteenth century Cambridgeshire has evidence on the number of vagrants passing to and from London on its section of the same road. At the border town of Royston there were 569 tramps in 1803, 540 in 1807–8, 1014 in 1811–12, 2894 in 1815–16 and 6689 in

---

[22] P. Dunkley, 'Paternalism, the Magistracy and Poor Relief in England, 1795–1834', *International Review of Social History*, 24 (1979), pp. 376–86; S. and B. Webb, *Parish and County*, pp. 544–47; J.R. Poynter, *Society and Pauperism: English Ideas on Poor Relief, 1795–1834* (London, 1969), p. 11.

1819–20, the two last dates falling in a period of postwar demobilisation and insufficient work. In 1817 there were said to be about 50,000 English vagrants. The working of the system may be illustrated by Hertfordshire, also crossed by the Great North Road, with its tramps from London. Here the 'rates and prizes' for passing vagrants were set out in April 1703 and repeated annually until 1707. From 1718 a contractor was paid £200 a year. After the office was ended in 1740, and ensuing complaints and difficulties, the treasurer took the job at £220 a year. A succession of contractors was then appointed until 1784. Subsequently, after a committee had considered the whole matter of the cost of vagrancy, it was decided to split the county into districts with a contractor for each part. Epiphany sessions 1786 provided an almost verbatim definition of vagrants from 12 Anne 2 c. 23 for the benefit of all constables, and laid down 'rules and regulations' for the conduct of contractors. This method continued until 1832, when the county reverted to one contractor, appointed at £610 a year, reduced to £500 when the contract was renewed in 1833.[23]

In the seventeenth century there were several other ways in which the counties dealt with or alleviated some of the poor. Each county provided money from the rates for the relief of poor inmates in the London prisons of the King's Bench and Marshalsea. Disability pensions were given to soldiers and sailors, and lump sums or pensions to their widows. Both practices were based on statutes. Occasionally, too, grants were made to individuals who had suffered misfortune. But these were special methods of helping a few poor. The second and third practices died out in the early eighteenth century.[24]

Roads and bridges took up much quarter sessions' time. Parishes were expected to maintain their own roads by labour provided by the occupiers of lands and other householders. In the later seventeenth century there was legislation enabling parishes to apply to the justices for permission to levy a rate for the upkeep of their highways. Thus at Trinity sessions 1736 in Wiltshire eight parishes or tythings were allowed to levy 6d. rates for highway repair, by separate orders.[25] If a parish neglected

[23] *VCH, Shropshire*, iii, p. 122; Cockburn, 'North Riding Justices', p. 512; *Victoria History of the County of Cambridgeshire*, ii, ed. L.F. Salzman (London, 1948), pp. 101–3; see note 21 above for Hertfordshire records.

[24] *The Poor*, ed. Melling, pp. 37–38; *Hertfordshire County Records*, 7, pp. xxvi–xxviii; 8, pp. xxxiv–xxxvi, 344–45; 9, pp. xx–xxi.

[25] *Wiltshire Quarter Sessions and Assizes, 1736*, ed. J.P.M. Fowle, Wiltshire Archaeological Society Records Branch, 11 (1955), pp. 74–76; S. and B. Webb, *English Local Government: The Story of the King's Highway* (London, 1913), pp. 51–53.

its duty to repair the roads, the remedy was effected by means of a judicial process, through taking legal action against the inhabitants. Under common law it was open to anyone to indict the inhabitants of a parish at quarter sessions or assizes whenever the king's highway became 'ruinous, miry, deep, broken and in great decay' so as to be 'to the great damage and common nuisance of all the liege subjects of our said Lord the King'. At quarter sessions a fine was imposed; it was usually deferred for three months, to give the parish time to put the road in repair. If the parish did the work, and one or two justices certified that the road was repaired, the fine was excused. If the repairs were not done, the sheriff was directed to levy the fine by distress on an occupier of the parish, paying it either to the parish surveyor of the highways or someone else for mending the road. Thus in Suffolk in 1765 the court ordered the sheriff to levy a fine of £50 set upon the inhabitants of the parish of Brent Ely for not repairing a road which had been presented for being out of repair, no certificate having been produced that it had been repaired pursuant to an order of 8 October 1764. The following year 'it appearing to this Court that the road in the parish of Westerfield, presented . . . for being out of repair, is duly and sufficiently repaired and amended, this Court doth therefore remit the fine of £40 set upon them for that offence'.[26]

Quarter sessions also tried to control nuisances committed by people on the public highways, again using the judicial process. There were frequent indictments for allowing animals to stray, not cutting hedges, permitting ditches to overflow, encroachment on the highways or waste ground on the edge, undermining highways, putting refuse in the streets and using them for slaughtering meat. At Manchester in April 1751 one justice, for example, made seven presentments of nuisances for obstructing the highway by placing on it varying quantities of manure.[27] A further way in which quarter sessions were concerned with roads was through legislation intended to preserve road surfaces by regulating the number and size of wheels on vehicles, the number of horses used, and the weight they carried. Sometimes the justices were asked to waive the regulations and allow the use of extra horses on certain hills.[28]

In the eighteenth and early nineteenth centuries the courts were also concerned with the diversion of roads. Originally the only legal way to divert a highway was by royal licence following a writ and inquisition of

---

[26] LSE, Webb Collection, Suffolk, vol. 230.
[27] S. and B. Webb, *The Story of the King's Highway*, p. 82.
[28] *Kentish Sources: Some Roads and Bridges*, ed. E. Melling (Maidstone, 1959), p. 36.

ad quod damnum, which enquired whether the king or his subjects would be harmed by the proposed alteration. From 1697 quarter sessions were involved. After the issue of a writ *ad quod damnum* and the ensuing inquisition, a right of appeal to quarter sessions was allowed. If no appeal was made the inquisition and return were deposited with the clerk of the peace. An act of 1773 increased the powers of the justices. An order made by two justices with the consent of the landowners was to be confirmed by quarter sessions at a public meeting, if there was no appeal. Thus in 1782 a small section of road was diverted in Bromley, Kent, so as to lie further from a house belonging to the landowner. Two justices made the order and received his consent the same day. In January 1783 they certified that the highway had been properly made; at quarter sessions at Maidstone on 16 January the order and certificate were publicly read in open court, then enrolled among the records. Diversions were almost innumerable. In Kent there were 257 between 1773 and 1830.[29]

Many of the main bridges in most counties were the responsibility of the justices, who had to order and pay for repairs or (if necessary) have the bridges rebuilt. Occasionally, they erected a new bridge in the place of a ford; more frequently, they widened bridges if there was an obvious public need. Bridges constituted an increasingly important aspect of the work of quarter sessions as the number for which they were responsible grew from the 1770s and 1780s, and particularly in the early nineteenth century. Bridges reparable by parishes or individuals were presented at quarter sessions in case of neglect so that judicial action might be taken.

Prisons and their inmates were another growing concern of the courts in the later part of the period. The justices were involved with two types of local prison: the county gaol and the house of correction (or bridewell). Gaols before the last quarter of the eighteenth century were primarily places of safe custody for those awaiting trial – or punishment in the form of execution, whipping or transportation; or in custody over debts. On an average half the prisoners were debtors, for the discharge of whom there were periodic orders. Until late in the century gaols were run by the gaolers as a business for their own profit: prisoners paid fees to the gaoler and also paid him for their board and lodging if they could afford it; they also bought liquor from his taproom. Justices could build and repair gaols and were also empowered to give poor prisoners who were unable to provide for themselves a small daily allowance of bread and beer. Houses of correction were basically criminal workhouses to which the vagrant poor and other minor offenders were sent for short sentences involving in principle

[29] Ibid., pp. 41–43; Centre for Kentish Studies, Q/RH2/1–257.

some work, with the costs of maintaining them (including the salary of the master) paid by quarter sessions.[30] Prison repairs were made periodically between the 1660s and 1760s and new prisons were occasionally bought or erected; the number of houses of correction increased particularly between about 1700 and 1720. From the 1770s and more especially in the 1780s the prison reform movement inspired by John Howard, the growing use of imprisonment for punishment and the general increase of population led to the reconstruction or enlargement of most county gaols and houses of correction, designed to put into practice the principles of the reformers. The reform movement brought salaried officials into county gaols, including chaplains (1773) and paid gaolers, in lieu of men receiving profits from the sale of liquors, under an act of 1784, and paid turnkeys varying in number according to the size of the prison. Detailed rules and regulations were introduced. Under an act of 1791 visiting justices were appointed for goals and bridewells. Peel's act of 1823 'for the first time made it peremptorily the duty of the justices to organize their prisons on a prescribed plan' and to make quarterly reports to the Home Secretary.[31] All this not only greatly increased county expenditure, it involved the courts in much more work.

Quarter sessions dealt with a variety of licensing and regulatory business in the later seventeenth century and the early and mid eighteenth century, and the amount grew steadily from the 1770s. In the first part of the period the implementation of statutes dealing with working life was a considerable part of the work of the justices, although sometimes done in a half-hearted way. The assize of bread was applied occasionally by quarter sessions, particularly in time of scarcity, though it was often treated as a dead letter. They continued to act under the Statute of Artificers (1563). In the East Riding, for example, the justices handled apprenticeship petitions involving masters wanting to discharge unsuitable apprentices and apprentices seeking discharge from their masters. People were still presented for trading without due apprenticeship, though the practice was dying out in the early eighteenth century; in the North Riding at Northallerton sessions on 28 July 1702 two bricklayers were presented for using the trade of plasterers without legal apprenticeship.[32] The regulation of wage rates by justices

[30] *Kentish Sources: Crime and Punishment*, ed. E. Melling (Maidstone, 1969), pp. 203–4.

[31] S. and B. Webb, *English Local Government: English Prisons under Local Government* (London, 1963), p. 74.

[32] G.C.F. Forster, *The East Riding Justices of the Peace in the Seventeenth Century* (York, 1973), p. 55; *North Riding Record Society Publications*, 7, *Quarter Sessions Records*, ed. J.C. Atkinson (1889), p. 187; E.G. Dowdell, *A Hundred Years of Quarter Sessions: The Government of Middlesex from 1660 to 1760* (Cambridge, 1932), p. 182; LSE, Webb Collection 141, 230; Norfolk and Norwich RO, Y/C12/1, 1719–28 (information from Dr R.G. Edrich).

in the seventeenth century continued into the early part of the eighteenth century. In Warwickshire it was continued by the justices at their Easter sessions down to 1779.[33] Since 1563, too, the clerk of the peace had been expected to keep a register of badgers, laders, kidders, carriers and drovers (who needed a licence), reflecting public hostility to middlemen who committed market offences.[34] Another duty, under an act of 1692, was the setting down of rates for the carriage of goods by road to prevent price fixing by carriers. Not all counties issued rates at first, and among those that did issue them there was a tendency to repeat them formally over the years without alteration. Thus the Derbyshire assessment of 1808 was the same as 1754, despite the price rises of the intervening years. Other rates were similar to actual charges for most of the period. The act was in force until 1827.[35]

Apprenticeship continued to be a subject for quarter sessions because it was still generally used to provide training for young people; the licensing of badgers was ended in 1772. Most quarter sessions were ceasing to issue wage rates by the mid eighteenth century because parliament was gradually ending trying to control various aspects of working life. On the other hand, the squirearchy in parliament were maintaining and extending the game laws with enthusiasm because it affected their own estates and personal pleasures: under acts of 1706 and 1710, for the better preservation of game, gamekeepers were licensed by the courts at the request of the lord of the manor.[36]

Other responsibilities inherited from an earlier period concerned religious and social matters. Briefs were issued to collect money for the rebuilding of churches or the relief of towns or villages which had suffered from fire. Although the lord chancellor issued the brief, quarter sessions assessed the value of the loss after taking expert opinion and drew up any petition to him. Collections, usually of a few pence at a time, were made all over England. Thus in Leicestershire at Michaelmas sessions 1758 a brief was sought for the steeple of Lutterworth church, the damage being estimated at £1162.[37] There were several more instances in the following years. Individuals could obtain letters of licence from

[33] Styles, *Development of County Administration*, p. 7.

[34] *Guide to the Kent Archives Office*, ed. F. Hull (Maidstone, 1958), p. 27.

[35] T.S. Willan, 'The Justices of the Peace and the Rates of Land Carriage, 1692–1827', *Journal of Transport History*, 5 (1962), pp. 198–202; W. Albert, *The Turnpike Road System in England, 1663–1840* (Cambridge, 1973), pp. 168–69.

[36] *Kent Guide*, pp. 31–32.

[37] Leicestershire RO, QS 5/1/3, fol. 44; Styles, *Development of County Administration*, pp. 7–8.

quarter sessions to beg for relief in the county after suffering heavy loss, such as that caused by a fire. In the North Riding at Thirsk sessions on 14 April 1702 two Grosmont men petitioned for a collection in respect of a loss totalling £478 6s. 8d. from a fire which had consumed a dye-house, storehouses, a press-house, a large barn, a cowhouse and an ox-house, with livestock, cloths, wool, dyes and corn and hay and imple-ments.[38]

In the later seventeenth century the fitful implementation of religious statutes gave the justices a great deal of work. Thus Sunday and religious offences were by far the most numerous matters dealt with by Hertfordshire quarter sessions between 1658 and 1683 (Table 2.2). Cases before justices at various county quarter sessions included prosecutions for Sunday offences, presentments and convictions of recusants, and of dissenters for attending conventicles. Prosecution of Protestants ceased after the Toleration Act of 1689 and by the early 1700s the enforcement of the recusancy laws had been relaxed. Yet in the eighteenth century the absence of full religious toleration meant the continued existence of legislation relating to dissenters and papists which involved quarter sessions in several sorts of business. Meeting houses were registered with quarter sessions under the Toleration Act of 1689, and the eighteenth-century order books contain numerous entries recording the licensing of chapels. The number grew with the spread of dissent from the 1770s and 1780s. Declara-tions against transubstantiation and certificates of having taken the sacra-ments were required of office-holders. Very many people took oaths of allegiance and supremacy under acts of 1689, 1702, 1714 and 1722; dis-senting ministers made oaths and declarations. In addition, papist estates were registered under an act of 1715.[39]

Social business included in the seventeenth century prosecutions for erecting a cottage without 'laying four acres of ground' under an act of 1589. In most cases of illegal building the justices found some ground for it to be 'continued'. The use of the act was rarely invoked in the eighteenth century and it was repealed in 1775. The licensing of alehouses, with the taking of recognizances for good behaviour, went back to an act of 1552. It was dealt with not by quarter sessions but by two local justices meeting in 'brewster sessions' each September; quarter sessions dealt with cases of disorderly and unlicensed alehouses. Until the 1780s it is thought that licensing was a formality. From 1787, following the forma-

[38] Styles, *Development of County Administration*, p. 8; *North Riding Quarter Sessions Records*, 7, p. 186.

[39] *Kent Guide*, pp. 29–30; *Hertfordshire County Records*, 7, pp. 465–563.

tion of the Society for the Reformation of Manners among Lower Orders and a royal proclamation obtained by Wilberforce, quarter sessions sought to adopt a comprehensive licensing policy, controlling the number and regulating the conduct of public houses. The Nottinghamshire justices declared their intention of refusing a licence at brewster sessions to any persons not selling wine, chocolate, coffee, tea, ale, beer or other liquors – to stop the exclusive sale of spirits.[40]

New legislation from the 1770s included two laws concerning crops. Under an act of 1770 quarter sessions appointed inspectors to make weekly returns to the Treasury of the prices of corn in the principal markets. An act of 1781 made the justices responsible for the payment, out of the land tax, of bounties to growers of hemp and flax, and for forwarding returns of such payments to the Board of Trade.[41] The act of 26 George III c. 71 tried to reduce horse and cattle stealing by enforcing the licensing of slaughter-houses (other than butchers) by quarter sessions.[42] Quarter sessions became responsible for collecting accurate information on some social matters. The inquiries into poor law expenditure in 1776, 1785 and 1803 (and into charitable donations in 1785) were made by constables, overseers and justices' clerks, under the superintendance of quarter sessions, which forwarded returns to the government and paid the costs from the county rates. The census returns from 1801 were handled in the same way.[43] Private asylums had to be inspected and licensed from 1775, theatres to be licensed from 1788. The rules of friendly societies had to be exhibited at quarter sessions under an act of 1793, and rules of savings banks and benefit societies deposited from 1817. Under the wartime Unlawful Societies Act (1799), freemasons' lodges had to submit annually lists of members. Notice of printing presses were also required.[44]

On the criminal side, the justices were concerned almost entirely with misdemeanours (especially assault) and petty larceny. In the later sixteenth and early seventeenth centuries the courts had dealt with cases of felony for which death sentences were imposed. This ended in the later seventeenth century, with the more serious charges going to the assizes. The growth of

[40] B. Osborne, *Justices of the Peace, 1361–1948* (Shaftesbury, 1960), p. 175; *Kent Guide*, p. 26; S. and B. Webb, *Parish and County*, p. 586; J.D. Chambers, *Nottinghamshire in the Eighteenth Century: A Study of Life and Labour under the Squirearchy* (London, 1932), p. 70; Moir, *Local Government*, p. 120.

[41] *Kent Guide*, p. 34; Styles, *Development of County Administration*, p. 9.

[42] F.G. Emmison, *Guide to the Essex Record Office* (Chelmsford, 1969), p. 43.

[43] Styles, *Development of County Administration*, p. 9.

[44] *Guide to the Kent Archives Office*, p. 31.

crimes punishable by death led to more reprieves recommended by the judges; it was also felt that capital cases were too serious matters for magistrates, and that such cases should be left to professional judges.[45]

Between 1650 and 1750 assault indictments were far more numerous than those for petty larceny. In rural areas stealing was mostly of livestock, crops and clothing. Larceny represented 17 per cent of Warwickshire sessions indictments between 1680 and 1690. In the North Riding the average between 1690 and 1750 was ten out of thirty. W. Le Hardy analysed the cases tried at Hertfordshire sessions (Table 2.2). Religious offences

Table 2.2

Offences Presented at Hertfordshire Quarter Sessions, 1658–83 and 1700–52

Offence	1658–83	1700–52
Assault	156	240
Presentments for repairs to roads, bridges, etc.	247	67
Larceny	63	63
Unlicensed and disorderly alehouses	226	44
Receiving inmates and undesirables	54	33
Nuisances and obstructions	63	28
Trading without due apprenticeship	117	24
Not attending juries	*	23
Building houses without four acres of land	46	15
Refusing to watch	*	15
Enclosure and encroachments	18	10
Sunday and religious offences	804	9
Rioting	33	9
Poaching	34	9
Trading without licences	142	8
Refusing to execute warrants	*	7
Swearing	7	7
Selling bad food	0	4
Refusing to assist in highway repairs	88	4
Drunk and disorderly	12	4
Fraud and false pretences	3	4
Libel	12	4
Refusing to assist constables	*	3
Burglary	0	3

(Offences marked * together amounted to eighty-four cases)

were the most numerous between the 1660s and 1680s, then almost disappeared. Presentments for assault were particularly prevalent and there were many larceny cases. Others were presented for conducting unlicensed and disorderly alehouses (to stop idleness and gaming which

[45] *Crime and Punishment*, ed. Melling, p. 3.

led to poverty), receiving inmates and trading without having served an apprenticeship or a licence. Prosecutions of parishes and individuals about road work seem to have become less necessary.[46]

The number of cases of assault and particularly of petty larceny was growing rapidly in the later eighteenth century. The most striking feature of the later eighteenth century in Hertfordshire was the growth of theft cases. In the years 1752–99, according to Le Hardy, there were 378 larceny offences compared with sixty-three between 1700 and 1752. Cases of assault and rioting rose from 249 to 362, and counterfeiting appeared for the first time. On the other hand, cases of non-repair of highways, of trading without due apprenticeship and of nuisance declined. All religious or Sabbath day offences, receiving inmates, building houses without four acres of land, and so on, disappeared.[47]

The number of larceny cases handled by quarter sessions grew everywhere in the early nineteenth century. In Hertfordshire between 1799 and 1833 there were 552 cases of assault and riot compared with 352 between 1752 and 1799, an increase which may be explained largely in terms of the growth of population; on the other hand, the number of larceny cases rose from 378 to 908. Crime was increasing particularly rapidly in urban areas, where there was much more shoplifting and theft of personal possessions and household goods, as retail trade expanded and people lower down the social scale had more possessions.[48] Juvenile delinquency was very noticeable in towns. In Warwickshire, where part of the population lay in the large and growing towns of Birmingham and Coventry, the number of larceny cases before the courts grew dramatically. There were 445 convictions for larceny, fraud and related crimes in 1837, nearly as many as in the whole period 1775–1800; in 1773 there had only been three.[49] Crime in rural areas was also believed to be on the increase in the 1820s. In the mainly rural county of Shropshire a huge number of larceny cases was handled in this decade compared with cases of assault and malicious damage: especially frequent were thefts of clothing, but household goods, farm produce, stable gear and saddlery and tools and hardware were also often stolen. Quarter sessions were also handling more larceny cases because of the greater efficiency in the catching of criminals. In London, where the problem of urban crime was obviously more acute, paid police began to be

[46] Cockburn, 'North Riding Justices', pp. 487–91; *Hertfordshire County Records*, 7, p. xxxiii.
[47] *Hertfordshire County Records*, 8, p. xxxi.
[48] *Crime and Punishment*, ed. Melling, p. 94.
[49] Styles, *Development of County Administration*, p. 6.

appointed in the later eighteenth century. The urban improvement acts of the same period often included powers to raise rates to pay a watch. Private local associations were formed to catch criminals. By the 1810s and 1820s courts were beginning to try crimes more serious than petty larceny, adding to their work.[50]

The number of larceny cases fluctuated in the short run. The major causes were the price of food; and war and peace. The evidence shows that larceny indictments varied in a general way with prices in the eighteenth century. The North Riding court handled exceptional numbers of offences in periods of hardship caused by bad weather and poor harvests, such as 1709–10 and 1728–29. They peaked at forty-four in 1729 compared with an annual average of thirty. Property crime in rural parishes in Surrey and Sussex was also affected by harvests throughout the century. London and rural areas had reduced property crime in wartime, when poor men enlisted, and were almost overwhelmed by offences when peace and demobilisation came. Thus London crime was low in the mid 1740s and at a peak about 1750. The Seven Years War and the American War had a similar effect. Later the Napoleonic Wars involved unprecedented enlistment, but there was heavy unemployment and crime in 1816.[51]

Meetings of sessions over several days involved not only the justices and county officials, but also jurors, lawyers, witnesses, prisoners, high constables and people with claims. The magistrates dined and drank together during the proceedings and met friends on business and pleasure. Increasingly, their wives and families travelled with them if the sessions was in a town, eager to visit shopkeepers, such as drapers, vintners, goldsmiths and booksellers, to make social calls and to go to assemblies or private parties. As a social festivity sessions were less important than assizes, the county's grand ceremonial occasion. From the early eighteenth century the wealthier gentry attended the assizes as grand jurors or to meet friends, and especially to see the judges who were their contact with the central government. Again relations and servants helped to fill the town, and there were entertainments such as dances and races. The judges advised the justices on government policy, particularly in rela-

[50] Ibid., p. 4; M. Ignatieff, *A Just Measure of Pain: The Penitentiary in the Industrial Revolution, 1750–1850* (London, 1978), pp. 180–83; M.C. Hill, *County of Salop: Abstract of the Quarter Sessions Records, 1820–1830* (Shrewsbury, 1974); M.D. George, *London Life in the Eighteenth Century* (1925; reprinted London, 1966), pp. 21, 28–31; W. Holdsworth, *A History of English Law*, xiii (London, 1952), pp. 188–89.

[51] Cockburn, 'North Riding Justices', p. 491; J.M. Beattie, *Crime and the Courts in England, 1660–1800* (Oxford, 1986), pp. 201–12.

tion to the punishment of crimes. Thus at Guildford (Surrey) assizes in August 1768 the judges emphasised the majesty of the law because authority seemed threatened by smugglers, corn rioters and radicals; but rioters and troops who had shot political demonstrators were to be tried. On other occasions, the judges complained about the state of the shire hall or the gaol to accelerate renovation, being able to impose a fine if no action was taken. In 1801 the Worcestershire gaol and bridewell were presented by the grand jury at the recommendation of the judges; from 1802 to 1808 the judges complained about the justices' neglect and threatened a fine. Some decisions by sessions were approved by the judges, such as regulations for the new prisons from the 1780s. The grand jury presented prisons or shire halls as unsuitable before they were rebuilt. The principal work of assizes was judicial, trying the more serious crimes such as murders, highway robbery, burglary, embezzlement and horse-stealing.[52]

The county meeting was the other official occasion linked to the work of the justices. Strictly it was summoned by the sheriff and comprised county freeholders. From 1779 these meetings were used by political reformers to organise local opinion. When acts were obtained for building, they followed petitions to parliament by county meetings. For example, Devon and Staffordshire received statutes for gaols by this means in the 1780s, and Gloucestershire and Herefordshire for shire halls in the 1810s. Throughout the period unofficial meetings were held or soundings of opinion taken on account of the cost of building. In 1675–76 the repair of the shire hall and rebuilding of the gaol and house of correction by the Warwickshire bench was authorised by the assize judges, grand jurors, most justices, high constables, lords of the manor, freeholders and inhabitants throughout the county. A meeting of gentry preceded the erection of the Warwickshire shire hall in 1753–58. Both needed special rates. A special Leicestershire sessions was held on 5 August 1789 before the building of the gaol; it was the first day of the assizes when all notables were in Leicester. The previous sessions advertised that 'we request the acting Justices, Grand Jury, and other Gentlemen of the county to attend, as the subject is of great importance to the county, and will be attended

[52] F.W. Jessup, *Sir Roger Twysden, 1597–1672* (London, 1965), pp. 163–68; Moir, *Local Government*, pp. 139–41; J. Brewer, 'The Wilkites and the Law, 1763–74: A Study of Radical Notions of Governance', in *An Ungovernable People: The English and their Law in the Seventeenth and Eighteenth Centuries*, ed. J. Brewer and J. Styles (London, 1980), pp. 133–36; Worcestershire RO, BA 3, 122, orders concerning the new county gaol, 1808–11 (one volume); A. Rosen, 'Winchester in Transition, 1580–1700', in *County Towns in Pre-Industrial England*, ed. P. Clark, (Leicester, 1981), pp. 152, 176–77.

with vast expense'. Meetings were also held before the building of prisons in Gloucestershire, Hampshire and Lincolnshire at this time, presumably because the expenditure was unprecedented. While some gatherings may not have been traced, it is likely that most buildings in the eighteenth and early nineteenth century were approved simply by sessions and assizes after presentment.[53]

Other less formal opportunities for discussion among groups of justices and other gentry existed. Some gentry lived in the county town or its neighbourhood, stayed there for part of the year, or visited it frequently for shopping or entertainment. In 1774 many Derbyshire gentry were spending much of the year in Derby. There were county societies in London and Bath. Much circulation of ideas and many unrecorded debate undoubtedly preceded the formal resolutions of quarter sessions about building. The principal reason was the cost. We must now discuss county income and expenditure.[54]

[53] B. Keith-Lucas, 'County Meetings', *Law Quarterly Review*, 70 (1954), pp. 109–12; Gloucestershire RO, Q/AS 1; Herefordshire RO, QS, shire hall minutes, 1814–19; *Victoria History of the County of Staffordshire*, vi, ed. M.W. Greenslade and D.A. Johnson (Oxford, 1979), p. 204; A.C. Wood, *The Rebuilding of the Shire Hall, Warwick in the Mid Eighteenth Century* (Warwick, 1983), pp. 5, 7; *Leicester Journal*, 17 July 1789; Lincolnshire RO, Lindsey QS sessions minutes concerning the county gaol, 1785, p. 25; *Salisbury and Winchester Journal*, 30 August 1784; J.R.S. Whiting, *Prison Reform in Gloucestershire, 1776–1820* (Chichester, 1975), p. 11.

[54] Langford, *Public Life*, pp. 379–84.

3

County Finance

Between the seventeenth century and 1830 county expenditure grew greatly on a changing and widening range of matters, although it always remained much less than parish poor relief or the land tax. The cost of criminal justice became increasingly heavy. In the later seventeenth century most counties rebuilt or altered a prison or shire hall. The upkeep of bridewells, payments for hospitals and other charitable needs came from the rate for the relief of prisoners in the King's Bench and Marshalsea. There was also a rate to support poor prisoners in gaol. Pensions given to 'maimed soldiers' were another major expense. The counties also spent varying but often considerable amounts on bridges, for which there was a separate bridge rate.

An estimate of total county income for these purposes in this period is impossible. About a quarter of English counties have no records for all or most of the time. Surviving order or minute books rarely state the rates; alternatively they record only the bridge levies. Perhaps £70 or £80 a year on average was spent by a shire on bridges, though sums varied from several hundred pounds to trivial amounts. Exceptionally Surrey was stated to levy £400 a year in addition to bridge rates by the end of the 1670s, and Devon received an average of £410 annually in 1632–39 inclusive (a total of £3284) for all except bridges. A little evidence survives for the principal maimed soldiers' rate: the North Riding raised £468 in 1662, Somerset spent £652 in 1673 and Kesteven £106 in 1687–88; Devon levied £565 in 1667, Shropshire £368 10s. for 201 pensioners in 1668, and Devon £376 (203 pensioners) in 1674. The Warwickshire bench voted £230 annually at Epiphany 1663; the smaller King's Bench and Marshalsea fund gave just £2 annually to these prisons; the rest was a general amount for county needs. In 1669–70 Somerset spent £193 on hospitals, compensation for property damaged by fire, people needing relief, and the salary of the keeper of the bridewell. An account survives of one of the Norfolk treasurers of this fund, collecting from eighteen out of thirty-four hundreds in 1672–73, which reveals the variety of payments. He levied £105 19s. 0d. and spent £117 10s. 0d. on keepers' wages and other costs for five houses of correction (£39 13s. 0d.), the salary of the doorkeeper (presumably a caretaker) at the shire hall, clerk's fees, repairs to bridges and bridewells, compensation for fire losses, release of prisoners in the Duchy of Lancaster gaol, and a surgeon's fee. The average county may have spent about £500 annually by the 1690s, so the income of the forty English counties was probably £18,000 or £20,000.[1]

For the period 1700–60 there is a little more evidence. Counties were responsible for passing vagrants, which was a major charge during the eighteenth century. There was now a vagrancy rate, which lasted until all the levies were amalgamated in 1739. Costs were high, particularly in counties crossed by main roads. The Hertfordshire bench paid a contractor £200 a year between 1718 and 1740, more than half its annual expenditure. In Norfolk, which was bigger but has the sea for more than half its county boundary, transporting tramps averaged about £130 or £140 a year in the 1720s, from a total outlay of about £1200 or £1300. In the North Riding, across the main road to Scotland, peak sessions expenditure on vagrants was between 1701 and 1716, the annual average being £338 from 1708 to 1714 when costs were greatest. From 1736 to 1749 the costs were £94 a year. In other counties expenditure was also high at the beginning of the century, when most existing vagrants were passed on. Wartime enlistment reduced outlay. The payment of pensions to maimed soldiers dwindled gradually in most shires; Norfolk was still giving over forty people sums in the 1720s. Out of an average total of about £1081 annual expenditure in 1721–28 (excluding bridges) Norfolk paid £223 on maimed soldiers and mariners, £136 on passing vagrants, £326 on prisoners in the Norwich Castle (with repairs), and £396 on the King's Bench and Marshalsea, the miscellaneous category. For most counties the cost of prisons and bridges was steady in the long run until the 1760s and 1770s. Prisoners' maintenance did not rise markedly, as hanging, transportation and whipping, not imprisonment, were the normal punishments for felons. On the other hand, the conveyance and prosecution of prisoners and coroner's fees became a cost from 1752, and the transportation of felons was a charge for the many counties that made use of it from 1718. For the decade 1730–39

---

[1] *Minutes of Proceedings in Quarter Sessions Held for the Parts of Kesteven in the County of Lincoln, 1674–1695*, i, ed. S.A. Peyton, Lincoln Record Society, 25 (1931), pp. lxxxi–lxxxv; *Warwick County Records*, 4, *Quarter Sessions Records, 1657–1665*, ed. S.C. Ratcliff and H.C. Johnson (Warwick, 1938), p. xxx; *Norfolk Quarter Sessions Order Book, 1650–1657*, ed. D.E. Howell James, Norfolk Record Society, 26 (1955), p. 15; *Surrey Quarter Sessions Records: Order Books and Sessions Rolls, 1659–1666*, ed. D.L. Powell and H. Jenkinson, Surrey Record Society, 35, 36, 39 (1934–35, 1938); Norfolk RO, C/Sba 2/2/5/15; Surrey RO, QS 2/1/3 p. 438; Devon RO, QS 1/7, Michaelmas 1639.

Gloucestershire spent £830 12s. 0d. and for three years 1730–39 Lincolnshire paid £379 17s. 0d. on this latter task. Militiamen's families were an additional cost during the Seven Years War. Altogether expenditure rose; although outlay on maimed soldiers' pensions gradually disappeared, vagrancy was a major charge from the 1700s, with costs growing in the 1740s and 1750s. Hertfordshire rates rose from £200 in 1701–10 to £600 in the 1750s. Shropshire's revenue probably doubled to £753 over the same period, and Gloucestershire's expenditure rose from about £400 in 1700 and £450 annually in the decade 1730–39 to £1139 in the 1750s. According to an estimate based on a statement in *Parliamentary Papers* (1839), total English county rates were about £46,000 in 1750. Probably the figure was between £55,000 and £60,000 by 1760.[2]

Bridge expenditure rose sharply in the mid 1760s and prison building outlay in the 1770s, particularly from about 1785. Prisoners increased from the mid 1770s, with the rising population and the end of transportation to America and, from about 1780, with the growing tendency of judges to award prison sentences. The introduction of staff salaries also increased outlay, but the growth of prison maintenance was the most expensive charge. Militiamen's families were also a cost during the war. The moving of vagrants now took a smaller percentage. High food prices, the making of peace and the consequent greater unemployment increased crime and vagrancy and hence outlay in two important respects; while the army and navy absorbed tramps and even criminals in wartime. On the other hand, the militia was a charge during war but not in peace. Over the whole century expenditure rose at least ten times in Hertfordshire and about fifteen times in Shropshire. In 1800 the forty English counties received £277,873, the annual average for 1796 to 1805 being £369,960.[3]

This represented a rise in rates of nearly five times in money – and probably nearly three times in real value – since 1760. According to

[2] Norfolk RO, C/Sba 2/2–5; J.S. Cockburn, 'The North Riding Justices, 1690–1750', *Yorkshire Archaeological Journal*, 41, p. 512; Lincolnshire RO, Holland QS minutes, 1732–50, fol. 204; *Hertfordshire County Records: Sessions Books 1700 to 1752*, 7, ed. W. Le Hardy (Hertford, 1931), p. xxvi; *Victoria History of the County of Shropshire*, iii, ed G.C. Baugh (Oxford, 1979), pp. 101–2, 122; LSE, Webb Collection: Gloucestershire 123; Gloucestershire RO, Q/FAc 1; *Parliamentary Papers* (1839), xliv: references to *Parliamentary Papers* follow the usual form, stating the year and volume number in the annual series, but no page number.

[3] *Hertfordshire County Records: Sessions Books 1752 to 1799*, 8, ed. W. Le Hardy (Hertford, 1935), p. xv; *VCH, Shropshire*, iii, ed. Baugh, p. 122; *Parliamentary Papers* (1839), xliv.

Baugh, while Shropshire's annual expenditure was about £750 in the 1750s, in the period 1768–89 the annual average was nearly three times as great at £2152; a similar rise (to £5769) happened in 1790–1809.[4] In Somerset the annual average expenditure per decade between 1760 and 1799 was as follows: 1760–69 £1149; 1770–79 £1694; 1780–89 £3219; 1790–99 £4731; 1800–9 £6940.

As was shown in Chapter 2, the growth of expenditure in this period arose from expanding activity by the justices in a number of ways. The pattern differed to some extent among the counties. This may be seen by a comparison of figures for Somerset, Shropshire and the West Riding. The detailed Somerset data is useful because of its early date. As one would expect to find in other counties, the variety of payments grew. There were generally rising sums paid to the coroners, the clerk of the peace and other officers. A growing outlay comprised the payments to the keepers of the prisons for the maintenance of prisoners; another lesser cost was expenditure on arresting and passing on vagrants until the 1790s. The support of prisoners took 27 per cent of total outlay between 1760 and 1769 (an annual average of £308), and 37 per cent in the 1780s (£1195 a year). Vagrants cost 12 per cent in the 1760s and 16 per cent in the 1780s. The smaller sums paid for conveying and prosecuting criminals rose in a similar way. Prison improvements were sizeable in the later 1780s and 1790s, taking about one-fifth of all expenditure over those years. Bridges absorbed 11 per cent in the 1760s, then a much smaller proportion until the 1790s, when bridge works took about 12 per cent of county expenditure. Thus the cost of building became moderately important only from the later 1780s, earlier growth of expenditure coming mainly from supporting and handling prisoners. Somerset was not responsible for any major bridge and two bridewells had been built earlier.[5]

For Shropshire rising costs in conveying vagrants (especially along the London to Chester road) largely accounted for growing total expenditure in the 1750s; in the next decade the prisoners became dearer. In the early 1760s bridges cost about 6 or 7 per cent of the average annual outlay; then between 1768 and 1782 they formed the largest item of expenditure, on account of the rebuilding of Atcham and Tern bridges, in many years exceeding that on vagrancy and gaol expenses. In the decade 1784–93 outlay on the shire hall and then the county gaol dominated expenditure, with bridge works important again in the 1790s.

---

[4] *VCH, Shropshire,* iii, p. 122; *Parliamentary Papers* (1822), xi.
[5] Ibid.

Outlay on construction was prominent despite the spreading of the works over thirty years. The sessions were responsible for major bridges, some over the Severn. The need for a shire hall was probably exceptional as the judge imposed a fine in 1782 to secure immediate action. The West Riding court's pattern of expenditure was unusual on account of its consistently large bridge outlay, the result of many county bridges. The vagrancy figures show high costs after the end of wars, in 1749–50, 1764 and 1784, none of these years having dear corn, then an immediate return to former lower expenditure levels.[6]

The charges on all counties continued to grow between 1800 and 1830; total outlay was about £271,100 in 1800 and £687,434 in 1830. Part of the increase in money terms during the French wars reflects the general price inflation, but expenditure grew more in the years after 1815 when prices were falling. In predominantly agrarian Berkshire, sessions were probably spending about £1500 annually on average in the early 1780s. Between the mid 1790s (when figures first became available) and the early 1830s amounts grew as follows (Table 3.1):[7]

Table 3.1

Average Annual County Expenditure in Berkshire, 1794–1833

	£	s.	d.
1794–1798	2269	11	8
1799–1803	2972	12	1
1804–1808	4343	18	10
1809–1813	5853	8	3
1814–1818	5870	10	2
1819–1823	7253	9	4
1824–1828	7848	0	0
1829–1833	9283	0	0

Altogether outlay probably rose about six times in money terms between the early 1780s and 1830. In the partly agricultural and partly industrial county of Cheshire expenditure was about £10,000 a year in the early 1790s; by the early 1820s the average outlay was over £30,000; it was more than £40,000 in the years around 1830.[8]

During the war years expenses relating to the militia contributed to

[6] *VCH, Shropshire*, iii, pp. 122, 125–26; H. Owen and J.B. Blakeway, *A History of Shrewsbury*, i (1825), p. 584.

[7] C.W. Chalklin, 'Prison Building by the County of Berks, 1766–1820', *Berkshire Archaeological Journal*, 69 (1979), p. 70.

[8] *Parliamentary Papers* (1825), vi.

the rising outlay of the counties, but these ended after 1815. It was the continued growth of crime which contributed most to the long-run increase of the county rates. The cost of the prosecution of prisoners was always a significant item of expenditure and naturally grew with the number of cases handled. Even more expensive was the maintenance of prisoners, involving such items as the provision of food and the salaries of gaolers. These costs rose sharply with the jump in crime rates in the later 1810s, and do much to explain the continued rise in total county expenditure after the end of the French wars and the end of militia expenses. In Berkshire about one-third of the total annual expenditure in the mid 1790s was devoted to the maintenance of prisoners (especially the provision of food), the salaries of gaolers, surgeons and chaplains, the conveyance of prisoners to trial and the costs of their prosecution. By about 1820 the handling of prisoners (especially food, costs of prosecutions and salaries) was taking half county expenditure. This continued in the 1820s, taking one year with another.[9] In England as a whole in this decade the maintenance of prisoners and prosecutions took about 46 per cent of expenditure.

Bridge construction also made heavy though uneven demands on the county rates and contributed to rising outlay between the 1790s and 1820s. From the 1770s and 1780s the rebuilding of gaols and houses of correction added considerably to county expenditure. In some cases the undertaking led to a doubling or even trebling of county expenditure during the period of construction. For example, Bedfordshire spent £6850 on a combined gaol and house of correction in 1798–1802. The effect on county expenditure may be seen from the accounts of annual financial outlay (Table 3.2).

Here, as a result of the prison building scheme, county expenditure doubled in 1799, increased further in 1800. By 1801 it was more than four times that of 1794–97. From 1803 it returned to a more normal level.[10] In other instances the raising of loans reduced the rate burden during the time of construction but the period in which the undertaking was a cost on the county was of course lengthened. In the whole period from 1780–1830 it was common for counties to spend as much as one-fifth or one-sixth of their rate income on prison building, or on prison, shire hall and lunatic asylum construction together. In the forty years 1781–1820 Berkshire raised about £150,000 in rates. During this period two new houses of correction and the county gaol at Reading

[9] Chalklin, 'Prison Building', p. 70.
[10] *Parliamentary Papers* (1825), vi.

Table 3.2

Average Annual County Expenditure in Bedfordshire, 1794–1805

	£	s.	d.
1794	964	13	6
1795	1140	2	5
1796	1136	9	8
1797	960	4	9
1798	1390	19	8
1799	2871	4	2
1800	3499	14	0
1801	4559	14	11
1802	3345	4	1
1803	1752	15	3
1804	1599	17	4
1805	1337	9	10

(added to in 1812) were built, which cost together about £38,000 or £40,000, or just over one-quarter of the total sum raised. Further improvements were made to the gaol in the 1820s, but the outlay was relatively small. Over the period 1780–1830 expenditure on prison building was probably about 20 per cent of the total county outlay.[11] To take a second case, in the West Riding of Yorkshire the bridewell was improved between 1799 and 1807 and rebuilt in the early 1820s; several courthouses were rebuilt partly or wholly with Riding funds in the years after 1806; a pauper lunatic asylum was erected in 1815–19, and in the later 1820s there were substantial contributions for gaol works at York Castle. Altogether between 1791 and 1830 the Riding spent about £180,000–£200,000 on new buildings out of a total expenditure of around £1,100,000.[12]

County costs were small compared with parish poor law outlay, and less than highway expenditure. Yet rates rose faster than poor law levies, particularly because of charges in handling crime. In 1748–50 the latter averaged £690,000 and the counties spent about £46,000 or about 6.5 per cent. In 1803 the proportion was similar, or £4,268,000 compared with about £273,000. Arthur Young wrote about Oxfordshire in 1813 that while the average poor rate was 4s. 8d. in the pound in 1803 'the county rates . . . by the extraordinary good management of the magistrates [and especially the chairmen for over twenty years] have been kept down in a manner that should be an example to other counties. It does not amount to 3d. in the pound; and yet a new gaol has been built in

[11] Chalklin, 'Prison Building', p. 70.
[12] West Yorkshire RO, QS order books, 1791–1822; *Parliamentary Papers* (1825), vi.

Oxford . . .' In the whole country the proportion rose in the 1810s and 1820s. It was about 9 per cent in the years 1813–17 and 1818–22, and 11 per cent in 1823–27 and 1828–32. Parish highway rates were £1,075,262 and church levies £540,971 in 1827, compared with county rates of £690,576.[13]

In the later seventeenth and early eighteenth centuries rates were collected by the high constables from the localities within their jurisdiction. The quota required from each hundred or parish was fixed. Within the localities the assessments were made in various ways, such as the pound rent or acreage estimates used for parish rates. In the seventeenth century there was usually no unified county levy, some counties developing a principal rate in the early eighteenth century. Levies were sanctioned by a variety of statutes. For example, rates for bridges were allowed under the acts 22 Henry VIII and 1 Anne c. 19; the county's contribution towards prisoners in the King's Bench and Marshalsea by 43 Elizabeth I c. 2; and towards those in houses of correction by 7 James I c. 4.[14]

In this period most county expenditure on construction concerned bridges. Bridge rates were levied when the money was needed. The North and West Ridings of Yorkshire levied relatively small sums for particular bridges. Thus at Easter sessions 1688 the North Riding justices ordered that £50 be estreated for building West Burton bridge, £40 for the repair of the ruined Dalton bridge, and £20 for another bridge in addition to money already held by two justices. More commonly a round sum such as £100 or £300 was levied to pay for more than one bridge and possibly to provide a balance for urgent future works. Thus in July 1689 the Suffolk justices ordered a £100 rate for building Kettleburgh bridge and repairing Wilford and Brandeston bridges.[15] The infrequent building or purchase of prisons and houses of correction and of the few shire halls were paid for either by drawing on an existing county fund or by a special rate. The second method was usual when a major sum was needed. Warwickshire levied four special rates for building the shire hall and house of correction between 1675 and 1696, totalling £2701 16s. 10d.[16]

[13] B.R. Mitchell, *Abstract of British Historical Statistics* (Cambridge, 1962), p. 410; *Parliamentary Papers* (1839), xliv, appendix 1.

[14] E Cannan, *The History of Local Rates in England* (2nd edn, London, 1912), p. 110.

[15] *The North Riding Record Society for the Publication of Original Documents Relating to the North Riding of the County of York*, 7, *Quarter Sessions Records*, ed. J.C. Atkinson (1889), p. 87; East Suffolk RO, 105/2/13, fol. 37, and HD 330/6.

[16] *Warwick County Records*, 7, *Quarter Sessions Records, Easter 1674 to Easter 1682*, ed. S.C. Ratcliff and H.C. Johnson (Warwick, 1946), p. cxxi.

Quarter sessions often met problems in enforcing payment of the rates. The difficulties lay sometimes in the unwillingness of the localities to pay, sometimes in the negligence of the constables in collecting or paying over the money to the county treasurers. For example, on 12 January 1696 the Hampshire court ordered a penny rate for the repair of Redbridge bridges. Michaelmas sessions 1699 found that the work had been delayed because the money had been largely uncollected by the constables, who were then ordered to get it; four years later several parishes or tithings had not collected or paid it, and legal proceedings were threatened.[17] In Middlesex obstruction to the payment of both bridge and vagrant rates reached a height in the 1730s. Out of a £200 rate ordered in January 1736, for the repair of Brentford bridge, only £70 was collected. The legality of several rates was challenged; some were removed by *certiorari* by their opponents to the court of King's Bench, where two were quashed.[18] This led to the act 12 George II c. 29 (applying to all counties), creating a unified rate which could be levied once three-quarters of the previous tax had been spent. The money was to be paid by the church wardens and overseers of each parish out of the poor rate to the high constables, who were to pass the money to the treasurer. The power to enforce collection was strengthened and, as the parish officers levied the poor rate on a regular basis, the problem of collection was obviously eased.[19]

Rates continued to be raised on the basis of the old hundred and parish quotas. According to the act, quarter sessions were to levy rates on the towns, parishes and places in the county 'in such proportion as any of the rates heretofore made . . . have been usually assessed'. The levy was a fixed sum; when more than the proceeds of a single rate was needed a multiple was levied. In Shropshire the levy was fixed at £278 13s. 0d.; in 1755 three rates were raised, and in the 1770s there were usually eight levies a year.[20] With the growth of rates at the end of the eighteenth century and in the early years of the nineteenth century, the shifting distribution of population and wealth made the levies seem increas-

[17] Hampshire RO, QO 8, fos 36, 140; for difficulties in the collection of rates for maimed soldiers' pensions, see B. Osborne, *Justices of the Peace, 1361–1948* (Shaftesbury, 1960), p. 173.

[18] Greater London RO, Calendar of Middlesex Sessions Books, January 1735 to December 1738, p. 64.

[19] E.G. Dowdell, *A Hundred Years of Quarter Sessions: The Government of Middlesex from 1660 to 1760* (Cambridge, 1932), p. 128.

[20] *Shropshire County Records: An Abstract of the Orders Made by the Court of Quarter Sessions for Shropshire, 1741–82*, ed. R.G. Venables (Shrewsbury, c. 1902), pp. 153–56.

ingly unfair to many payers. The burden was uneven between occupiers of land in different parishes. Those with other forms of wealth often did not pay. Decaying market towns were increasingly burdened, while the householders in new or rapidly growing urban centres paid little or nothing. Under the act 55 George III c. 51, parliament directed the counties to tax according to a pound rate of the full annual value of every property. In the following years many counties set up committees to prepare new rate assessments and adopted them as a basis for the new levy. In 1817 a Wiltshire committee 'determined to make the new rate upon the basis of schedules A and B of the old Property Tax . . . By Michaelmas 1818 the rate had been completed on this basis for the whole county . . . The new rate was finally adopted in January 1819'. This allowed the increasingly burdensome rates of the 1820s to be levied in a more equitable way. In some counties the old assessments were still being used in the early 1830s.[21]

Sometimes when acts provided special powers for the building of prisons and shire halls the rates were levied in a different way. For example, the land tax was used as the assessment for the rate for a new Staffordshire gaol under the act 27 George III c. 60, and for that for the Staffordshire courthouse (34 George III c. 97). The income tax assessment was used in the case of the Sussex shire hall (48 George III c. 107). When the poor rate was the basis, special levies were sometimes raised, as for the Nottinghamshire shire hall (9 George III c. 62), and the Durham gaol and house of correction and courts (49 George III c. 139). Alternatively, the money was allocated out of the normal county stock, so that there was no special rate. The new gaol, prothonotary's office and other accommodation at Chester Castle were paid for in this way in the 1790s under 28 George III c. 82. These various means of raising money for building reflected local preferences. When Herefordshire decided to rebuild its shire hall in 1814 the county meeting's opinion stopped the use of the income tax assessment as the basis of the rate.[22] The land tax was obviously well known to the justices and other gentry as a leading direct tax, and the same was true of the unpopular income tax in the beginning of the nineteenth century.

The burdens imposed by building undertakings aroused opposition

[21] *Victoria History of the County of Wiltshire*, v, ed. R.B. Pugh and E. Crittall (London, 1957), p. 191; B. Keith-Lucas, *The English Local Government Franchise: A Short History* (Oxford, 1952), p. 91.

[22] Herefordshire RO, QS shire hall building minutes, 1814. Berkshire borrowed £3486 12. 0d. towards building Marlow bridge under an act of 1829, *Parliamentary Papers* (1835), xliv; Cornwall RO, QS M 4 (15 April 1779), concerning the building of Bodmin gaol.

both among some of the justices and among the ratepayers in the counties. In the mid 1780s the novelty and size of the prison building schemes under the influence of the prison reformers aroused opposition in several counties, although its extent among the many counties that either rebuilt their county gaol or one or more houses of correction cannot be accurately determined. This opposition was in spite of the fact that gaol fever and overcrowding in 1783 and 1784 gave an urgency to the extension and improvement of accommodation. In Lancashire the leading magistrate behind the scheme for a new house of correction at Salford, T.B. Bayley, met with strenuous initial opposition from some of the justices.[23] In Sussex plans for building a new house of correction at Petworth, embodying the proposals of the 1782 act relating to houses of correction, were accepted by the justices meeting at Petworth in February 1783. No action was taken on them that year and in 1784 they were again approved. In the summer of 1784 there was strong opposition and a petition from occupiers in the three western Rapes of the county was prepared at a meeting at Arundel on 23 June, requesting that the new building should not cost more than £1000. Yet the justices went ahead with a much larger scheme and accepted a tender for £5724 in January 1785.[24]

In later years the rebuilding of prisons seems to have been accepted more as a matter of course by the county magistrates and the county ratepayers. There is occasional evidence of disagreement about decisions to build. Considerable opposition arose to the new Kent prison at Maidstone in 1812 on account of its great size. It was the most expensive prison undertaking before the mid 1820s, costing about £200,000. An account of the campaign by some of the justices in East Kent and by local meetings which organised a petition to parliament is given elsewhere. The escalating cost of the Durham county courts, gaol and house of correction erected between 1809 and 1819, which amounted ultimately to £134,684, led to complaints about the special county rates, and even to an invitation to refuse to pay the rate by a meeting of landowners and occupiers of Darlington.[25] A decision to improve the Beccles gaol in 1820 also aroused ratepayers' opposition, on account of the agricultural

[23] T. Percival, *Biographical Memoirs of the Late Thomas Butterworth Bayley* (Manchester, 1802).

[24] West Sussex RO, QAP/5/W1; *Salisbury and Winchester Journal*, 7 June, 19 July and 9 August 1784; this newspaper also records the opposition to the new Hampshire county gaol in Winchester in 1784 and 1785.

[25] *New Maidstone Gaol Order Book, 1805–23*, Kent Records, 23, ed. C.W. Chalklin, (Maidstone, 1984), pp. 19–21; W. Fordyce, *The History and Antiquities of the County Palatine of Durham*, i (Newcastle, 1857), p. 292.

depression and the cost of the works in progress at the county gaol at Ipswich. It delayed work for over a year.[26] These instances of opposition to prison building were probably exceptional; the Kent and Durham projects were particularly expensive. Schemes to build pauper lunatic asylums under the permissive legislation of 1808 also met with opposition from some justices and ratepayers, because the asylums seemed less necessary than prisons. Opposition reduced the number of asylums erected in the next twenty or thirty years, as a result of effective protest.[27]

Although the county rates were rising rapidly, especially from the last quarter of the eighteenth century, there were two ways in which the burden on the county ratepayers was sometimes reduced when building was undertaken. While the rates were paid normally by occupiers of property, an act was sometimes obtained to shift part or all of the burden onto the landlords. This was done in the case of the building of some county gaols: both the act for building a new county gaol and house of correction for Shropshire (26 George III c. 24) and that for the Staffordshire gaol (27 George III c. 60), besides limiting the total amount to be levied and fixing a maximum annual levy, laid the burden of payment on the landlords not the tenants. It was also used to pay for new shire halls. The Sussex shire hall act (48 George III c. 107) allowed tenants to deduct half the rate payment from their rents, while the Gloucestershire and Herefordshire shire halls were erected on the basis of two-thirds of the cost being paid by the landlords. The justification for this procedure was that county buildings were expected to be used permanently, while tenants held property for a limited time. The other way of reducing the burden of payment for county buildings was by borrowing on the security of the rates and spreading the debt repayment over a number of years.

Money was rarely borrowed for bridge construction, presumably because the amount spent on individual bridges was relatively small compared with most prisons. Nor was there much borrowing for erecting buildings before the 1780s. The acts of 1784 relating to gaols and houses of correction allowed quarter sessions to borrow money for rebuilding on security of the county rates if the estimate of the cost exceeded half the annual ordinary county rate assessment, with the proviso that the money was repaid within fourteen years. The majority of building undertakings were financed partly or wholly in this way in order to spread the cost over a longer period, the sums being borrowed piecemeal as payments

[26] East Suffolk RO, 105/2/56 fos 161–62.
[27] See below, Chapter 11.

became due and being repaid as money became available to the treasurer. Most though not all of the projects paid for immediately from the rates were among the smaller new buildings. As an example, North-amptonshire's gaol and house of correction cost about £15,000, most of which was spent in 1791 and 1792; £13,450 was borrowed and repaid between 1792 and 1807 in various sums between £600 and £1150 (except in 1798 when the repayment was only £300).[28] In two cases, those of Gloucestershire and Surrey, legislation in 1785 and 1791 respectively enabled the commissioners responsible to repay over a twenty-five year period, receiving a fixed annual sum out of the rates; in the case of Gloucestershire this was £2000, of Surrey £2427. The money was used first to pay the expenses of the act, then interest on the money borrowed, then to discharge the cost of building, and finally as a sinking fund to discharge the principal of the loan.

The loans generally took the form of £50 or £100 bonds or mortgages secured on the county rates. They were usually advertised. Repayments were made in succession, usually according to numbers arranged by lot. The use of annuities and tontines were sometimes also considered, but in practice mortgages were generally used. In the case of Gloucestershire Sir G.O. Paul told the ratepayers that 'it was the first object of your Committee to consider the areas by which the burthen might be properly relieved. The best opinions were consulted, and various plans of annuities, tontines submitted to them . . .' The Gloucestershire act (25 George III c. 10) allowed quarter sessions to raise money either by mortgages or annuities, but in fact the latter were never used. One exceptional case in which a tontine was used was that of the Middlesex house of correction, erected between 1788 and 1795: £62,000 was raised between 1788 and 1794 by this means.[29]

There was generally little difficulty in either raising money or, in the later 1780s and beginning of the 1790s, in borrowing at or below the maximum legal rate of 5 per cent. This was partly because of the attraction of the loan, providing complete security for the lender; nor was there any danger of capital loss from oscillations in price, as in the case of the Funds. In the later 1780s and beginning of the 1790s the supply of capital was particularly plentiful. The current yield on government stock was one of the factors affecting the rate of interest offered by a

---

[28] *Parliamentary Papers* (1825), vi.

[29] *Call of a General Meeting of the Nobility, Gentry and Other Contributors to the County Rate of the County of Gloucester, with an Address Delivered by Sir G.O. Paul* (Gloucester, 1792), p. 33; Greater London RO, MA/G/CBF 1.

county, and in the later 1780s it was falling. Lancashire had to pay 5 per cent on the £14,000 it borrowed for the New Bayley prison at Salford between 1788 and 1790, but this reflected greater pressure on capital resources in the northern industrial areas.[30] On 26 April 1786 the Gloucestershire commissioners decided that 4½ per cent be allowed for money advanced to them but that, considering the state of the national funds and the peculiar advantage of the proposed securities, no higher rate of interest ought to be permitted. In May 1789 they borrowed at 4½ per cent and in July they obtained further money at 4 per cent; in November 1790 they borrowed from two sources, half at 4½ and half at 4 per cent. In July 1791 they tried unsuccessfully to borrow at less than 4 per cent: an advertisement in the *Gloucester Journal* that 'any persons inclined to advance money on credit of gaol securities at a lower rate of interest than 4 per cent are desired to make their proposals in writing to the Clerk to the Commissioners before 9 July' received no reply. After enquiries by the treasurer established that money was unobtainable at less than 4 per cent, they came to the decision to borrow at this figure. Berkshire paid 5 per cent in 1785 and 1786 for the £5600 it borrowed to build its Reading house of correction, and 4 per cent for £3000 needed for the gaol in 1792, reflecting the fall in the current rate of interest in the intervening years.[31]

In the tighter financial circumstances of the mid 1790s 5 per cent became the normal rate of interest. In April and May 1794 the committee for building the new county gaol at Newington in Surrey received no replies to their advertisements for £4000, so the money was obtained from existing mortgagees on condition that the rate of interest was raised from 4½ per cent to 5 per cent.[32] This rate of interest, the maximum permitted under usury law, remained the normal price paid by counties for money for the next thirty years. In the mid 1820s the Exchequer Bill Loan Office advanced money at 4 per cent to Holland quarter sessions for building the Spalding house of correction. By the later 1820s private lenders in general were accepting less than 5 per cent. The Middlesex justices borrowed at 4½ and 4 per cent for building their lunatic asylum in 1828 and 1829.[33]

Loans were only difficult to obtain in some years during the French

[30] Lancashire RO, CTM/1.
[31] Gloucestershire RO, Q/AG 7, pp. 26, 79, 82, 100, 107; Berkshire RO, QS 0 5, pp. 261–62, QS 0 7, p. 130.
[32] Surrey RO, QS 5/4/2, 16 April to 11 August 1794.
[33] Lincolnshire RO, Holland QS, B5/15; Greater London RO, MJ/OC 23, pp. 70, 435.

wars. Quarter sessions anxious to borrow money for building in the mid
and later 1790s shared the problems faced by borrowers generally in
this period. When Herefordshire in 1794 received hopelessly inadequate
replies to advertisements for money to pay for the new county gaol,
premiums were offered to local attorneys to persuade them to advise
their well-to-do clients to lend to the county. When advertisements for
£4000 in August and £2800 in September produced only £500 the justices
offered a 2 per cent commission to attorneys to make loans available –
and by the end of November £2600 had been obtained. Surrey received
no reply to advertisements for £2000 in 1797. On the other hand, Cheshire
borrowed sums in each year from 1792 until 1810, including £6200 in
1796.[34] The tighter money market at the end of the French wars also
affected borrowing by the justices. For the building of the new Kent
county gaol at Maidstone begun in 1811 the West Kent justices decided
not to borrow 'from the circumstances of the times', that is the difficulty
of raising large amounts of money at a time of high government borrowing.[35]

The loans were mostly provided by the well-to-do: gentry, women of
private means, professional people and prosperous tradesmen. In the
predominantly agricultural counties landowners were a major source of
capital. The thirty-seven people who lent £4000 to the North Riding in
1785 and 1786 to build a bridewell and sessions house were mostly gentry,
clergy, women, farmers and 'gentlemen' who may have been attorneys.
Tradesmen and women were also important lenders for prison and court
house building in rural areas. The loans for the Herefordshire shire hall
between 1815 and 1818 included modest sums from a builder, shoemaker,
grocer and stationer, a larger amount from a victualler and small sums
from seven widows and spinsters; much of the money came from two
Hereford men who were probably attorneys.[36] In urban and industrial
areas tradespeople and professional men were naturally numerous among
the lenders, with women also strongly represented. The creditors of
Lancashire quarter sessions in respect of the New Bayley prison (for
£14,000) included seven spinsters and widows, a doctor, surgeon and
clergyman and at least two local merchants.[37]

[34] Herefordshire RO, QS minutes, 1792–97, pp. 108–26; Surrey RO, QS 5/4/2, 28
September 1797 to 27 March 1799; *Parliamentary Papers* (1825), vi.

[35] *Maidstone Journal*, 2 March 1813.

[36] North Yorkshire RO, QS agreements for loans to finance building of new house
of correction and sessions house, 1785–86 (one volume); Herefordshire RO, shire hall
mortgages (one volume).

[37] Lancashire RO, CTM/1.

Money was supplied sometimes by people with a personal involvement in the process of building or its finance. The chairman of the North Riding quarter sessions was among the subscribers to the loan for the new house of correction and sessions house in 1785–86.[38] When it was difficult to borrow money on the open market the surveyor, treasurer and even craftsmen lent money or accepted payment in bonds. In the case of the new Surrey county gaol, the surveyor George Gwilt lent £3100 between 1793 and 1799, and the treasurer, John Pardon, £6500 between 1791 and 1799, out of a total borrowing of £22,600.[39]

Apart from private lenders, during the 1820s several counties borrowed from the Exchequer Bill Loan Office. In Lincolnshire, in addition to the loan to Holland for the Spalding prison, Lindsey quarter sessions borrowed £20,000 for building Spilsby house of correction in 1824; and £12,000 for improving the Louth bridewell in 1825.[40] Insurance companies were not used before the 1830s. These loans from the 1780s greatly reduced the burden of the rates during the years of construction. The 1784 acts marked the beginning of a long history of county borrowing.

[38] North Yorkshire RO, QS agreements.
[39] Surrey RO, QS 5/4/1.
[40] Lincolnshire RO, Lindsey QS minutes, 1823–24, 1824–25.

4

Surveyors, Engineers, Architects and Builders

In the long period between the later seventeenth century and 1830 build-ing works were organised by the justices in various ways. There was a growing tendency to use a regular surveyor paid on a salary basis, instead of appointing a surveyor for a particular job or even using the contrac-tor to provide plans. Individual craftsmen sometimes contracted for all the work, or they provided the materials and did the work just in their own trade, such as bricklaying or carpentry. On other occasions they did the work in their particular skill, while the justices and their surveyor bought the materials separately. Work gradually became handled more professionally, with the growing use of advertising for tenders and increas-ing care with the preparation of specifications.

From the mid seventeenth century nearly all counties handled their surveying work in one of two ways. One method was to deal with all building undertakings, large or small, on an ad hoc basis, appointing someone to draw plans and supervise construction as needed. The other way was to employ one or more surveyors to handle all or most bridge works, while other county building was dealt with by surveyors appointed for particular tasks. In some counties the absence of a general surveyor of bridges reflected the fact that quarter sessions was only responsible for a handful of bridges. With six or eight (or even fewer) bridges to maintain, repair or rebuilding was only occasional, and a surveyor (most conveniently a local workman) could be found when need arose.

Nevertheless, some counties with considerable bridge works employed surveyors for at least part of the early and mid eighteenth century, although dissatisfaction with the appointment sometimes led to a return to a more ad hoc arrangement. In several northern counties bridge surveyors were appointed and the arrangement either became a permanent one or was revised or abolished if it proved unsatisfactory. In the East Riding of Yorkshire quarter sessions handled bridge repairs for most of the seventeenth century, but 'by 1708 the East Riding justices of the peace were employing a permanent surveyor of bridges at £10 per annum for his salary and riding charges'. He inspected all the eight county bridges periodically; when repairs were needed he set men to work, provided materials and presented the account to quarter sessions for approval and payment.[1] Durham first appointed a surveyor of county bridges in 1732, when Thomas Shirley was commissioned to see that they were kept in repair and to report their condition at each quarter sessions for a salary of £20 a year.[2] Lancashire had a permanent system of bridge 'supervisors' for each hundred and sometimes for individual bridges, some of whom were paid money periodically and presented accounts of their expenditure.[3] Another county, the North Riding of Yorkshire, changed its procedure for bridge maintenance several times in the early eighteenth century, reflecting the fact that it was difficult to find a satisfactory way of caring for the bridges. From the 1680s in most years the court employed a surveyor with general responsibility for their bridges. In 1709 a new surveyor was appointed at £8 a year, helped by four undersurveyors, each in charge of a division of the county, at £3 a year each. Then in April 1714 the four undersurveyors were dismissed and John Bartlett, the principal surveyor, was given full responsibility at £20 a year. This lasted until Bartlett's death at the end of 1727, when the Riding was divided between two surveyors at £15 each. The new method was short-lived; in October 1728 the surveyorships were abolished. For the next fifteen years the justices made orders for bridge works on the evidence about the state of bridges supplied to them by the chief constables in each wapentake. In 1743 the cost of bridge works again led to the consideration of the use of a surveyor: at the July sessions it was recommended that a general surveyor of county bridges be appointed, instead of the chief constables, as 'it would save the Riding money', though no action was taken.[4]

In southern England Devon had an organised system of bridge supervisors in each of three grand divisions of the county from the seventeenth century. Each supervisor had responsibility for a group of bridges in his particular division.[5] Essex appointed a public surveyor between 1704 and 1706, 1711 and 1715, and permanently from 1718.[6] Elsewhere in the south, in the midlands (apart from Derbyshire) and in East Anglia,

[1] G.C.F. Forster, *The East Riding Justices of the Peace in the Seventeenth Century*, East Yorkshire Local History Society (1973), p. 64.

[2] Durham RO, QS order book (OB) 8, p. 557.

[3] Lancashire RO, QS order books (O) 2.

[4] *The North Riding Record Society for the Publication of Original Documents Relating to the North Riding of the County of York*, 7 (1889), *Quarter Sessions Records*, ed. J.C. Atkinson, pp. 54, 73, 87, 91, 108, 127, 159, 179–220, 230; London School of Economics, Webb Local Government Collection, vol. 251.

[5] LSE, Webb Collection, vol. 108.

[6] LSE, Webb Collection, vol. 119; N. Briggs, 'The Evolution of the Office of County Surveyor in Essex, 1700–1816', *Architectural History*, 27 (1984), p. 298.

the justices worked with the advice of workmen appointed for the occasion. In Gloucestershire the important Chepstow bridge was handled by a 'surveyor' under contract at an annual salary, out of which some of the repairs had to be paid (probably those of a routine nature).[7] In counties such as Suffolk, Hampshire and Kent, where bridge expenditure was a regular occurrence by the early eighteenth century, no attempt was made to appoint a salaried surveyor.[8] When a bridge was presented, the justices in that division of the county were ordered to initiate and supervise the repairs or rebuilding. Workers were often asked to survey and estimate the work which was needed. In some counties, such as Nottinghamshire (where bridge repairs were only occasional) and Westmorland, the chief or high constables handled the bridges in conjunction with their other tasks. Benjamin Brown of Troutbeck, as high constable of Kendal ward between 1711 and 1732, was responsible for thirty-four bridges under the general supervision of the local justices. He had to view the bridges periodically, assess the need for repairs, find workmen, contract and check the progress of the work. Occasionally there seems to have been no surveyor. None is mentioned at the rebuilding of Sussex gaol in 1651–53 and, perhaps understandably, there were difficulties in 1658.[9]

As the salaries (£8, £10, £12 or £20) paid to surveyors suggest, most of them devoted a relatively small part of their working time to the care of bridges. Some of them were building craftsmen, such as the two masons, John Watson and Robert Carr, appointed as surveyors of the West Riding bridges in April 1743 at a salary of £15 each.[10] Others came from a variety of occupations: two of the three surveyors appointed at Devon quarter sessions in 1742 were farmers, and the third may have been a gentleman farmer or an attorney.[11]

---

[7] LSE, Webb collection, vol. 123; at the beginning of the eighteenth century two other bridges were handled by a surveyor.

[8] See quarter sessions order books for each county; it was also the case in Surrey, Norfolk and Dorset, and probably Staffordshire.

[9] M.A. Logie, 'Benjamin Browne of Troutbeck, High Constable of Kendal Ward, 1711–1732', *Transactions of the Cumberland and Westmoreland Antiquarian and Archaeological Society*, new series, 71 (1971), pp. 86–87. In R. Burn, *Justice of the Peace and Parish Officer* (London, 1755), the office of surveyor was said to be attached to that of high constable; Greater London RO, MJ/OC 19, p. 58; W. Albery, *A Millennium of Facts in the History of Horsham and Sussex, 947–1947* (Horsham, 1947), p. 341.

[10] LSE, Webb Collection, vol. 252.

[11] Devon RO, QS 1/18; the county treasurer was used occasionally for particular tasks. The Worcestershire treasurer acted as surveyor for the bridewell erected in 1716–18, and received a fee: Worcestershire RO, QS, order book 2, fol. 68.

The decision to appoint a surveyor followed usually from a conviction that they were at the mercy of workmen where charges and the quality of materials were concerned. Money would also be saved if bridges were regularly inspected and by repairs being done on many occasions while damage was still slight. Essex decided to appoint a surveyor of county bridges in April 1718 because 'the county hath been notoriously abused and put upon by the workmen of severall trades employed in the repairs of the public bridges . . . and in other public works and repairs done at the charge of the county for want of a proper officer to take care therein . . .'[12] As already noted, the North Riding considered the appointment of a general surveyor of county bridges in 1743 to save money.[13] On the other hand, the salaries had to be paid and it placed a wide responsibility in the hands of people whose efficiency and reliability were sometimes uncertain. Justices living in the neighbourhood of a bridge could normally be relied upon to report, or have presented by the grand jury or a constable, any damage or decay when it became noticeable, and would also be likely to know which local worker's opinion and work were reliable. Probably for these reasons the majority of counties with considerable bridge works outside the north of England continued to rely on local justices and ad hoc surveyors for most of the eighteenth century.

In the later eighteenth century several counties which were already employing bridge surveyors also used their services for the increasing amount of prison building which was now being undertaken. They became county surveyors in a full sense – in fact as well as name. The West Riding employed its two surveyors of bridges in 1765 to prepare plans and estimates for the new house of correction at Wakefield. In August 1766 they were appointed to superintend the work for an additional fee.[14] In 1774 its surveyor of bridges (Robert Carr) prepared a plan and estimate for an infirmary in the prison; in 1775 he was appointed to superintend the building of an additional room for the register office.[15] In the 1780s John Gott (surveyor of bridges until 1793) handled alterations to the house of correction, apparently as a matter of course, sometimes with the additional title of surveyor of public works.[16] More counties, including Middlesex and Norfolk, ceased to rely on small groups of justices and (when required) ad hoc surveyors. They began to pay surveyors with a general responsibility either for just bridges, or, as in the case of

[12] LSE, Webb Collection, vol. 119.
[13] LSE, Webb Collection, vol. 251.
[14] West Yorkshire RO, QS 024, fos 126, 285.
[15] West Yorkshire RO, QS 028, fos 3, 110.
[16] West Yorkshire RO, QS 030, 031.

the West Riding, for all types of construction. For Middlesex Thomas Rogers claimed in 1778 that he 'hath had the honour of being considered as surveyor to the county of Middlesex upwards of seven years in which time he has had the planning and surveying of the several very considerable works done by the justices', including the extension of the new prison.[17] He then designed the sessions house (1779–82) and was county surveyor until 1802. In at least two cases, Shropshire and Surrey, the first county surveyor was a man who was appointed to survey particular works and later came to be treated as the regular county surveyor. In Surrey George Gwilt handled prison building at Southwark in 1771–72 and Kingston in 1774–75; in south-west Surrey a Guildford surveyor, Thomas Jackman, surveyed the rebuilding of Guildford house of correction in 1767, its enlargement ten years later, and the repairs to Wonersh bridge (costing £426 13s. 5d.) in 1774–75. Other men were used for the important bridge works during the decade. From the early 1780s Gwilt dealt with all or most bridge matters as well as prison construction, plus the preparation of plans for courts of justices at Guildford in 1787 and the direction of repairs at Guildford house of correction in 1789. Within about twelve years his work increased from the care of the Southwark prisons to a general responsibility for all the county's public works.[18]

In the first three decades of the nineteenth century a surveyor responsible in name or in fact for all county works was common, but it was far from being invariable. Worcestershire and Sussex still had no surveyor in the 1830s. Dorset only appointed a bridge surveyor in 1809, despite the fact that bridge works had been considerable during the course of the eighteenth century. In some counties the appointment of a surveyor reflected the late development of a responsibility for bridge maintenance. Thus Berkshire appointed a county surveyor in 1812 as the justices began to devote more time and money to bridge works. In some cases the surveyor dealt with county bridges only, and not county buildings in general. Herefordshire had a surveyor of bridges in fact though not in name before 1800, but it appointed a separate surveyor of public buildings in 1824 and the two offices only combined on the death of the surveyor of bridges in 1831.[19] In at least two cases the appoint-

[17] Norfolk RO, C/S1/14,15; Greater London RO, MA/S/312.

[18] Briggs, 'County Surveyor in Essex', p. 303; Surrey RO, QS 2/1/20–27. For the case of Thomas Telford in Shropshire, *Victoria County History of Shropshire*, ed. G.C. Baugh, iii (London, 1979), p. 127.

[19] Herefordshire RO, typescript 'County Surveyors of Herefordshire'; Howard Colvin, *A Biographical Dictionary of British Architects, 1600–1840* (3rd edn, New Haven and London, 1995), p. 399.

ment of one or two surveyors of bridges replaced the practice of giving responsibility to five or six or as many as ten surveyors, each handling a small part of the county. Whereas in 1783 Northumberland had ten bridge surveyors, in 1799 they were replaced by two men, one for the north and the other for the south of the county.[20]

The increasing tendency to employ a surveyor of bridges or a general county surveyor reflected the growing amount of county building work, on prisons, bridges and courthouses, and the emergence of professional surveyors wholly or largely concerned with surveying rather than contracting (or other employment not necessarily concerned with building). With the large number of county building responsibilities, it saved time to have a regular surveyor on call who kept all works under surveillance. Where his skill was established it was more efficient to employ him rather than a succession of different men. A few counties were prepared to pay large salaries to recognised civil engineers to improve the quality of bridge works, and also to save money on repairs. Devon bridges were handled by six surveyors at the opening of the nineteenth century: at Epiphany sessions 1808 it was reported that a bridge erected in 1806 had been washed away because the surveyor had not enforced the terms of the contract and the mortar had been defective. It was recommended that 'a civil engineer of approved talents and ability' be appointed to take charge of county bridges; despite the considerable salary to be paid, it was thought that this would reduce county bridge expenditure.[21]

The payments made to surveyors continued to reflect their part-time role. Several of the surveyors in the later eighteenth century were paid on a fee basis, not by salary, at a time when the use of a general surveyor by a county was still at an experimental stage. Nevertheless, the payment of a salary was usual, necessarily related to the amount of bridge work undertaken, and (at least in the early nineteenth century) to professional skill and reputation. Hertfordshire, where bridges were relatively small both in number and size, agreed to pay its first 'county surveyor of buildings, bridges and works' £20 a year in 1798.[22] Northumberland paid its two surveyors £40 each between the 1800s and the 1820s.[23] These

[20] Northumberland RO, 'Handlist of Northumberland Quarter Sessions Papers and Order Books from 1663 to 1834' (1960)'; LSE, Webb Collection, vol. 211.

[21] LSE, Webb Collection, vol. 108.

[22] *Hertfordshire County Records: Calendar to the Sessions Books, 1752–99*, ed. W. Le Hardy, 8 (1935), p. xxviii. Middlesex paid on a fee basis: Greater London RO, MJ/OC 19, p. 59 (referring to 1819).

[23] LSE, Webb Collection, vol. 211.

were clearly employments involving work on one or two days a week. The Staffordshire justices appointed a county surveyor in 1792 at £52 12s. 0d. a year to work for two days a week.[24] Yet even the experienced civil engineers or architects sometimes employed by counties in the early nineteenth century at a salary of several hundred pounds were active in other fields. Thus Thomas Evans of Wimborne in Dorset, appointed county surveyor in 1824 for £200 a year, was active as a church builder in the county in the later 1820s.[25]

The early nineteenth-century bridge surveyors had to inspect periodically the growing number of county bridges, attend sessions and report about them, prepare plans and estimates and superintend all work. This was agreed by James Green, civil engineer, when he was appointed bridge surveyor of Devon in 1808 at £300. Some idea of the distances travelled and the probable amount of time spent during the year may be gathered from the appointment of the architect G.A. Underwood as surveyor of bridges and other public works in Somerset in 1818. He was to attend the first day of each quarter sessions (for which he was paid £20 a year). He later estimated that he travelled generally about 2000 miles for the county; this probably involved the equivalent of not more than between ninety and one hundred days' work. During the two years after his first appointment in 1818, he not only supervised numerous bridge works but also dealt with alterations to the Shepton Mallett house of correction and Ilchester gaol (which included the preparation of plans and valuation of property to be bought). He also set up a clerk's office in Wilton house of correction.[26] In addition, surveying the site for a new building, its valuation and the negotiation of its purchase was sometimes an important task.

In the later eighteenth century some of the surveyors employed by the justices were still building craftsmen, such as carpenters and joiners, bricklayers or masons. Of the five bridge surveyors appointed by Devon in 1787, four were described as builders, three being joiners by trade.[27] John Best, appointed surveyor of Hertfordshire in 1798, was a carpenter who had contracted for county bridge and prison works in the 1780s and 1790s.[28] Nevertheless, the choice of a practising surveyor or architect

[24] A. Bayliss, *The Life and Works of James Trubshaw, 1777–1853* (Stockport, 1978), p. 6.
[25] Colvin, *British Architects*, p. 356; LSE, Webb Collection, vol. 115.
[26] Dorset RO, QS 07, fos 109–10; Somerset RO, CQ 2.2/6 (2) and (3). He told the Dorset justices in July 1821 that his usual daily charge was two guineas and that his annual bill never exceeded £200.
[27] Devon RO, QS 1/21, Midsummer 1787, and QS 88/84.
[28] *Hertfordshire County Records*, 8, pp. 433–78.

was becoming more common. The county surveyor of Staffordshire in the first four decades of the nineteenth century, Joseph Potter, had previously supervised alterations and repairs to Lichfield and Hereford Cathedrals, becoming the established architect at Lichfield Cathedral. G.A. Underwood, appointed surveyor to Somerset in 1818 and Dorset in 1821, had been trained in the office of Sir John Soane and had been practising as an architect in Cheltenham.[29] Architects were still prepared to take on bridge works but, with the development of the professions of architect, surveyor and civil engineer, several of the county surveyors appear to have been primarily civil engineers concerned with transport undertakings such as bridges, canals or docks and harbours. Thomas Telford, the county surveyor of Shropshire responsible for several notable Shropshire bridges in the 1790s, was also a road-builder and canal-maker and an improver of harbours. He had designed the important Menai and Conway suspension bridges in North Wales.[30] James Green, the Devon surveyor after 1808, was also involved in several west country canal schemes. At least two other county surveyors before 1820 described themselves as 'engineers'. Telford became the first president of the Institution of Civil Engineers in 1820. Thus county surveying work made at least a small contribution to the emergence of a new profession.

Despite the regular use of the same surveyor, whether or not with an official title, counties often called on the help of an architect or surveyor of repute for works of particular magnitude, taste, skill or difficulty. In 1819 a committee of Middlesex justices said that the office of surveyor had formerly been treated as consistent with the station of a person in the rank of clerk of the works, leaving them free to engage an architect when needed.[31] Some of the most celebrated surveyors and architects of the time were involved in this manner with the types of building handled by the justices. The architect Smirke designed the Cumberland county courts, Gloucestershire and Herefordshire shire halls, the Lincolnshire county courts and the Maidstone sessions house in the 1810s and 1820s. In the 1780s ten counties and boroughs engaged in rebuilding their prisons consulted William Blackburn, regarded as the leading prison architect of the time; he designed, for example, Staffordshire gaol, erected from 1788, despite the appointment in 1785 of a surveyor of bridges.[32] Hampshire employed Robert Mylne to design and superintend a new

[29] Colvin, *British Architects*, pp. 774–76, 1000.
[30] Ibid., p. 970; L.T.C. Rolt, *Thomas Telford* (Harmondsworth, 1979), chapters 3–12.
[31] Greater London RO, MJ/OC 19, p. 58; Colvin, *British Architects*, p. 877–78.
[32] Colvin, *British Architects*, pp. 128–29; Staffordshire RO, QS 018, fol. 204; William Salt Library, 'Staffordshire Gaol Accounts, 1788–93', M605.

bridge at Romsey in 1782, despite its use of a regular bridge surveyor named George Hookey. Mylne was recommended as 'an experienced architect conversant in bridge building' by one of the justices to see if the bridge should be repaired or rebuilt, and to give a plan and estimate; at £3039 the rebuilding was the most costly bridge undertaking by Hampshire justices during this period.[33]

Sometimes the selection of a design was based on a competition, the winner superintending the building. For example, the York architect John Carr produced the winning design for a bridge at Ferrybridge in January 1797, following an advertisement in the *Leeds Mercury* that 'such persons as think proper' could submit plans and offering a 'proper gratuity' for the most approved scheme. In this case, while Carr did not provide constant supervision, he prepared virtually all the working drawings and issued copious written instructions to the regular West Riding bridge surveyor on matters of construction and design. On the other hand, justices sometimes did not advertise for designs because they preferred to employ an architect or surveyor whom they had used previously, rather than an unknown person. This is well illustrated by the comment of a leading Kesteven justice in April 1828:

> With respect to the Sleaford sessions house, I am quite sure, the best plan would have been to have employed Mr Smirke at once . . . The competition scheme is far better in theory than in practice, and after the experience we have had of Mr Smirke's character and talent [in building the county hall], there was no reason for being thus exposed to the speculations of minor architects.[34]

In these cases it was common to pay the architect or surveyor a commission of 5 per cent of the money spent on the building. In addition, he was often paid a fee for attendance and for plans relating to the choice of the site and the building before the contractors or craftsmen began work. His travelling expenses were also paid if he lived some distance from the building work. Particularly in this case, and if his attendance was only expected intermittently, a clerk of the works was appointed to provide day-to-day direction and supervision of the building. Surrey, for example, employed the London surveyor Kenton Couse for the construc-

---

[33] Hampshire RO, QO 19 and bridge committee minute book, 1782–1817, fos 1–29.

[34] A. Booth, 'Carr of York and the Book of Bridges', *Yorkshire Archaeological Journal*, 38 (1954), p. 370; R.B. Wragg, 'The Bridges of John Carr', *Transactions of the Hunter Archaeological Society*, 10 (1979), p. 328; Lincolnshire RO, Kesteven QS, clerk's papers, 5 (1828), no. 27.

tion of Chertsey bridge with Middlesex between 1779 and 1784. At Translation sessions 1785, out of a total outlay by Surrey of £6813 4s. 11d. on the building, Couse was paid by the county for surveying the old bridge, making drawings of the new stone bridge with land arches and abutments on the Surrey shore, forming contracts, directing the works and settling the accounts at a figure of £364 16s. 0d.; this represented 5 per cent of the total expenditure, including the expenses of journeys and sundry attendances.[35] When Berkshire employed the architect Robert Brettingham, as surveyor of a new gaol in 1791, it paid him a fee for his travelling expenses and plans before building began, and 5 per cent on the building works; in addition a clerk of the works was paid £1 2s. 0d. per week.[36] Less often a fee or salary was paid.[37]

The gradual tendency to begin employing a regular county surveyor was partly a consequence of the more general use of surveyors before the making of a contract and in superintending the construction. Procedure in the later seventeenth century and early eighteenth century tended to be relatively informal and very varied. In some instances surveyors were employed to prepare a plan and perhaps an estimate; the justices then negotiated a price with one or more workmen. On the other hand, it was not uncommon for justices to ask workmen to deliver a plan and perhaps specifications with a proposal of the price at which they would be prepared to build. This was the case, for example, with the construction of the Surrey county gaol in 1720–23 according to the plan, scantling and price put forward by a local carpenter, Edward Oliver; no independent surveyor appears to have been used beforehand or to have superintended construction, but two craftsmen, 'being persons usually employed in surveying building', were asked on completion to measure the building and compare it with the plan and scantlings.[38] The act of 1739 required that county bridge works be advertised, and that the most reasonable proposal be accepted, but bridges continued to be built on the basis of plans and proposals put forward by intending contractors following advertisement. Some bridges

[35] Surrey RO, QS 2/1/26, p. 377.

[36] Berkshire RO, QS 07, pp. 51, 181.

[37] Shropshire paid the surveyor of the shire hall £60 in October 1783 and agreed to pay the surveyor of the new gaol and house of correction £60 a year in July 1787: Shropshire RO, minutes of commissioners to build shire hall and gaol, 1783–94, fos 13, 38. In the case of the building of the Wakefield lunatic asylum in the 1810s, a fee of £750 was agreed to be paid to the architects, Watson and Pritchett, for superintending (6 July 1815); later the clerk of the works was to be paid two guineas weekly, West Yorkshire RO, Wakefield Hospital, minutes of the committee for building a lunatic asylum.

[38] Surrey RO, QS 2/1/12, p. 344; compare also the building of the Hertfordshire county gaol, *Hertfordshire County Records*, 7, *1700–52* (Hertford, 1931), p. 17.

were being built in Yorkshire in this way in the 1760s and early 1770s. The same was true of other types of county building: in Hertfordshire James Adams designed and built the shire hall in 1768–70; and the county gaol was designed and built by a local bricklayer and builder in 1776–80. In general by the 1770s the prior drawing of plans, the making of surveys and the preparation of estimates before tenders were obtained was becoming increasingly usual.[39] As late as 1798 and 1809 Bedfordshire contracted with a local builder for a gaol and for an asylum on the basis of the plans he submitted.[40] This, however, was an exceptional case.

In the first two or three decades of the nineteenth century many counties tightened up their procedure for handling building works in such a way as to increase the work of the surveyor. Several courts issued orders making the preparation of estimates standard practice. In April 1803 the West Riding justices decided that when in future plans of new bridges or of alterations were laid before sessions, the surveyor was to produce estimates.[41] The bridge act of 1803, which required that new bridges erected otherwise than by the county should, as a condition of their becoming reparable by the county, be constructed as the justices might approve, led the courts to order careful supervision by the bridge surveyor. The Northumberland justices in January 1827 ordered

> that in future when any person shall be desirous to erect or build a bridge within this County at their own expense, and shall in pursuance of the statute of 43 George III c. 59 apply for one of the Bridge Surveyors of this county to inspect the same, such Bridge Surveyor shall report to the next Quarter Sessions in writing, whether he approves of the site, foundation and detail of the same, and that when such bridge shall be completed to his satisfaction he shall deliver in a report in writing to the then next Quarter Sessions which shall be entered in the records of this County.[42]

[39] Hampshire RO, QM 6, pp. 366, 377, QO 17, fol. 361; West Yorkshire RO, QS 024, fos 29, 54 (relating to Ferrybridge, 1764); *York Courant*, 1771–72 (advertisements of bridge works for North and West Ridings); A.L. Thomas, 'Geographical Aspects of the Development of Transport and Communications Affecting the Pottery Industry of North Staffordshire during the Eighteenth Century', *Collections for a History of Staffordshire Edited by the William Salt Archaeological Society, 1934* (1935), pp. 86–87; *Hertfordshire County Records*, 8, pp. 155–58, 231, 248.

[40] E. Stockdale, 'Bedford Prison', *Bedfordshire Historical Record Society*, 56 (1977), pp. 87–88; Bedfordshire RO, QGE 1/1.

[41] LSE, Webb Collection, vol. 252. Devon's committee of expenditure recommended similarly in Easter 1821: Devon RO, sessions order book 1/25, p. 286.

[42] Quoted in S. and B. Webb. *English Local Government*, v, *The Story of the King's Highway* (London, 1963), p. 111. For a similar Dorset order in October 1831, LSE, Webb Collection, vol. 115.

By the end of the period concern about rising costs and the desire for high standards of construction led to the normal use of a surveyor at all stages of county building and repair work.

Before 1739 when the justices and sometimes their surveyor sought to contract work they enquired personally of one or more craftsmen about the task and its price. Often, after discussion with several workmen, they received a number of proposals in order to have the job done as cheaply as possible. In April 1723 the North Riding court ordered the surveyor of bridges (John Bartlett) to contract with such workman or workmen as he should judge would well (and as cheaply as possible) build News-ham bridge of wood; two named justices were 'to assist and direct the said Mr Bartlett in making a bargain for building the said bridge'.[43] When the Ipswich division of the Suffolk court wanted to convert some rooms for the county gaol in April 1719, the magistrates were asked to receive proposals from several craftsmen, and to agree with those offering the most reasonable proposal for up to £100.[44] These examples are exceptions, as unfortunately little documentary evidence survives about the way contracts were made in this period. The extent to which justices secured a number of proposals or even tried to bargain with craftsmen cannot be known. In some cases they were probably content to agree with a workman whom the county had used before, or whom they had employed themselves on their own estates, rather than make thorough inquiries for the cheapest price.

The act of 1739 required justices engaged on bridge works to accept 'the most reasonable price or prices' after public notice had been given at quarter sessions. This was done by newspaper advertisements and the distribution of handbills. The Gloucestershire justices at Easter sessions 1741 received a presentment of Over bridge. The clerk was ordered to advertise in the *Gloucester Journal* that the justices at the next quarter sessions would contract 'with any person or persons for repairing amend-ing and altering the said bridge piers and arches at such price and prices and in such manner as shall be thought most reasonable and expedi-ent'.[45] When the Shropshire justices decided to rebuild Atcham bridge, in February 1768, they ordered that 'notices be printed and dispersed'.[46] When the plans and specifications had been prepared in advance by the

---

[43] *North Riding Quarter Sessions Records*, 8, p. 168; see also Essex RO, QS 04, p. 223 (6 April 1714), concerning the new nisi prius court.

[44] East Suffolk RO, 105/2/14, fol. 147.

[45] Gloucestershire RO, QS 06, fol. 215.

[46] Shropshire RO, QS bridge book, 1741–1827, fol. 14.

surveyor, as became increasingly usual during the following decades, newspaper advertisements tended to follow a similar form. For example, on 21 July 1772 the West Riding justices advertised as follows in the *York Courant*:

> BRIDGES to be contracted for.
>
> NOTICE is hereby given, That all Workmen willing to contract for the building of Breasley Bridge, and widening Sowerby Bridge, both over the River Calder, near Halifax, in the County of York, may attend the Referees [the Justices] appointed for the Purpose of contracting for the rebuilding and widening the said Bridges, at the Old Cock in Halifax, on Thursday the 23d Day of July inst., by Ten o'clock in the Forenoon of that Day, to deliver in Estimates with the lowest terms for which they will undertake the Work according to the Plans and Elevations, which may be seen at any Time before the said Meeting, at the House of John Holroyd at Sowerby Bridge.

Prison buildings and the construction of court houses were being advertised in a similar way by the 1760s. Newspaper advertisement and the distribution of handbills remained the normal way of seeking tenders for the rest of the period. Occasionally, in the case of a large building, a selection of builders were asked by letter to tender to prevent offers at too low a price.[47] Sureties were normally required from men performing substantial contracts; the occasional failure to produce them led to the work being given to another person. By the early nineteenth century craftsmen were used whose work was known locally or could be checked by oral or written enquiry. When the North Riding received tenders for a new gaoler's house at the bridewell in May 1827, and three craftsmen were chosen, letters were written to an architect, a house owner, a parish committee and two estate agents about a bricklayer.[48]

Throughout the period a common means used by the justices for the erection of prisons and sessions houses was the single contract for the whole undertaking with one builder; or with two or more builders acting in partnership. Among the many instances of this method of contracting were the building of Hertfordshire gaol in 1702–3; Nottinghamshire shire house in 1770; Folkingham house of correct-

[47] For example, see *Oxford Gazette and Reading Mercury*, 18 January 1768; *York Courant*, 1 July 1766. For invitations to tender by letter, see the case of the Middlesex lunatic asylum, Greater London RO, MA/A/J1, p. 323; the idea for it may have come from the Office of Works, which employed it on all new building in the 1820s, M.H. Port, 'The Office of Works and Building Contracts in Early Nineteenth-Century England', *Economic History Review*, second series, 20 (1967), p. 102.

[48] North Yorkshire RO, QAG, 1825–28.

ion in Kesteven, 1808; Cambridgeshire gaol, 1803–9; and the Middlesex lunatic asylum in 1829–30.[49]

An alternative was to use one principal contractor, but to provide for some of the materials or individual skills in other ways. It was common to organise separately the supply of some of the building materials, particularly stone or bricks.[50] Devon contracted for the carcass of its new county gaol in 1790 with a single builder, John Fentiman of Southwark; in this case, some of the bricks had already been made, and there were separate contracts for the cast ironwork, the smith's work, slating, plumbing and glass.[51]

Again the various tasks might be carried out under contracts with the different craftsmen. In some cases the tradesmen continued to supply the materials, in the same way as the contractor, for the whole building. Although this method of multiple contracts was not used as often as the single contract, numerous examples of it may still be found among the building works of the justices. They include the Middlesex sessions house, 1779–82, the Surrey county gaol in the 1790s, the Nottinghamshire house of correction at Southwell (1807–9) and the West Riding lunatic asylum (1815–19).[52] Even more frequent was the 'direct' method, by which contracts were made with the various craftsmen, with some or all of the materials, such as timber, bricks and stone bought by the justices and their surveyor. An early eighteenth-century case of the justices buying in at least some of the materials is that of the building of the Buckinghamshire county gaol and courthouse after 1721. Later examples include several courthouses, such as Essex (1789–91) and Cumberland (1808–22).[53] Among other buildings erected in this way were the Berkshire house of correction at Abingdon (1805–16), the Gloucestershire lunatic asylum (1814–24) and the enlargement of the Sussex county gaol at Horsham (1819–21).[54]

[49] *Hertfordshire County Records*, 7, p. xxiii; K.T. Meaby, *Nottinghamshire: Extracts from the County Records of the Eighteenth Century* (Nottingham, n.d.), p. 54; Lincolnshire RO, Kesteven QS minutes, 1802–8, p. 617; Cambridgeshire RO, QS 011, p. 190; Greater London RO, MA/A/J1, pp. 329–31, and MA/A/J2, pp. 150–51.

[50] E.g. Bury house of correction, 1786–88, East Suffolk RO, 105/2/47, fos 124, 125.

[51] Devon RO, QS gaol building committee minutes, 1787–95.

[52] Greater London RO, MA/S/439; Surrey RO, QS 5/4/2; *Nottingham Journal*, 31 January 1807; West Yorkshire RO, Wakefield Hospital building minutes.

[53] *Records of Buckinghamshire*, 12 (1927), supplement, p. iv; J. Hughes, 'The Building of the Courts, Carlisle, 1807–1822', *Transactions of the Cumberland and Westmoreland Antiquarian and Archaeological Society*, 70 (1970), pp. 210–11.

[54] C.W. Chalklin, 'Prison Building by the County of Berks, 1766–1820', *Berkshire Archaeological Journal*, 69 (1979), p. 67; Gloucestershire RO, HO 22/1/1; West Sussex RO, QAP/4/WE3 (1).

There were also different ways of paying for building work. The contract for payment for an agreed sum (subject to any alterations made in the course of building, particularly additional items) was the typical method when the whole task was given to one contractor. Payments were made by instalments as the work proceeded, with extras paid at a valuation, a bond and sureties being required from the contractor. Presumably the undertaker either sub-contracted the work which he was unable to do with his own labour to various craftsmen; or bought the materials himself and paid the craftsmen for their labour. Since the justices only employed and paid the contractor, there is generally no record of how the contractor himself organised the construction. Only in two instances has any evidence been found on this point. The two Shrewsbury builders who contracted for the Shropshire county gaol in 1788 themselves obtained the timber and stone and made the bricks, paying the bricklayers, carpenters, masons and labourers on a weekly basis; the more specialised skills, such as slating, appear to have been sub-contracted.[55] The contractor for the Middlesex asylum in 1829, William Cubitt, who tendered at £63,200, was a permanent employer of about 700 men with his own 'large workshops and ample accommodation for the workmen'; however, as a large London builder of the 1820s, Cubitt was hardly typical of the men who contracted for county building works.[56] Many country builders obtaining a contract for a new prison or large bridge needed a temporary expansion of their workforce. On the award of the contract for a new bridewell at Reading for £5073 in January 1785, the Reading builder William Collier (who was also a brickmaker) advertised in the *Reading Mercury* on 31 January as follows: 'To brick and tile makers. Wanted, ten or twelve brick makers for a season or two, who may have immediate employ in digging clay etc. and to begin making bricks as early in the spring as the weather will permit of.' Agreements with a contractor for payment by prices fixed in the contract for various types of work, which were measured during the course of construction (known as 'measure and value' or 'measure and prices'), were rarely used by the justices when the building was given to one man or a partnership.[57] The method was used extensively in other types of public building, particularly barrack construction during the French wars from 1793.

[55] Shropshire RO, 348/353.
[56] Port, 'The Office of Works', pp. 96, 109.
[57] Apparently it was used for building the Durham county gaol, *Newcastle Courant*, 5 November 1808. For an unusual instance of the method being used to construct a bridge, see Montford bridge on the Severn, 1790–93, Shropshire RO, QS bridge book, 1741–1827, fol. 58.

When the justices contracted with the various craftsmen it was usual – though not invariable – for payment to be made according to measure and value. The craftsmen tendered for the work on a price basis and the prices were fixed in their contract. In cases where the materials were bought by the county, craftsmen might be paid either on a daywork basis or by piece-work according to periodic measurement; where alterations were concerned the former might be preferred, because of the difficulty of measuring the new work.[58]

Most bridges were built by a single contractor. In some counties this method seems to have been used almost as a matter of course. This practice is observable, for example, in Cumberland, Nottinghamshire and Devon in the eighteenth and early nineteenth centuries.[59]

In some instances accessory work was handled separately from the main contract; in Staffordshire in the 1810s and 1820s it was common to make payments to different men for such work as digging, road making, embankments and even for materials such as timber and lime.[60] The 'direct labour' method was used much less frequently for new bridge building than the single contract, though it was often used for repair work. Several of the forty bridges built or widened by the North Riding while John Carr was surveyor of bridges between 1772 and 1803 were erected by direct labour,[61] although most were erected by a single contractor. The method was also used by the Essex justices for some of its new bridges in the later eighteenth century.[62]

There was some tendency for smaller, simpler and less costly building to be contracted with a single person; a higher proportion of the more ambitious undertakings were erected by agreements with the various craftsmen on a measure and value basis. The smaller work was relatively straightforward and was less likely to involve the contractor in financial problems during construction. In April 1819, when Surrey was considering the building of a new house of correction at Brixton, the committee of justices approving the plans and specifications recommended that, as the works were of great

[58] The West Riding lunatic asylum was built by contracts with craftsmen at a lump sum. On the use of day work and piece rates, Port, 'The Office of Works', p. 102.

[59] Cumbria RO (Carlisle), QAB 4–5; Nottinghamshire RO, QAB 2 and 4; Devon RO, QS 88 and QS 1/18–21.

[60] Staffordshire RO, FAa 1/6–8.

[61] Wragg, 'Bridges', pp. 332–33; York Georgian Society, *The Works in Architecture of John Carr* (York, 1973), pp. 1–36.

[62] Essex RO, Q/FAa 4/2, FAc 6/1; under the direct labour system for bridge building the money was paid to the craftsmen and suppliers of materials by the surveyors or supervising justices.

extent and beyond the means of many persons to contract for the whole building, advertisements should invite proposals both for the whole works and for the work of particular trades.[63] The tendency for the justices to give the more modest projects to a single contractor but to use individual craftsmen for a larger undertaking is illustrated by the case of Surrey in the later eighteenth century when Gwilt was surveyor. In 1771 the county gaol was enlarged for £689 13s. 0d. a new house of correction in Southwark was erected in 1772–73 for £2682 and rebuilt in 1781 for £2009 5s. 4d.; all these buildings were handled by a single contractor. On the other hand, the new county gaol built between 1792 and 1799 for £39,019 10s. 8d. was contracted to nine different trades.[64] Presumably almost all county bridges were handled by single contractors because the task was relatively straightforward and the cost small in comparison with the majority of county gaols and courthouses.

Opinion is known to have varied among leading architects and surveyors in the early nineteenth century about the best method of contracting. This was no doubt paralleled in the outlook of the surveyors and architects who advised the justices. Their influence is well illustrated in the case of the celebrated prison architect William Blackburn in the 1780s. Most of the prisons for which he provided the design and advised the county were erected on the basis of a main contract for the carcass, with smaller contracts for ironwork, plumbing, slating etc., as in the case of the Devon county gaol already quoted.[65] In some counties there may have been a tendency to follow a similar practice of building in successive works. All the building projects by Middlesex in the 1770s and 1780s, including the extension of the New Prison, the great house of correction at Clerkenwell (costing £65,000), and the new sessions house were built by arrangements with the different trades.[66]

In general a single contract was simpler and it appeared to have the advantage of determining the cost beforehand. It passed the responsibility for choosing the craftsmen and buying the materials and directing and coordinating the work of the craftsmen to a contractor who was anxious for financial reasons to secure completion as soon as possible.

[63] Surrey RO, QS 2/1/41, p. 109.

[64] Surrey RO, QS 5/4/2; QS 2/1/22, pp. 561–63; QS 2/1/23, pp. 13, 337; QS 2/1/25, p. 637.

[65] Port, 'The Office of Works', p. 94; see above p. 80. For Staffordshire county gaol, William Salt Library, M605, and typescript of a history of the gaol by Mr Standley. On replacing Cliffe house of correction, East Sussex RO, QS proceedings, 1788–94 etc.

[66] Greater London RO, MA/G/GEN 1, 28 June 1773; MA/S/319–61; MA/G/CBF 1, 16 January 1788.

Because of the possible difficulties of independent craftsmen working together, and of the savings their enterprise would achieve, contractors sometimes thought that one person executing the whole was simpler and cheaper. A Lincolnshire builder who was considering making a tender for work on the Sleaford sessions house in October 1828 wrote of 'the great disadvantages when a number of contractors are employed on the same business . . . I venture to assert that one person under an aggregate sum for the whole of the works would be enabled to execute from 5 to 7½ per cent lower than when the same works are given to a number'. These works were to do with relatively small buildings which cost about £7000.[67]

It is understandable that some surveyors and justices disliked one contract for a major structure. They felt particularly that the builder was tempted to skimp work; it also demanded capital resources and organising skill on the part of the builder. The contract was difficult to change when alterations were proposed during work. They felt that better workmanship and a fair price for both tradesmen and county came from splitting the work and paying by measure and value. Direct purchase of materials by the county economised by eliminating the contractor's or the craftsmen's profit on the purchase.

Naturally the views of the justices and their architectural advisers have survived rather than those of the builders. When it built its great Maidstone gaol in the 1810s, Kent's architect Daniel Alexander chose payment by measure and value. In his words:

> contracts made in this manner for the *price* of the work rather than for a *lump sum* for the work is the most fair and reasonable to both parties. It admits of less liability of being misunderstood on the part of the proposer and by consequence deters such practices as contractors are tempted to resort to reimburse themselves, and it is therefore the method (except in very simple and particular cases) I always recommend.

He arranged at least twenty contracts between 1810 and 1816 for materials or works, from fencing and excavating to the main brickwork and masonry. The arguments urged by William Parsons, the Leicestershire county surveyor, in January 1826 when the building of a bigger gaol was discussed were wider. He preferred payment by measure and value to a fixed-sum contract, partly because the justices might make changes during construction without the great inconvenience of altering the contract for a sizeable building. He had found great disadvantages in an agreement for a lump sum 'for large buildings of an unusual character and description, viz. the Custom House which was so altered and varied from the contract by constant additions and improvements that the *whole* of the work was obliged to be measured and left to a value price and the contract abandonned'. The other advantage was that 'by a contract for quantities the work is equally put into competition and there is always a greater anxiety and willingness on the part of the contractor to do his work in the best style because he is satisfied that he has his price for the quantity he give, which in a general contract let him make his estimate ever so carefully, he is not'. Worcestershire, Derbyshire and Rutland gaols were built conveniently in this way. It allowed sessions to alter prices when the local cost of materials or labour changed during the work. Leicestershire altered prices at Easter 1827; it agreed to an increase in the carpentry charges, and to let the ironfounders continue on tendering reduced prices. The widespread use of the method at the time on substantial buildings is understandable, although opinion in some quarters was beginning to change.[68]

The employment which the justices made available to craftsmen comprised such different items as contracts for major building works costing as much as £10,000 or £20,000; smaller buildings and bridges for several hundred pounds; the specialised work of a single craft (such as ironwork or glazing) at possibly a similar figure; and repairs to buildings and bridges for £20 or £50. As a result, jobs were available to building tradesmen working at a very varying level of operation. Some were basic craftsmen, such as bricklayers or carpenters, whose main employment came from repairs, alterations and enlargements to farm buildings, country houses or urban dwellings and public buildings. Smiths and plasterers, painters and glazier did their more specialised work in new and older houses and in public buildings. Men who took the larger contracts from the justices worth several thousand pounds were often among the leading builders of their district. They typically had a variety of business interests, dealing in building materials, architects' work, speculative house erection, country house improvements, bridge construction, church and other public building. The absence of builders' records makes it impossible to reconstruct the business careers of any of the craftsmen and contractors involved on one or two or on many occasions in justices' work. Some of the builders who took the larger contracts are

[68] *New Maidstone Gaol Order Book, 1805–1823*, ed. C.W. Chalklin, Kent Records, 23 (1984), p. 23; Leicestershire RO, QS 6/2/1, 32/2/1, 32/3/15/2,4; C.G. Powell, *An Economic History of the British Building Industry, 1815–1979* (London, 1980), p. 28.

also known in connection with other building activities; a little may be said about them, although it is impossible to give a comprehensive account of the work for which they contracted. Nearly all the smaller men, whether they were smiths, plumbers or jobbing carpenters or bricklayers, must remain mere names.

Most local building firms that handled quarter sessions work only took a sizeable contract on one or two occasions. Such work was clearly incidental to business activities which were predominantly concerned with other types of building. This is true, for example, of John Carline of Shrewsbury (1761–1835), who had a long career as builder, statuary mason and architect. He and his sons executed numerous monuments over several decades from the end of the 1780s and he is known to have handled the construction of a terrace and a cottage estate in Shrewsbury. He built and altered country houses and churches, including the erection of St Alkmund's church, Shrewsbury, in 1794–95. He and his partner John Tilley both designed and built the large Welsh Bridge over the Severn at Shrewsbury in 1793–95 at a contract price of £6600 for a committee of subscribers. So far as the Shropshire justices were concerned, Carline and another partner, John Sheltock, built the new county gaol between 1788 and 1794; their cashbook records the payment by Carline of £14,030 1s. 4d. They also contracted for the work of building Montford bridge between 1790 and 1793, receiving about £1968 10s. 0d., the supply of the stone being separate. Carline did further bridge work for the county in the 1810s.[69]

A rather similar case was that of Appleton Bennison of Hull, whose principal work for quarter sessions was the contract to build the sessions house, gaol and keeper's house for the East Riding justices in December 1804 at a price of £8550 and on which a total of about £22,000 was spent in the next eight years. He had been previously employed by the Riding on lesser building work, including the register office at Beverley, and continued to be used for various works in the years after 1812. A treasurer's voucher records that he received £2244 in instalments between 1814 and January 1816, comprising work at the register office at £174 3s. 9d.; building four new cells at the house of correction by contract for £1260; raising the prison walls at £370 17s. 5d.; and jobbing work at the county hall for £438 19s. 9d. He also contracted for works at Bridlington harbour

[69] Colvin, *British Architects*, p. 215; R. Gunnis, *Dictionary of British Sculptors, 1660–1851* (London, 1951), p. 80; A.W. Ward, *The Bridges of Shrewsbury* (Shrewsbury, 1935), p. 147; Shropshire RO, 348/353, and general accounts, 1788–96; M.C. Hill, 'Iron and Steel Bridges in Shropshire, 1788–1901', *Transactions of the Shropshire Archaeological Society*, 56 (1959), pp. 113, 115.

over eighteen years (1792–1810), and built at least one bridge, that over the River Hull, at Tickton in the East Riding, in 1804–5. He was also an architect and monumental mason. On 31 January 1801 he advertised in the *Hull Advertiser* 'PLANS and ELEVATIONS drawn at the shortest notice; MARBLE CHIMNEY PIECES and MONUMENTS, EXECUTED in the neatest manner'. His most important activity may still have been house building; he was extensively concerned in the erection of substantial terrace housing in the Sculcoates district of Hull. He is also known to have built at least one large town house in Beverley in about 1815.[70]

James Trubshaw (1777–1853), who did work for the Staffordshire justices, differed from Bennison in that much of his county building involved bridges, but again most of his work was done for other employers. His father James (d. 1808) was a mason and builder who was appointed county surveyor of Staffordshire in 1793 and handled bridge repairs during the ensuing years; with his two sons John and James he took over the contract for Wolseley bridge in 1799 at £2118 13s. 8d. After his father's death, in 1808, the younger James did a variety of county building work in the next fourteen years. In 1811 he was paid for work to six county bridges and for two more in 1812–13. At least three involved the payment of a large sum: he received £1575 for Cheddleton bridge (1811–12); £1430 for Weston bridge (1811–12); and contracted to build Hopwas bridge early in 1813 for £639 10s. 0d. He also won the masonry contract for the lunatic asylum, being paid £3100 12s. 0¾d. for work between 1814 and 1819. He also did some minor masonry work at the county gaol. However, he was also occupied as a church builder and on country house work. His two celebrated buildings were the Royal Manchester Institution (1827–29); and Grosvenor Bridge at Chester, with its single arch of 200 feet span.[71] Trubshaw regarded himself as primarily a builder and civil engineer, and 'as far as possible avoided that which he considered as interfering with the professional architect'.

As a final example of a provincial building firm Robert Cornish and Robert Stribling Cornish, his son, of Exeter, are interesting in their combined function as builders and architects. So far as the county is

---

[70] *Parliamentary Papers* (1825), vi; C.W. Chalklin, *The Provincial Towns of Georgian England: A Study of the Building Process, 1740–1820* (London, 1974), p. 121; Colvin, *British Architects*, p. 107; Humberside County RO, CT2, p. 137, and treasurers' vouchers, 1816; G. Poulson, *Beverlac: or the Antiquities and History of the Town of Beverley*, i (Beverley, 1829), p. 426; I. and E. Hall, *Historic Beverley* (York, 1973), p. 76.

[71] Colvin, *British Architects*, pp. 992–93; A. Bayliss, *The Life and Works of James Trubshaw* (Stockport, 1978); Staffordshire RO, QS 025, Epiphany sessions 1813, Q/FAa 7/6, Q/Alc, box 1, QS B1, Translation sessions 1819.

concerned, the elder Cornish did repair work as a joiner on the Exeter prisons and shire hall in the 1790s; in 1799 he was appointed general surveyor at £10 a year with the care of the county buildings in Exeter; and in 1806 he received the contract for repairing the gaol walls. He also advised on the financial burden of the building of the new bridewell in 1809. Later father and son designed the new city prison in 1818–19. They both designed, and were awarded the building contract for, the sheriff's ward, a prison for debtors for the county, at £8000. Finally, in 1825 the younger Cornish received the contract for altering the gaol and house of correction at £13489 17s. 0d. Yet this county work for between thirty and forty years was only a part of their business. The elder Cornish was surveyor to Exeter Cathedral from 1800 to 1838. Holy Trinity, Exeter, was rebuilt in 1820–21 by 'Cornish and Sons, architects and builders'; and the firm of Cornish and Julian were later involved in other designing and building work for churches and parsonages. In 1818 the younger Cornish also had premises in Fore Street, Exeter, where he sold Roman cement and various types of paint supplied from London.[72]

It was common for London builders to tender for county work in the home counties. For example, three of the seven men who tendered for the new house of correction in Reading in 1784 were based in London. The contractor of the large Essex gaol at Chelmsford in the 1770s was a builder based in St Giles, Cripplegate.[73] On account of the great size and continued expansion of London, and also because of its unequalled credit resources, its builders had exceptional opportunities to develop the experience and financial resources to enable them to compete successfully against local builders in the neighbouring county towns. In the rest of England the local men still usually provided the winning tender.

The one London contractor to obtain a series of contracts over much of the country was a Southwark builder, John Fentiman. In 1773 and 1774 he tendered for small works at the Surrey house of correction and county gaol in Southwark.[74] He obtained five contracts to build the carcasses of county gaols or houses of correction between 1787 and 1790:

[72] Devon RO, QS 1/22, 23, QS 95/20, QS 104/1, QS 1/26, p. 133; Colvin, *British Architects* pp. 271; *Trewman's Exeter Flying Post*, 12 February 1818. John Wing of Bedford also combined designing and building for his county, being responsible for both the new county gaol for £6850 between 1799 and 1801 and for the lunatic asylum in 1809–12 at a contract price of £9585, see n. 40 above.

[73] Berkshire RO, QS 05, p. 255; Essex RO, Q/AGb1/1.

[74] Surrey RO, QS 5/1/1, pp. 176, 196.

31 March 1787	Gloucestershire: Lawford's Gate,	
	Bristol, bridewell	£2165
26 May 1788	Monmouthshire: county gaol	£2600
21 April 1789	Dorset: county gaol	£8060
3 December 1789	Sussex: Lewes bridewell	£4116
15 January 1790	Devon: county gaol	£12,560

He also completed the other three new Gloucestershire houses of correction built in these years, after the original contractor, Gabriel Rogers, went bankrupt. In all these cases the London prison architect William Blackburn prepared plans based on the principles of the prison reformer John Howard and presumably encouraged Fentiman to tender. Fentiman also built a Unitarian chapel at Bristol in 1788 at the same time as the Lawford's Gate bridewell. He followed up the building of Dorset county gaol by building the barracks at Dorchester for about £24,000 in 1794–95, presumably in the latter case using some of the same labour.[75] Fentiman's contracts may be paralleled by those of the barrack contractors who erected one barracks after another in various parts of England during the French wars.[76] Presumably they did so at least in part because these were buildings of the same design erected by the same employer, the barrack department, just as Fentiman was working with the same architect. There was no county contractor similar to Fentiman in the sustained period of building in the decades after 1800. Hugh McIntosh of Bloomsbury Square, 'contractor of public works', who handled bridges and roads for Middlesex in the later 1820s, won the Brentford bridge contract for £7,277 7s. 8d. in 1824 and the Stone bridge (Gloucestershire) work for £1550 in 1825, after Thomas Telford had advised the counties on the bridges. He also provided the embankment and abutments at the Mythe bridge, Tewkesbury, designed by Telford (1823–26). He had begun his working life as a canal navvy, and was now at the peak of his career as a contractor for roads, dockyards, gas works and water works.[77]

[75] K. Kissack, *Monmouth: The Making of a County Town* (Chichester, 1975), p. 216; East Sussex RO, QS proceedings on replacing Cliffe house of correction (one volume), 3 December 1789; Devon RO, QS county gaol building minutes, 1787–96, 15 January 1790; Dorset RO, county prison, 1/9, p. 11; J.R.S. Whiting, *Prison Reform in Gloucestershire, 1776–1820* (Chichester, 1975), pp. 102–3, 139; W.W. Ison, *The Georgian Buildings of Bristol* (London, 1952), p. 82; J. Hutchins, *The History and Antiquities of the County of Dorset*, ii (London, 1873), p. 374.

[76] *Parliamentary Papers* (1806–7), ii.

[77] Greater London RO, MA/D/Br10; Gloucestershire RO, QS 105, fol. 299; J. Bennett, *The History of Tewkesbury* (Tewkesbury, 1830), pp. 286–90; M.M. Chrimer, 'Hugh McIntosh (1768–1840), National Contractor', *Transactions of the Newcomen Society*, 66 (1994–95), pp. 175–92.

Much of the smaller county repair work was done by craftsmen employed regularly by the justices. They were sometimes referred to as 'county carpenter' or 'county bricklayer'. Although the payments they received at any one time tended to be small, these men were often leading local builders. In Hertford a bricklayer and builder named John Kirby was doing repairs to the gaol and house of correction for more than thirty-five years between the late 1740s and the 1780s. Thus in October 1749 he was paid £5 5s. 10d. for work on the gaol; in April 1752 he received £8 3s. 6d. for repairs to the gaol and £21 0s. 7d. for the house of correction; two years later he and a carpenter submitted estimates for gaol repairs totalling £186 4s. 10d. Over the whole time he was working for the justices he obtained only one important contract for a new building, that for the new gaol in 1776 at £5012. His other business included the supply of bricks and tiles to local customers, and repairs to houses and other local public buildings; he may also have built houses in Hertford, for among his papers is an estimate of the bricklayers' work for two houses to be built in Fore Street in 1788 at £5344.[78] Very similar in his work for county justices over several decades in the later eighteenth century was William Middleton of Beverley, whose tasks included repairs and alterations to the house of correction in 1791–92. Middleton was an architect and builders' merchant who erected many houses in Beverley, as well as being employed by the corporation on repair and rebuilding work over about thirty-five years.[79] Nevertheless, most craftsmen employed by the justices on repairs to prisons and the building of small bridges were probably men whose main work consisted of modest jobbing tasks for house owners, farmers and landowners, and who never took on any sizeable contract work or speculative building.

There is almost no evidence about the number of workmen employed in county building. A very large labour force was needed in excavating works such as canals. Its size might be in thousands, or at least hundreds. In March 1805 three thousand men were sought for digging the Royal Military Canal; and in January 1829 'upwards of 600 men are expected to be set to work in the course of a fortnight' making the River Medway navigable from Tonbridge to Penshurst.[80] Even very small transport works might involve many workers for a short time. Twenty-two men with barges

[78] *Hertfordshire County Records*, 7, pp. 353, 371; ibid., 8, pp. 16–362; PRO, C 114/131, bundle inscribed 'the late John Kirby's papers'.

[79] Humberside County RO, CT1, 2; K.A. MacMahon, 'William Middleton: Some Biographical Notes on an Eighteenth-Century Beverley Builder and Architect (1730–1815)', *Georgian Society for East Yorkshire Publications*, 4 (1953–55), pp. 70–80.

[80] *Kentish Gazette*, 4 March 1805; *Maidstone Journal*, 13 January 1829.

were paid £8 15s. 3d. by sessions for 'cleaving' Houghton bridge near Arundel, Sussex, in 1751. During the summer of 1773 after the collapse of Ribchester bridge, Lancashire, forty-one labourers got building stones out of the water for periods of between eighteen and thirty-seven days for £56 5s. 0d. paid by the county.[81]

Building works needed far fewer men, though they had to be at least partly skilled. Some indication of the size of the labour force used on county buildings survives for the 1810s. The construction of the Kent gaol at Maidstone (1810–23) may have drawn on 200 or 300 carpenters, bricklayers and stonemasons at its peak, but the size of the building was exceptional.[82] There was a rise in the number of the workmen at Lancaster Castle between 1817 and 1823, when a female penitentiary and other projects including repairs were undertaken and at least £25,000 was spent. In March 1817 five masons and two joiners were used; in August it was decided that not more than twenty masons should be employed on the new works. This was apart from the labourers. Probably there were at least one hundred men in periods such as the second half of 1819 and from February 1820. At about the same time Lancashire was building a pauper lunatic asylum which by June 1820 cost £42,000. In 1814 the foreman had about thirty-six labourers. Some jobs were done by master craftsmen (plastering, joinery, ironwork, painting, plumbing and glazing); men were also paid for carting.[83] Perhaps the average prison or shire hall used about twenty or thirty skilled men.

[81] West Sussex RO, QR/W/436; Lancashire RO, QSP 2008/4.
[82] *New Maidstone Gaol Order Book*, p. 26.
[83] Lancashire RO, CTA2, pp. 29–31, CTA4, pp. 9–10, 40–43, QAM 1/7, 1/23.

Fig. 5.1. Corbridge Bridge, Northumberland. Rebuilding was finished in 1674 after the justices had claimed in 1666 that £3000 would be needed and following several thousand pounds spent earlier. It was probably the most expensive county bridge work in the seventeenth century.

5

Bridges, 1650–1760

Early modern England inherited almost innumerable bridges from the middle ages, and especially from before about 1350. The major rivers were almost always bridged less than ten miles apart, and often under five miles apart. Main roads, such as those leaving London for the north, west and south, had a bridge at every river crossing. Local roads were also usually tied by bridges. Ferries supplemented the dense bridge network across the lower parts of wide rivers. Fords often linked minor roads, or were alternatives to bridges in dry weather. As well as being vital for trade and personal mobility, bridges were sometimes important landmarks. The famous traveller Celia Fiennes wrote of Ripon in 1697: 'a pretty little Market town mostly built of Stone. There is a good large stone built Church well carved they call it a Minster . . . A pretty large Bridge with several arches called Hewick Bridge, the middle arche is very large and high'.[1]

The number of bridges for which a county was responsible in this period varied. Some quarter sessions with numerous bridges listed them once or twice; most did not. I have counted those mentioned in the surviving records, which may mean an underestimate. Four counties in midland and southern England did negligible bridge work: Lincolnshire and Rutland did not maintain bridges, according to the records; in the eighteenth century Berkshire only repaired two bridges, both shared with other counties; and there was only one county bridge (or possibly two) in Worcestershire.[2] In eighteen counties the courts did significant work with relatively few bridges (see Table 5.1a)

---

[1] D.F. Harrison, 'Bridges and Economic Development, 1300–1800', *Economic History Review*, 2nd series, 45 (1992), pp. 241–46; *The Illustrated Journeys of Celia Fiennes*, ed. C. Morris (London, 1984), p. 95.

[2] *Minutes of Proceedings in Quarter Sessions Held for the Parts of Kesteven in the County of Lincoln 1674–1695*, ed. S.A. Peyton, vols 1 and 2, *Lincolnshire Record Society*, 25 and 26 (1931); Lincolnshire RO, Kesteven QS minutes, 1696–1703, 1724–59, Lindsey QS minutes, 1665–78, 1704–12, 1729–48, Holland QS minutes 1683–1765; Leicestershire RO, Rutland QS minutes, 1742–74 (the first minute or order book); Berkshire RO, QS 01, 02; J.W. Willis-Bund, 'Worcestershire Bridges', *Transactions of the Worcestershire Archaeological Society*, 31 (1911–12), pp. 286, 301; Worcestershire RO, QS 01–3 (1693–1756).

Table 5.1

The Number of County Bridges, 1650–1760

County		Period or Date of Evidence	Number
A. Shires with between Three and Fifteen[3]			
Bedfordshire		Seventeenth, early and mid eighteenth centuries	5
Buckinghamshire		1678–1768	6
Cambridgeshire		1664–65	3
East Riding		*c.* 1650	8
Gloucestershire		1689–1749	4
Hampshire		1680–1725	*c.* 13
Hertfordshire		1682	10
Huntingdonshire		1672, 1752, 1769	3
Lancashire		1646	3 (and roadway)
Leicestershire	(1)	1696, 1705	5
	(2)	1761–85	11
Middlesex		1660–1785	3
Monmouthshire		1789–1800 (earliest date)	10
Northamptonshire		1669–99	3 or 4
Nottinghamshire		Seventeenth century	5 or 6
Oxfordshire		1691–1747	7
Shropshire		Seventeenth century (end)	6
Surrey		1660–1750	8
Wiltshire	(1)	Mid seventeenth century	6
	(2)	By 1720	15

[3] Bedfordshire RO, 'Lock Gate', i, p. 220, ii, p. 157; QBM 1, pp. 1, 3, and P.L. Bell, 'The Office of County Surveyor', 1984 (typescript); Buckinghamshire RO, 'County of Buckingham ... Calendar to the Sessions Records', ii, '1694–1705' (1936), ed. W. Le Hardy and G.L. Reckitt, pp. xxii-xxiii, and iii, '1705–12' (1939), p. 79 (typescripts); Buckinghamshire RO, Q/FB1 (Midsummer 1761), QS 015, p. 474; Cambridgeshire RO, QS 01, pp. 75, 79, 98; G.C.F. Forster, *The East Riding Justices of the Peace in the Seventeenth Century*, East Yorkshire Local History Society (1973), p. 64; Humberside RO, QSV 1/1; LSE, Webb Collection: Gloucestershire; Hampshire RO, Q06, fos 16–17, 19, 23, 39, 76, Q07, fol. 94, Q08, fos 200, 212, 226, 232, 240, 355, 360, and QT15, fos 4, 5; *Hertfordshire County Records: Calendar to the Sessions Books, 1658–1700*, 6, ed. W. Le Hardy (Hertford, 1930), p. 163; *Royal Commission on Historical Monuments (England): Huntingdonshire* (London, 1926), p. 234; E. Jervoise, *The Ancient Bridges of Mid and Eastern England* (London, 1933), p. 96; Huntingdonshire RO, county treasurers' accounts, 1769–85; *Proceedings of the Lancashire Justices of the Peace at the Sheriff's Table during Assize Week, 1578–1694*, ed. B.W. Quintrell, Record Society of Lancashire and Cheshire, 121 (1981), p. 98; Leicestershire RO, QS 5/1/1, 111/1/1; J. Rider, *Report of the Committee of Magistrates Respecting the Public Bridges in the County of Middlesex* (London, 1826), p. 4; Monmouthshire RO, T. Acc. B.0001; Northamptonshire RO, Misc, QS 197; H. Hampton Copnell, *Nottinghamshire County Records in the Seventeenth Century* (Nottingham, 1915), pp. 81–83; Oxfordshire RO, Oxfordshire QS, minute books, 1688–1788; *Victoria*

Table 5.1 Continued

The Number of County Bridges, 1650–1760

County		Period or Date of Evidence	Number
B. Shires with between Twenty and Fifty[4]			
Cumberland	(1)	1665	32
	(2)	1753	67
Dorset		1720s	28
Herefordshire		1665–94	35
Kent		1625–1750	29
Norfolk		1720	39 or 44
Staffordshire	(1)	1620–65, 1687–1700	23 or 24
	(2)	1701–50	45 or 46
Suffolk		1740	33
Sussex		1650–1750	20
Warwickshire	(1)	1625–57	14 or 15
	(2)	1657–74	23
	(3)	1697–1723	34
	(4)	1764	34

continued

History of the County of Shropshire, iii, ed. G.C. Baugh (Oxford, 1979), p. 101; *Surrey Quarter Sessions Records: Order Book and Sessions Rolls, 1659–1661*, ed. D.L. Powell and H. Jenkinson, Surrey Record Society, 35 (1934), pp. 15, 30, and *1661–1663*, ibid., 36 (1935), p. 57; O. Manning and W. Bray, *History and Antiquities of the County of Surrey*, iii (London, 1814), pp. xxxiii, xxxviii; Surrey RO, QS2/1/13, 12 January 1730/1; Wiltshire RO, A1/150/6, 17; A1/160/1, 3, 5/6.

[4] J.B. Bradbury, *A History of Cockermouth* (Chichester, 1981), p. 233; Worshipful Chancellor Ferguson, 'Ancient and County Bridges in Cumberland and Westmorland', *Transactions of the Cumberland and Westmorland Antiquarian and Archaeological Society*, 15 (1899), pp. 118–23 (sixty-seven county bridges in 1753, the rest parish bridges); W.T. Jackman, *The Development of Transportation in Modern England* (2nd edn, London, 1962), p. 152; E. Boswell, *The Civil Division of the County of Dorset* (Sherborne, 1795), pp. 76–86; Dorset RO, QS 1/1; Herefordshire RO, QS 01–3; C.W. Chalklin, 'Bridge Building in Kent, 1700–1830', *Studies in Modern Kentish History*, ed. A. Detsicas and W.N. Yates (Maidstone, 1983), p. 52; Centre for Kentish Studies, U442 Q7, QS Ow3, fol. 46, QS Ow6 (4 April 1706); Norfolk RO, C/S2/7 (12 January 1720); A.L. Thomas, 'Geographical Aspects of the Development of Transport and Communications Affecting the Pottery Industry of North Staffordshire during the Eighteenth Century', *Collections for a History of Staffordshire Edited by the William Salt Archaeological Society, 1934* (1935), pp. 46, 81; Staffordshire RO, QS 02–14 (for the names of further county bridges); East Suffolk RO, 105/2/19, fol. 146; West Sussex RO, QAB/3/W1; East Sussex RO, QAB/3/E1, QR/E397/23; *Warwick County Records*, 3, *Quarter Sessions Order Book Easter 1650 to Epiphany 1657*, ed. S.C. Ratcliff and H.C. Johnson (Warwick, 1937), p. xlix, and ibid., 5, *Orders Made at Quarter Sessions Easter 1665 to Epiphany 1674* (Warwick, 1939), p. lviii; Warwickshire RO, QS order book, 1697–1723, QS 24/22/1.

Nine more county quarter sessions handled between twenty and fifty (see Table 5.1b). Finally there were eleven quarter sessions with between fifty and 200 bridges. No county in the midlands or eastern England had more than fifty bridges apart from Essex, which had about fifty-eight in the later seventeenth century. The majority of county bridges were in the south west, and in the north and the north midlands. Somerset had approximately fifty-five shire bridges (1650–1750), while in Cornwall there were more than fifty between 1737 and 1770, when evidence is first available. The Devon court handled the huge number of over 200 bridges in the seventeenth century. Among the northern shires, Westmorland had about 110 county bridges; as in Devon many were very small. Durham had fifty-two shire bridges in 1688 and Northumberland fifty-three or fifty-four (1687–1750). The North Riding of Yorkshire was responsible for seventy-nine in 1676. West Riding county bridges totalled forty-eight in 1601–2, 112 in 1702, and 113 or 115 in 1744. Derbyshire had sixty-four in 1729. After Devon, Cheshire had the most shire bridges in the eighteenth century: 131 were listed in 1727; 127 in 1741.[5]

All counties which handled bridges gave grants for the repair or building of structures which were the responsibility of hundreds, parishes or individuals. These gifts were less frequent and on average smaller than major charges for county bridges, being mostly under £50. Between 1681 and 1710 the North Riding quarter sessions spent sums on about seventy-five of its bridges, giving gratuities for the exceptional number of approximately fifty non-county bridges. The grants were justified usually on the ground of lack of money on the part of the locality or individual, and the importance of the bridge for trade and passage.[6]

Counties normally had hundred bridges. Their number differed sharply,

[5] *Essex Quarter Sessions Order Book, 1652–1661*, ed. D.H. Allen (Chelmsford, 1974), pp. 30, 42, 64, 96, 118, 185, mentions over forty county bridges and another seventeen or eighteen had work done to them between 1671 and 1700: Essex RO, Q/FAc1; W. Goddard, *An Extract from the Sessions Rolls of the County of Somerset* (London, 1765), pp. 76–91; Cornwall RO, QS 1/1–3; Devon RO, QS 1/5–15; J.F. Curwen, *The Later Records Relating to North Westmorland or the Barony of Appleby* (Kendal, 1932), pp. 14–16; Cumbria RO (Kendal), WQ/01–07; Durham RO, QS OB 7 p. 92; Northumberland RO, Calendar of Northumberland QS order books, 2, Michaelmas 1687 to Midsummer 1697, QS 03–8; *North Riding Record Society Publications*, 6, *Quarter Sessions Records* (1888), ed. J.C. Atkinson, pp. 262–63; Jackman, *Development of Transportation*, p. 151; E.C. Ruddock, *Arch Bridges and their Builders, 1735–1835* (Cambridge, 1979), p. 26; West Yorkshire, RO QD1/461; S. Glover, *The History, Gazetteer and Directory of the County of Derby* (Derby, 1829), p. 258; Cheshire RO, QJB3/8; *Victoria History of the County of Chester*, ii (1979), ed. B.E. Harris, p. 71.

[6] *North Riding Record Society Publications*, 7, *Quarter Sessions Records*, ed. J.C. Atkinson (1889), pp. 49–224.

such as eight in Staffordshire and at least fifty-five in the West Riding. Lancashire, where the six hundreds were exceptionally large, had the huge figure of 491. Six quarter sessions (Kent, Lancashire, Staffordshire, West Riding, Warwickshire and Worcestershire) ordered and recorded levies or payments for work on hundred bridges. These bridges are included in this study. As they were on average smaller than county bridges, being sometimes just for horses and often wooden, charges tended to be lower. Many of the Lancashire hundred bridges were comparable in size with shire bridges in other counties, being bigger than many of the Westmorland county bridges. Some Devon county bridges were probably of the same size as the more sizeable hundred bridges in Kent.[7]

The number of bridges which a county maintained is naturally in part explained by the total for the shire, the latter being decided by its location, size and configuration, being affected by the number and width of its rivers, and the amount of land traffic. Coastal Sussex and Lincolnshire with sizeable rivers had more and more substantial bridges than inland Northamptonshire and Hertfordshire, which were also smaller. Some coastal counties, especially Cornwall, had more seaborne trade than others, while inland shires naturally had none. Counties with much industry or large towns had a denser communications network than others.

The number of county bridges grew considerably between the later sixteenth century and about 1690. From 1531 quarter sessions maintained bridges, both by common law and statute, when there was no other liability to support them. At this time justices' work of all kinds was growing and bridges were increasingly used. There is evidence of bridges which were maintained, or believed to be maintained, by parishes or individuals in the sixteenth and sometimes the early seventeenth centuries later becoming a county responsibility. In 1580 the crown as successor to the local abbots was liable for Chertsey Bridge, Surrey's most important bridge responsibility between 1650 and 1830. One or two counties such as Wiltshire show no bridge work in their later sixteenth-century records, despite activity in the early seventeenth century. The earliest record of sessions work is in the 1560s and 1570s, for the North Riding of Yorkshire and Norfolk respectively. Counties such as Devon and Staffordshire repaired and rebuilt bridges by the beginning of the seventeenth century, as their oldest surviving relevant documents show. Bridges across major rivers such as the Thames, Severn and Trent were usually maintained by income from property or tolls, as had been the case since the middle

[7] Thomas, 'Geographical Aspects', p. 45; West Yorkshire RO, QD 1/707; Lancashire RO, QS G 1/1, p. 70.

ages. Counties with few or no shire bridges lay mainly in a group across the midlands between Gloucestershire and Lincolnshire. These had been among the wealthiest shires in the early fourteenth century, when they had been supplied with many relatively strong bridges by local property owners and institutions to handle their own trade. Presumably their quality enabled those responsible to continue to maintain them. In the seventeenth century counties that adopted bridges were often in poorer regions, particularly the north, which were now beginning to show signs of economic development. It is likely that counties had to repair, improve or build bridges in these areas because the localities themselves could not afford to support or build them; yet growing trade made the need especially great. The many shire bridges in one or two wealthier counties, such as Devon, Essex and Cheshire, may in part be explained by relatively zealous and efficient sessions; their small numbers or absence in counties such as Berkshire and Worcestershire by weaker benches. Further, in contrast to the West Riding of Yorkshire with its rapid industrialisation, Lincolnshire was now relatively backward and its market of farm produce grew only slowly. Economic, social and administrative influences therefore help to explain the differences in the number of bridges for which counties were responsible.[8]

The immediate reason for the adoption of a bridge was often the need to repair combined with the fact that prescriptive responsibility for it was unknown, as no work had been done for many years. This was often the case as, until the seventeenth century, nearly all goods on the roads went by packhorse and there was less trade than later. Landowners who were justices sometimes persuaded quarter sessions to take over their private bridges, though references are too sparse to estimate the extent of this practice. Sir John Reresby of Thrybergh attended West Riding sessions at Barnsley in October 1696:

> I gott ther an order for £10 to be raised upon the weapontack of Strafford and Tickil, for the repair of Saddle Brige or New Brige . . . built about 100 years before by the family for their own convenience . . . And though the use of it was now publique, yet the charge of repairs was still the families bycaus we built it, till by this £10 being given or raised upon the weapon-

---

[8] H.J.M. Stratton and B.F. Pardoe, 'The History of Chertsey Bridge', *Surrey Archaeological Collections*, 73 (1982), p. 116; *Wiltshire County Records: Minutes of Proceedings in Sessions 1563 and 1574 to 1592*, ed. H.C. Johnson (Devizes, 1949); *North Riding Record Society Publications*, 2, *Quarter Sessions Records*, ed. J.C. Atkinson (1881), p. 298; D. Dymond, *The Norfolk Landscape* (London, 1985), p. 232; Norfolk RO, C/Sea 1/1; R.S. Schofield, 'The Geographical Distribution of Wealth in England, 1334–1649', *Economic History Review*, 2nd series, 18 (1965), p. 504.

tack it will now be entitled to be so repaired for the future. I gott also ten pounds to make Dern Brige passable for coach and carriage, which was only before used for horses.

A county may sometimes have assumed care for a hundred bridge which needed costly work because the hundred was a division of the county.[9]

Quarter sessions in the northern and north midland counties, and occasionally in the south, expressed their concern for communications as a justification for bridge works. This reflects the fundamental reason for the growth of county bridge maintenance in the seventeenth century, the fact that transport demands were growing. Inland trade was expanding and wheeled traffic in the form of carts, waggons and coaches were creating serious problems. Existing bridges, which had been adequate for pedestrians, riders or groups of packhorses, were unsuitable for heavy, wheeled transport. While packhorses carried loads of up to 500 pounds weight, a heavy waggon drawn by five or six horses sometimes held twenty or thirty hundredweight. Waggons were a very substantial component of the growing services between London and the rest of England by 1700. Thus there was pressure to widen or rebuild bridges. The growth of transport also explains the demand for the building of bridges to replace fords, impassable after heavy rains, or damaged by waggons.[10]

By the 1690s and especially during the early eighteenth century the attitude of courts was hardening towards bridge responsibilities. They wished to keep down costs, and particularly to avoid more county bridges, although the latter policy reversed previous practice in at least some counties. The reasons probably included a desire for economy generally and the urge for greater efficiency; perhaps also less interest in administrative business. The desire to cut expenditure in other fields is seen in the legislation to reduce poor rate costs and transport expenses. Some counties appointed surveyors or contractors to reduce costs; the biggest spender, the West Riding, appointed contractors in 1712 which greatly lessened outlay. Justices in the early eighteenth century were satisfied with carrying on existing administrative functions. Numbers attending declined in some counties. Four complaints by quarter ses-

[9] Cheshire RO, QJB 3/2 (11 July 1671); Staffordshire RO, QS 0 11, Translation 1710, Easter 1711, QS 0 12 Epiphany 1725/26, Translation 1727; D. Hey, *Packmen, Carriers and Packhorse Roads: Trade and Communications in North Derbyshire and South Yorkshire* (Leicester, 1980), p. 78.

[10] Cheshire RO, QJB 3/2 (4 October 1670, 15 July 1673); Northumberland RO, QS 0 7, p. 439; Jackman, *Transportation*, p. 155; J.A. Chartres, 'Road Carrying in England in the Seventeenth Century: Myth and Reality', *Economic History Review*, 2nd series, 30 (1977), p. 82.

sions about bridges have been traced. Warwickshire court at Easter 1675 noted the great charge of county bridges; to stop the expense being laid on the county or a hundred unless it was obliged to repair, the chief constables were to find out the number of county, hundred and private bridges; and to report on the dimensions and state of the county and hundred bridges and the cost of necessary repairs. However, the county continued to adopt bridges in the following decades. In 1693 the Lancashire court complained of mounting bridge charges: 'what great sums of money are estreated upon this country upon pretence of Bridges, and how forward some persons are to demand and exact great sums for the repair of bridges, whereas much small[er] sums were sufficient' in the past. It was said that the money was converted to private uses, or extravagantly spent. Accounts were to be made by the treasurers and surveyors and only accepted if proved and reasonable. Sums not spent by officials on bridge works were to be returned. Devon and Essex quarter sessions decided that they were being forced to maintain bridges for which others were responsible. The Devon court at Michaelmas 1706 mentioned that 'many endeavours and sinister practices have of late been made whereby to lay the burden of severall bridges at the publique charge of this county which formerly have been, and of right ought to be repaired at the charge of the inhabitants and owners of particular hundreds, parishes etc.'; rewards were offered for discoveries of such practices. On 12 January 1720 Essex quarter sessions noted that obligations by prescription to maintain bridges were being forgotten and, because of the residuary duty of the county to repair, 'many private bridges and causeways have come upon the county to be repaired, and many others are out of repair, and some altogether down and demolished, the reparation of which in time may become a charge to this county'. As the financial burden of bridge repairs and rebuilding was often heavy for a parish or individual, there was a temptation to escape responsibility by this means. While both Devon and Essex seem to have assumed care for many more bridges in the previous century, there is almost no evidence of further bridge adoption.[11]

---

[11] G.W. Oxley, *Poor Relief in England and Wales, 1601–1834* (Newton Abbot, 1974), p. 21; T.S. Willan, 'The Justices of the Peace and Rates of Land Carriage, 1692–1827', *Journal of Transport History*, 5 (1962), p. 198; LSE, Webb Collection: West Riding; N. Landau, *The Justices of the Peace, 1679–1760* (Berkeley and Los Angeles, 1984), pp. 259–61; *Warwick County Records*, 7, *Quarter Sessions Records Easter 1674 to Easter 1682*, ed. S.C. Ratcliff and H.C. Johnson (Warwick, 1946), p. 36; A. Langshaw, 'The Hundred Bridges of the Hundred of Blackburn in the Seventeenth Century', *Transactions of the Historic Society of Lancashire and Cheshire, 1946*, 98 (1948), p. 27; LSE, Webb Collection: Devon; Essex.

Dislike of more expensive bridge charges and particularly of growing bridge responsibilities increased by mid century. Counties, such
as the West Riding of Yorkshire, Warwickshire, Derbyshire and Dorset,
which had adopted bridges earlier, nearly all stopped by the 1720s
and 1730s. The attitudes of most counties to bridge works is illustrated
by the case of Westmorland. Its quarter sessions ordered repairs to be
done in the 1730s and 1740s at as 'moderate' or as 'low' a rate as possible; on receiving a petition from Stainton to rebuild and adopt a
bridge in 1750, the court declared itself 'intirely avers to increase the
number of county bridges, but compassionating the hardships which
ye said inhabitants have laboured under and the great expence' gave
a £4 gratuity.[12]

To some extent it is misleading to discuss the extent of the involvement of quarter sessions in bridge works in terms of the number of
county bridges. They differed in their size and use and hence in the
amount of necessary work. Some stone bridges were no more than
seven, eight or nine feet wide; the majority were between ten and
fifteen or sixteen feet. Most of the West Riding bridges in the mid
eighteenth century had a width of between nine and fifteen feet, with
twelve feet being the median (and most common) size (Fig. 5.2). The

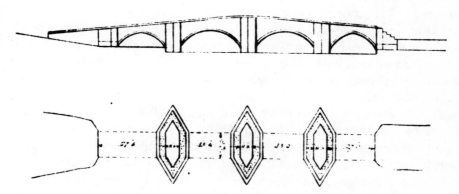

Fig. 5.2. Sowerby bridge, West Riding, built in the sixteenth century and partly
rebuilt in 1674 for about £200, when the central semicircular arches were erected;
it was fourteen feet wide.

[12] Cumbria RO (Kendal), Westmorland QS order books, 1724–37, 1738–50 (Kendal
and Appleby).

normal length was between fifty and 150 feet. One, two or three arches were typical, though four, five and perhaps six were found sometimes. Bridges of seven or more arches (perhaps with some on land to deal with flood water, or of two or three structures) were unusual. Occasionally land walls ('landstalls') or causeways, needed on floodplains, were attached. Bridges on main roads were under growing pressure as the amount of wheeled traffic increased. Crossings on minor routes, on the other hand, needed little attention. Middlesex had only three county bridges; one was an important Thames crossing at Chertsey (shared with Surrey); another was at Brentford on the road from London to Bath and Bristol, both needing frequent expensive maintenance; the third was no more than a local bridge and was seldom repaired by the county.[13]

Rebuilding or partial improvement sometimes involved the widening of a horse bridge. Pedestrians and horses had used the existing bridge, while carts and waggons had passed through the water when it was at a normal level. Recurring floods and more wheeled traffic encouraged the conversion to a cart bridge. However, works are often either not described, referred to as repairs, or less often as rebuilding or building. References to widening (or to any other alteration) are rare, and it is impossible to estimate its extent. Arches destroyed by floods were, nevertheless, rebuilt and causeways altered or added.

The rebuilding and new construction of whole bridges was even more important. Building was occasional in comparison with sizeable repair works in most counties. In a few shires and at particular times new work was considerable. Periodically severe floods destroyed county bridges, which had to be rebuilt. The arches were often too narrow to allow the flood water to pass through freely and the piers were too weak to withstand the exceptional pressure. Some bridges collapsed more than once because of flood action. Exceptionally there was much new work replacing Lancashire and Cheshire fords in the 1670s, and some in Northumberland in the mid eighteenth century. The Lancashire and Cheshire construction followed a clause in the highway act of 1670 allowing their courts to erect new bridges, and rebuild others destroyed during the Civil War, for ten years; in both counties there were 'many and sundry great and deep Rivers which runn cross and through the[ir] common and publique Highways and Roads . . . which many times cannot be passed over without hazard and losse of . . . Lives and Goods . . . for want of convenient god and sufficient Bridges'. The justices of the two counties mentioned

[13] West Yorkshire RO, QD 1/461; Ruddock, *Arch Bridges*, p. 207.

road communications when ordering new bridges. Economic development compelled the erection of bridges in central and northern
Northumberland where there was an insufficient number as late as the
1730s and 1740s. The need for bridges to replace fords is illustrated by
the exceptional surviving account of a Derbyshire crossing in 1718, related
by J.C. Cox. 'The question of Alport ford, over the Lathkil, came before
the Court in July 1718. It was stated that the king's highway from
Manchester and Stockport to Derby and London passed over it, and
that, lying in a bottom, the river there often overflowed . . .' Recent
heavy rains had torn up the channel and rendered it impassable for
eight or ten days together. 'Carriers with loaden horses and passengers
cannot pass the said road without great danger of being cast away . . .'
It was argued that a horse bridge was most urgently needed, for 'great
gangs of London carriers' horses as well as great drifts of malt horses,
and other dayly carriers and passengers use the ford. The bridge was
ordered'.[14]

Local pressure was obviously important in persuading benches to pay
for enlarged or stronger bridges, or a bridge replacing a ford, though
evidence seldom survives. New bridges and the reasons for their erection, like their varying number, are among the most interesting aspects
of the history of county bridges in this period.

The number, size and importance of bridges, and the extent of repair
and rebuilding, naturally affected costs. Materials were also a factor. They
were usually wooden or stone (more often stone) but the use of bricks
was spreading.

Wooden structures were cheaper but more ephemeral than stone, as
they needed repair often. During this period a number were replaced
by stone or brick bridges. Stone was used if it was available locally or the
justices were prepared to pay the extra money at the time to save the
trouble and expense of repairs in future years. Two cases illustrate these
matters. At the Derbyshire court in Michaelmas 1693 it was stated:

that whereas by an order of last Sessions at Bakewell the sume of forty
pounds was given for the repairs of Yorkshire Bridge within the Hundred
of High Peake that the said bridge being a wood bridge stood in frequent
need of such large sumes to repair it. And that it was much more for the
Countyes interest to convert it into a stone bridge there being plenty of

[14] Quintrell, *Proceedings*, pp. 23, 135; Cheshire RO, QJB 3/2 (e.g. 14 January 1672);
R. Newton, *The Northumberland Landscape* (London, 1972), p. 226; J.C. Cox, *Three Centuries
of Derbyshire Annals* (London, 1890), p. 223.

stone near at hand and the masons that have viewed it beinge willinge to undertake to make it with three turned arches for one hundred and thirty pounds.

It was ordered that the stone bridge be erected. When the Kent and Sussex justices decided to rebuilt Lamberhurst bridge in 1753 estimates were obtained both for a timber and for a stone structure. The clerk of Sussex hoped that the Kent court would want a stone bridge on account of its durability 'and then it may be made a very handsome noble little bridge and last for ever'. In September a craftsman estimated the cost of a stone and brick bridge at £331 3s. 10d., the major items being 7342 feet of stone work at 6d. per foot (£183 11s. 0d.) and six rods of brickwork 'if the arches be turned with brick' at £8 8s. 0d. per rod (£52 16s. 0d.). This compared with an estimate of £193 17s. 8d. for a timber bridge. The latter would in fact have been about 40 per cent cheaper than the stone structure which was built.[15]

Brick was being used increasingly in the eastern counties on account of cost and durability. Buntingford timber bridge in Hertfordshire was too badly decayed for repair in 1719. It was rebuilt in brick (of one arch) because it was cheaper.[16]

Bridge rates may have averaged £70 or £80 a year per shire. Quarter sessions of some inland counties, such as Berkshire and Northamptonshire, handled only a few bridges. Charges were trivial, consisting of an outlay in an occasional year or a small annual sum. Other courts did not spend normally more than £20 or £30 a year. In Hertfordshire, where none of the ten bridges was large, the treasurer of the bridge money paid £340 12s. 6½d. between Christmas 1690 and Easter 1703, an average of about £26 a year. Probably in about a quarter of the counties annual expenditure averaged between £100 and £500. The largest bridge spender before the mid eighteenth century was the West Riding: between 1698 and 1712 £7545 19s. 4½d. was laid out on bridges, or about £530 a year. Information is available about bridge rates in eight counties for at least four decades between 1650 and 1760. These shires were among those most concerned with bridge works. The levies for Cheshire and Devon reveal the exceptional importance of new projects and rebuilding after flood damage respectively. Otherwise the rates varied between £450 a decade for Herefordshire and £4974 for the North Riding (Table 5.2).

[15] Cox, *Three Centuries*, p. 220; Chalklin, 'Bridge Building in Kent', p. 57.
[16] *Hertfordshire County Records*, 7, p. 176.

Table 5.2

County Bridge Rates, 1651–1760*

Decade	Cheshire	Devon	Essex	Hereford-shire	Norfolk (incom-plete)	North Riding	Suffolk	Warwick-shire
1651–1660			1220 (9 years)		761	2587		1043
1661–1670	1613			392 (6 years)	1030	2738	730	812
1671–1680	7821 (new works)		3250	506	1277	4974	1835	650
1681–1690	1616		2800	1070	1620	2445	1300	895
1691–1700	1644		4500	2025	1800	1535	1470	704
1701–1710	3174	2270 (8 years)		450	1200	1692	1100	1317
1711–1720	3333	6475 (after floods)		450	1500		1150	1019
1721–1730	4585	3783	4500	665	3000 (7 years)			850
1731–1740	1945	2689 (9 years)		450 (9 years)		4000 (7 years)		1400 (9 years)
1741–1750	2109							
1751–1760	2148[17]							

*in pounds

Many of the payments for £20 or less were for minor repairs to bridges; much less often they concerned partial rebuilding of small structures, or were grants towards repairs or construction by a parish. Many bridge payments were of this small size. Between Easter 1699 and Michaelmas 1702 Essex spent £2174 on bridges; forty-eight payments were made for works on at least twenty structures; thirty-five were for less than £50 and twenty were under £20.[18]

Works costing between £20 and £100 were frequent. They involved new arches, widening, adjoining road improvements, paving or new battlements (Fig. 5.3). Sometimes horse bridges or one-arch structures for wheeled traffic were erected, particularly in shires with many county

[17] Berkshire RO, QS 0 1, fos 14, 22, 37, 90, 124, 168, 182, QS 0 2, 1735–36; *Hertfordshire County Records* 6, pp. 39–40, 163; LSE, Webb Collection: Yorkshire, West Riding (17 July 1712); Cheshire RO, QJB 3/1–12; Devon RO, QS 1/14–18; Allen, *Essex Quarter Sessions*, pp. 30, 42, 64, 96, 118, 185; Essex RO, Q/FAc 1; Herefordshire RO, QS 0 1–6; Norfolk RO, C/S2/1–9; *North Riding Record Society Publications*, 5–7, *Quarter Sessions Records* (1887–89), ed. J.C. Atkinson; J.S. Cockburn, 'The North Riding Justices, 1690–1750: A Study in Local Administration', *Yorkshire Archaeological Journal*, 41 (1963–66), p. 503; East Suffolk RO, 105/2/5, 7, 10–14, HD 330/6; *Warwick County Records* 3, 5, 7, and 9 (1937–64); Warwickshire RO, order books, 1697–1723, and QS 40/1/10.

[18] Essex RO, Q/FAc 1.

Fig. 5.3. The tiny new King's bridge between Rainford and Billinge, Lancashire, was estimated to cost £59 1s. 9d. in 1710, including £20 for carting the stone, sand and materials. The old bridge was decayed and too narrow for a cart. It was to be seven feet four inches wide between the battlements, the arch fifteen feet wide and the land walls forty-five feet long. It was typical of the smaller Lancashire hundred bridges costing between £10 and £60. (Lancashire Record Office, QSP 1004/56.)

bridges, such as those in the north. Among the few surviving contracts from the early eighteenth century, four for Cheshire made between 1708 and 1721 concerned work costing between £27 and £100: Hartford bridge was rebuilt with one stone arch twelve feet wide and thirty-five yards long for £100 in 1708; and Wybunbury bridge, also of one stone arch, was erected twelve feet wide and twenty-two yards long in 1711 at a cost of £60; a cart causeway 100 yards long was constructed on one side of a bridge for £27 10s. 0d. in 1718. Three years later improvements were made at Booth Mill bridge at Mobberley, a stone structure of several arches: battlements were raised, a new buttress erected, paving done on the bridge, and a new causeway ascending gradually built 100 yards long, three and a half wide on one side, for £70. As another example of a small carriage bridge, in 1747 a new structure was ordered to be built at Dawlish, Devon, for £80 (and the materials of the old bridge); it was to have a stone arch twenty-six feet wide, 120 feet long including the pavement at each end, and ten feet broad from wall to wall. Particularly in Westmorland, and occasionally in other counties, new structures, perhaps just foot or horse bridges, or without battlements, cost as little as £20 or £30. The price of a bridge naturally varied according to the size of the arch, its length including the walls and pavements at each end, and of course the width.[19]

County bridge works often cost between £100 and £500 (Table 5.3). About 640 undertakings in this price range have been traced in the surviving shire records between 1640 and 1760. Probably over one quarter of the courts ordered more than twenty bridge works, and over a half at least ten undertakings costing more than £100. On the other hand, about a quarter of the counties, chiefly in the midlands, did not spend such a sum, or not more than once or twice. The biggest spenders of this type were among the counties with the most numerous bridges, the West and North Ridings of Yorkshire, Cheshire and Essex. The West Riding appears as ready to undertake considerable bridge works as it was to accept more county bridges in the seventeenth century. It built or repaired substantially about a quarter of bridges, costing over £100. Sums of several hundred pounds were spent up to three or four times on bridges such as Ilkley and Hewick, often on account of floods and probably inadequate foundations. The stock of bridges may have been especially inadequate earlier. Trade and prosperity were expanding as the cloth industry grew with diversification into worsteds (bays), though this period probably saw less textile growth than the early eighteenth century. Westmorland's numerous bridges hardly produced any expenditure over £100, presumably because they were small. Devon and Lancashire had many costly bridge projects, but the evidence is insufficient to decide their number.

In the whole of England expenditure was reasonably balanced between the later seventeenth and early eighteenth centuries. In some counties there were more works between 1700 and 1760 than between 1640 and

[19] Cheshire RO, QAR 1–4; Devon RO, QS 1/19; Cumbria RO (Kendal), WQ/0 1, p. 134, 25/4/1695; WQ/0 2, pp. 88, 108, 221.

Table 5.3

County Bridge Works Costing between £100 and £500, 1640–1760

County	1640–1700	1700–1760
Yorkshire, West Riding	90	20 or 30 (at least)
Yorkshire, North Riding	29 or 30	44 (at least)
Essex	33 (from 1671)	32
Cheshire	27 (from 1660)	19
Suffolk	*c.* 24 (except 1652–58)	10
Norfolk	19 (from 1650)	9 (except 1735–49)
Somerset	16 (except 1640–46 1660–65)	10
Warwickshire	10	14
Wiltshire	7 (except 1654–70)	18
Dorset	6–16 (except before 1663)	8 or 9
Kent	6	19
Sussex	6 (from 1649)	10
Hampshire	4	11
Surrey	6 (from 1662)	8
Staffordshire	8 (at least)	8
Durham	9 (from 1650)	7
Middlesex	7 or 8	7
Derbyshire	8 (from 1683)	8
Northumberland	(not available)	9
Hertfordshire	3	9
Cumberland	(not available)	7
Herefordshire	3 (from 1665)	4
Shropshire	0	4
Yorkshire, East Riding	(not available)	3
Cambridgeshire	1 (from 1660)	1
Westmorland	0?	1
Northamptonshire	1 (from 1669)	0
Bedfordshire	(not available)	1
Oxfordshire	(not available)	1
Leicestershire	(not available)	1?
Lincolnshire	0 (from *c.* 1670)	0
Buckinghamshire	0 (from 1678)	0
Nottinghamshire	0	0

Figures for Berkshire, Cornwall, Devon, Gloucestershire, Huntingdonshire, Lancashire, Monmouthshire, Rutland and Worcestershire are not available.

1700, but their greater number is balanced by the huge outlay in the West Riding between the 1660s and the 1680s. In contrast, at least four other counties had fewer works after 1700. The great bursts of repairs and building in the West Riding and to a lesser degree in Cheshire in the earlier period may have reduced the necessary work in the early eighteenth century. To a small extent the rise in the number of county bridges explains the greater number of undertakings in several counties such as Warwickshire and Wiltshire. Unexpected flood damage also increased bridge works. In 1696 'great water floods' destroyed Bungay bridge on the border of Norfolk and Suffolk, damaged at least two other Suffolk bridges and hit Norfolk bridges similarly; Suffolk quarter sessions were charged £235 for its share of the rebuilding of Bungay bridge, while the repair of two other structures was estimated at £170 and £100. Political events influenced work in the seventeenth century, as has been shown. There was little bridge expenditure during much of the 1640s on account of the Civil War, which made rate collecting difficult. Destruction for military reasons led to more building in the next decades, not only in Lancashire and Cheshire. In the 1680s, during the royalist revival, judges pressed for work in Norfolk and probably other counties.[20]

Expenditure between £100 and £500 involved a bridge typically of several arches in stone, or occasionally of wood or brick. The work was either major repairs, building of part of the bridge or of the approach, or a wholly new bridge. Sometimes one or two arches were erected on old or new piles, or the foundations and arches strengthened, or a causeway erected. Alternatively the paving and battlements might be rebuilt, or the whole bridge repaired and improved. The Devon court ordered the repair of Taw bridge in 1668, and a mason, Nicholas Arnold, agreed at £110. In 1672 he was paid another £22 when his account was settled as 'he hathe done a great deale of worke about the bridge beyond his agreement by wallinge all the old arch of the said bridge and layed the foundation of the arches 3 feet deeper and one arch made 8 feet and the other 3 arches each 1½ feet broader'. In July 1673 the West Riding justices agreed with four masons for the partial reconstruction of Bolton bridge, Skipton, recently 'thrown down' and made impassable 'by ye violent swelling current and inundacon' of the River Wharfe. For £310 they were to build a new western arch of hewn stone with sufficient support, ensure that the pavement over the old arch was as high as the part over the new one and that it gave an easy ascent on both sides, and that the battlement was at least a yard high. Two years later this sessions raised £200 to rebuild the two middle arches of Sowerby bridge destroyed by floods; it was done in hewn stone, the piers framed and the road paved. The proposals of two masons to rebuild St Thomas bridge near Salisbury for the Wiltshire court in 1746 constitute a rare survival of bridge estimates at this time in southern England. They stated that it was to be fifteen feet wide, fifty-two feet long and to have three arches, and they provided measurements of the different types of stonework in

[20] East Suffolk RO, 105/2/13, fos 36, 51; Norfolk RO, C/S2/5 (12 January 1697), C/Sea 1/1.

their valuation. The contractors received £189 for the bridge and £71 for repairing and finishing the causeway.[21]

Most of these 640 works between 1640 and 1760 cost nearer £100 than £500. Only about ninety, approximately 15 per cent, were for more than £300. Structural works for more than £500 were few. Twenty-six or twenty-seven have been traced costing up to £1000. They were in counties which undertook numerous works or in those with important crossings. West Riding quarter sessions handled six and Essex three. The Northumberland court paid for four in this price range between 1714 and 1730 (all full rebuildings); and there were two major repairs and a rebuilding by Hampshire quarter sessions (1745–46, 1755–56, and 1758–59). They involved at least a partial reconstruction and the majority were in the north.[22]

Finally, between eighteen and twenty undertakings costing between £1000 and £3350 have been traced in the period 1640–1760. These are listed. They consisted of two new causeways (in Cheshire), two bridges replacing a ford (Ribchester and Barton-upon-Irwell in Lancashire). The rest were rebuilding and several repairs (Table 5.4).[23]

Corbridge bridge was a major expense for the Northumberland court until 1674. It stands on the River Tyne at the crossing of the major north road (Ermine Street) with an east-west route linking Newcastle with Cumberland and Westmorland towns much used by traders. Over £5000 was levied and it was rebuilt twice in stone over several decades before 1661. It then needed to be reconstructed because the pillars were too small and decayed for such a powerful river; a gravel bed above it wanted

[21] C. Henderson and E. Jervoise, *Old Devon Bridges* (Exeter, 1938), p. 81; West Yorkshire RO, QS 1 1681 (23 July 1673); H.P. Kendall, 'Sowerby Bridge and Stirk Bridge' *Halifax Antiquarian Society* (1915), pp. 65–75; Wiltshire RO, QS bridges (bundle, 1746–1841).

[22] West Yorkshire RO, QD1/707; Essex RO, Q/FAc1, Q/FAa4/2; Northumberland RO, QS 03, 6–7; Cumbria RO, Kendal WQ/AB1; Durham RO, Q/F1; Cheshire RO, Q/JB3/10, 11; *Middlesex County Records: Calendar of Sessions Books, 1689–1709*, p. 136, *1727–29*, pp. 7, 12; East Sussex RO, QAB/3/E1; West Sussex RO, QAB/3/W1; Norfolk RO, C/S2/9; Humberside RO, CT1; Hampshire RO, QT15, fos 17–18, 34–35, Q016, fol. 169; North Yorkshire RO, QS minute and order book, 1748–66; Lancashire RO, QSP 464/12.

[23] Ed. Atktinson, *North Riding Record Society Publications*, 6 pp. 185, 213; *Northumberland County History: The Parish of Corbridge* (Newcastle, 1914), pp. 226–29; Cheshire RO, QJB3/2 and 6, 7; for Ribchester bridge, see below p. 117; Northumberland RO, calendar of QS order book 2, 1687–97; Hampshire RO, Q06, fol. 39, QT15, fol. 5; West Yorkshire RO, QD1/707, QS 022, fos 170, 191, 232; East Sussex RO, QAB/3/E1; Dorset RO, QS orders, 1727–35 p. 78; Greater London RO, MF1; North Yorkshire RO, QS minute and order book, 1748–66.

Table 5.4

County Bridge Works Costing £1000 or More, 1640–1760

Date	Bridge	Type of Work	Cost (£)
1673–74	Ulshaw, North Riding	rebuilding	1000
1674	Corbridge, Northumberland (seven arch bridge)	rebuilding	(presumably over 1000)
1674–75	Latchford, Cheshire (including causeway)	building	c. 1067
1674–76	Ribchester, Lancashire	building	c. 1000
c. 1677–79	Barton, Lancashire	building	c. 1200
1680	Redbridge, Hampshire	repairs	1000
1684	Loyn, Hornby	rebuilding	1250
1687–93	Chollerford, Northumberland	rebuilding	1033
1696	Redbridge	rebuilding or repairs	?1400
1698–99	Tadcaster, West Riding	rebuilding	1144
1718–22	Wilderspool, Cheshire (causeway)	building	1653
1725	Redbridge	partial rebuilding	1125
1726–27	Lewes, Sussex	rebuilding	2250
1728–29	Longham, Dorset (contract)	rebuilding	2000
1741–42	Brentford, Middlesex	rebuilding	3350
1743–45	Chertsey, Middlesex and Surrey	repairs	1355 and 1507
1753–55	Masham, North Riding	rebuilding	c. 2500
1757–59	Penwortham, Lancashire	rebuilding	2000
1759–60	Leeds, West Riding (contract)	widening and rebuilding	1450

removing and jetties and protecting walls were required. In 1666 the justices claimed that the cost would be £3000. A bridge of seven wide arches was finished in 1674. The well-founded Ulshaw bridge reconstructed in the same year had four segmental arches with a total span of sixty-five feet and was twelve feet wide between the parapets.

In southern England the rebuilding of Redbridge bridge on the main road west out of Southampton was exceptionally expensive for a county. It consisted of at least two horse bridges and a foot bridge, as well as the main stone bridge. In the later seventeenth and early eighteenth centuries the bridge was damaged in various ways. Bridges in a tideway are liable to damage with the violent scouring up and down stream, and the great variations in the level of the water; according to J.S. Furley, 'barges damaged the piers at Redbridge by mooring to them, timber floated downstream and was allowed to drift on to them'. At January Sessions 1682 a Fordingbridge mason was said to have finished repairs to Redbridge bridge according to agreement with the justices for £1000. In 1696 £1400 was needed but, as there were great difficulties in collecting the rate, it is not clear how much work was done. In 1725 'great rains and flouds' destroyed two stone arches and damaged the rest of the bridge; works then cost over £1100. Smaller sums were also spent between 1700 and 1760. Brentford bridge on the Bath Road outside London was periodically repaired and reconstructed. Its rebuilding by the Middlesex justices in 1741 and 1742, for about £3350, included £406 for a temporary structure. It was a one arch brick and stone bridge, built as wide as thirty-four feet on account of the traffic, but the court did not align it with the main road because of the additional cost (£1255) of buying the land on both banks. While the considerable charge of Corbridge bridge may owe something to the previous rebuilding of Berwick bridge, and that of Brentford bridge to the new Fulham and Westminster bridges, both lay on crossings where traffic size was probably exceptional.[24]

In sum, on the rising number of county bridges (about 1330 by 1750) there were innumerable outlays of between £20 or £30 and £80 or £90 for repairs and rebuildings between 1640 and 1760. About 135 works have been traced costing more than £300. The typical major bridge undertaking was for between £100 and £300. About 550 works have been found in this category, involving the reconstruction, alteration or repair of what were frequently stone structures of more than one arch for carts or waggons. Expenditure was widely distributed, but it totalled probably only between £250,000 and £350,000. It was an age of bridge repair rather than bridge building. The reasons were the huge number and wide distribution of bridges (except low down major rivers) in 1650, their stone construction, and the steady but not dramatic growth of trade before 1750.[25]

---

[24] *Northumberland County History: Corbridge*, pp. 226–39; Hampshire RO, QT15, QM5 fos 71, 84, Q06, fol. 39, Q07, fos 7, 223, 225, Q08, fos 53–4, Q09 p. 113, Q012, fol. 188, Q013 pp. 104, 141; J.S. Furley, *Quarter Sessions Government in Hampshire in the Seventeenth Century* (Winchester, n.d.), p. 33; M. Dowdswell, *A Hundred Years of Quarter Sessions: The Government of Middlesex from 1660 to 1760*, (Cambridge, 1932), pp. 128–29; Rider, *Report of the Committee of Magistrates*, p. 221; Greater London RO, Middlesex County Records: calendar of sessions books, 1738/9–1741, pp. 119–20.

[25] Harrison, 'Bridges and Economic Development', pp. 240–61, for the explanation, Harrison agreeing that bridge building was subdued in this period.

6

Bridges, 1760–1830

From the 1760s county bridge work was growing. The rise is sharp from the middle of the decade. In the early eighteenth century work had increased in some counties but in others it had declined. There is evidence of only a tiny growth in a small number of counties in the 1750s (including Hampshire, Essex and the North Riding), but not in other shires (including Cheshire, Middlesex and Dorset). This was a time of rising expenditure in many areas. A minority of counties had more public bridges by the 1770s, and the number of shire bridges grew more generally in the 1780s and 1790s, but the greater outlay was particularly the result of many more improvements and repairs to existing bridges. There was more expenditure on building compared with repair than in the previous century. In addition, bridges of unprecedented cost were erected from 1765 (Fig. 6.1).

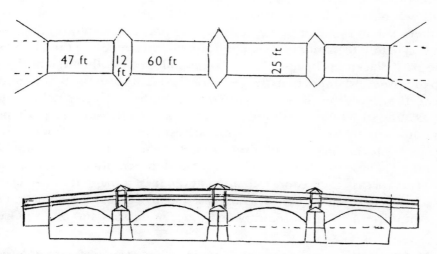

Fig. 6.1. Ferrybridge bridge, West Riding, built 1765. Costing £3950, it was the largest Yorkshire county bridge erected before the 1790s; the material was chiefly local ashlar and the contractor a mason who became a bridge builder and surveyor, John Gott of Calverley near Leeds. (West Yorkshire Record Office, Q/AB15.)

The explanation for the growth in bridge works lies partly in the continued growth of road transport, as epitomised by the great expansion of the turnpike road system in the 1750s and the 1760s. There was an increasing number of regular long-distance coach and waggon services between London and provincial centres, and of services between provincial towns. Cart or carriage bridges were increasingly liable to damage on account of the great volume of wheeled traffic, particularly as the standard of workmanship sometimes left much to be desired. Awkward approaches which were dangerous to unwary drivers needed improvement; and with more vehicles and the provision of footways and widening to take two waggons or coaches abreast this became more pressing. At Derbyshire sessions in Michaelmas 1776, Ashford county bridge (of three low stone arches, probably sixteenth century) was said to be 'so extreame narrow that it is dangerous for carriages to pass over the same, and that the battlements are very frequently knocked off by carriages which renders the bridge dangerous for passengers'. Foot and horse bridges used with fords for wheeled traffic (where the bridge might be opened to vehicles in time of flood) were found increasingly inconvenient and dangerous, so the rebuilding of the carriage bridges seemed to be urgent.[1]

At the same time counties were becoming more ready to raise sums as rates for special or new undertakings, as seen in the rebuilding of a number of shire halls in the 1770s and the construction of new prisons and houses of correction. So far as bridges were concerned, the justices had before them the examples of undertakings by bodies of commissioners, set up by act of parliament, relying partly or wholly on the collection of tolls to pay for construction and maintenance. On the Thames the great Blackfriars Bridge (1768–70) was followed by other new bridges up the river, and important bridges were also erected on the Severn and Tyne. Previously the justices had often been contented with patching up an existing structure or building a relatively narrow new bridge, perhaps with inadequate foundations or approaches. They were now sometimes prepared to undertake building projects to a modern professional standard. These new bridges were wider, at between fifteen and twenty-five feet (occasionally more), to allow at the least a waggon or carriage to pass a pedestrian or rider. The increased span of the arches, sometimes one hundred feet or more, provided wider waterways and often more

---

[1] E. Dawson, *Transport and Economy: The Turnpike Roads of Eighteenth-Century Britain* (London, 1977), appendix I; D. Gerhold, 'The Growth of the London Carrying Trade, 1681–1838', *Economic History Review*, 2nd series, 41 (1988), pp. 408–9; D. Hey, *Packmen, Carriers and Packhorse Roads: Trade and Communications in North Derbyshire and South Yorkshire* (Leicester, 1980), p. 84, for the Derbyshire reference.

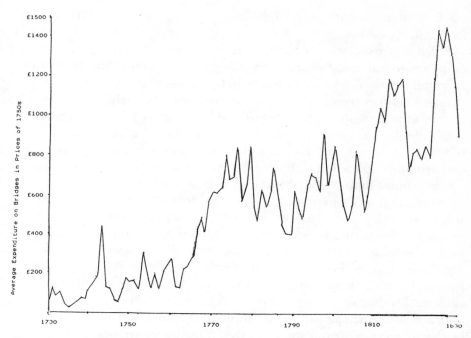

Fig. 6.2. County expenditure on bridges, 1730–1830. The graph shows the great rise in the late 760s and 1770s and the years after about 1810, with a brief peak in the late 1820s.

headroom for boats. Gradients were flatter partly because segmental or semi-elliptical arches were used for long spans. Structures were aligned with the road, which had wider approaches. Deeper or more secure foundations prevented future flood destruction. A well-known surveyor was employed sometimes to design and supervise the construction. Robert Mylne who designed Blackfriars bridge was used for the rebuilding of Tonbridge bridge in 1775–76 and Romsey bridge in 1782–83; he reported on Hexham bridge in 1783. Knowledge of, and interest in, the science of bridge building was spreading, deriving particularly from France. Several books were published on the geometry and mechanics of construction, by writers who had studied the art of bridge building on the Continent, or who wished to improve the quality of building in England. S. Riou, author of *Short Principles for the Architecture of Stone-Bridges, with Practical Observations, and a New Geometrical Diagram to Determine the Thickness of the Piers to the Height and Base of Any Given Arch* had studied architecture abroad and drew on French treatises. Charles Hutton published *The Principles of Bridges* in

1772 after an exceptionally high flood had destroyed the Tyne bridge in the previous year.[2]

Brick was used widely because it was cheap. Naturally its cost in comparison with stone varied, depending on the accessibility of the stone. Normally we do not know by how much, as estimates for both brick and stone structures are rare. Shropshire contracted for Ashford Carbonell bridge to be rebuilt, largely in brick with an eighty foot span eighteen feet wide, by a Ludlow mason for £680 in 1795. A collapse happened before he finished and, after temporary communication by 'the slight construction of a wooden bridge', the contract was altered to make it more 'commodious' and 'durable' for £150 more in 1797. The use of stone made it more expensive. A local justice noted that 'the common size of our brick is insufficient to lie in the work, and to insure strength and duration it must be built of stone unless it is the opinion of Sessions that it should be built of wood: a very scarce article now with us, considering the length, and depth of timber which would be requisite for that purpose. . .' The mason proposed to erect 'a stone arch with stone of such quality that Mr Tilford [Thomas Telford, the county surveyor] shall approve of anywhear within the limits of six or seven miles from the bridge as there is proper stone for that purpose within that distance on the demintions from four to six inches thick the lenth and bredth at pleasance'. Telford had proposed stone which would be dearer because it came from a more distant quarry. His advice may have been taken finally, as altogether over £1500 was spent on the two building attempts and the temporary wooden structure between 1795 and 1798. Counties differed in their preference regarding material. Essex used timber on fourteen bridge rebuildings, brick on fourteen and stone on one between 1762 and 1812. Timber was regarded by the Essex surveyor John Johnson as suitable for long spans, avoiding the flood destruction

---

[2] S. Lewis, *Topographical Dictionary of England*, iii (London, 1831), p. 144; J.W. Walker, *A History of Maidenhead* (London, 1909), pp. 14–17; D. Whitehead, 'Georgian Worcester' (unpublished M.A. thesis, University of Birmingham, 1976), pp. 112–16; H. Colvin, *A Biographical Dictionary of British Architects, 1600–1840* (3rd edn, New Haven and London, 1995), pp. 441, 682; C. Riou, *Short Principles for the Architecture of Stone Bridges, with Practical Observations, and a New Geometrical Diagram to Determine the Thickness of the Piers to the Height and Base of Any Given Arch* (London, 1760); C. Hutton ('Mathematician'), *The Principles of Bridges: Containing the Mathematical Demonstrations of the Properties of the Arches, the Thickness of the Piers, the Force of the Water against Them etc. Together with Practical Observations and Directions Drawn from the Whole* (Newcastle, 1772); see also G. Semple, *A Treatise on Building in Water* (London, 1776); L.T.C. Rolt, *Thomas Telford* (Harmondsworth, 1979), pp. 48–49; E.C. Ruddock, *Arch Bridges and their Builders, 1735–1835* (Cambridge, 1979), pp. 132–34, 149.

of brick piers. Lincolnshire, when it began finally to do bridge work after about 1810, used mainly brick; the most expensive county bridge to that date, Brigg in 1827, cost £2100, in a typical use of stone adding £650 to the price. An alternative material, iron, became available from the 1770s, after the erection of the Coalbrookdale bridge. It appeared ideal for single-arch bridges needing a long span. Its first use by a county was by Shropshire on Buildwas and Cound bridges in the mid 1790s, but it was not widely employed by counties instead of brick or stone until the 1820s.[3]

Greater aggregate expenditure on bridges occurred in many of the counties for which there is available evidence. In some cases the rise was considerable, as in Kent and Surrey and several northern counties. The outlay of the biggest bridge spender, the West Riding of Yorkshire, rose several times from the 1750s, reaching an average of over £4000 a year in the 1770s before falling to under £2600 in the 1780s. The North Riding spent over £1000 in most years after 1766. Cheshire spent more than £1000 usually after 1776, averaging over £2000 a year in the 1790s. For most counties an annual expenditure of a few hundred pounds was typical.[4] The growth of the West Riding outlay is matched by that on Lancashire's mainly hundred bridges. Their rapidly rising expenditure reflects the great industrial and commercial growth of these two regions.

About half the counties spent unprecedentedly large sums on individual works. Such outlays were particularly significant in Lancashire, the West and North Ridings, Northumberland, Shropshire and Surrey. Lancashire and Yorkshire had always had considerable bridge crossings which had often needed substantial expenditure on widening and strengthening. In Lancashire there were three major county rebuilding projects, relating to Ribchester bridge (1770–71 and 1775), Ribble bridge (1779–80) and Lancaster bridge (1783–87). Widening was an important component. Ribchester bridge cost £1900 in 1770 and 1771; after flood destruction, at least £2750 was spent on a new structure in 1775. The new Ribble bridge cost £3950 after the county was indicted for not repairing and widening it (Fig. 6.3). Lancaster (Skerton) bridge needed repair, widening (as two carriages could not pass each other safely) and a better position and approach. The basic impetus for rebuilding was the increased

[3] N. Briggs, *John Johnson, 1732–1814: Georgian Architect and County Surveyor of Essex* (Chelmsford, 1991), pp. 72, 162–64; Shropshire RO, DP4 and QS accounts 1768–1883; Lincolnshire RO, Kesteven treasurers accounts, 1802–37, LQS A2/27–44.
[4] Cheshire.RO, QJ8 3/14–17; see below pp. 119, 20.

Table 6.1

County Bridge Works Costing at Least £2000, 1760–1800

(all rebuilding)

Date	Bridge	£
1765–66	Ferrybridge, West Riding	3950
1766	Whitby, North Riding	2991
1768–77	Atcham, Shropshire	8647
1772–73	Chollerford, Northumberland	2578
1773–76	Hexham, Northumberland (unfinished)	over 5500
1775	Ribchester, Lancashire	at least 2750
1775–78	Wareham South, Dorset	3050
1777–81	Hexham (contract)	5700
1778–81	Tern, Shropshire	4676
1779–80	Ribble, Lancashire	4150
1779–85	Chertsey, Middlesex and Surrey	at least 15,000
1782–83	Romsey, Hampshire	3040
1784–88	Skerton, Lancaster	up to *c.* 17,000
1787–93	Ridley Hall, Northumberland	4075
1788–89	Frodsham, Cheshire	2063
1789–95	Hexham	8069
1790–92	Montford, Shropshire	5800
1792	Catterick, North Riding	2980
1792–94	Barford, Warwickshire	2413
1795	Croft, North Riding and Durham	6530
1795–97	Stratford, Suffolk	2772
1795–97	Swarkeston, Derbyshire (contract)	3550
1795–97	Belper, Derbyshire (contract)	2180
1796	Buildwas, Shropshire	6444

with five feet footpaths additionally, being given five elliptical arches each sixty-eight feet long. It is notable architecturally and structurally as the first large English bridge with a level road surface from bank to bank. The contract price was £10,400; the order book evidence suggests that additional stone costs and water damage may have brought charges to as much as £17,000. Contemporary estimates included £12,000 and £14,000.[5]

Special reasons explain the bursts of construction in Northumberland, Shropshire and Surrey. Nearly all Northumberland bridges on the Tyne were destroyed by floods in 1771 and 1782. They had to be replaced at

---

[5] Lancashire RO, QS 02/130–56, QS P 2008/4, DDX 51; 22 George 3, c. 57; Colvin, *British Architects*, p. 466; J. Dugdale, *The New British Traveller*, iii (London, 1819), p. 303; Lewis, *Topographical Dictionary*, iii, p. 20; Mannex and Co., *A History, Topography and Directory of Westmorland, Lonsdale and Amounderness in Lancashire* (Beverley, 1851), p. 487.

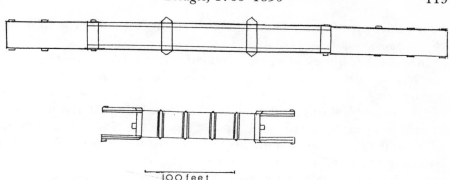

100 feet

Fig. 6.3. Ribble bridge, Lancashire, and Eye Kettleby bridge, Leicestershire, erected 1780 and 1822 respectively. Ribble bridge, nearly 500 feet long with three wide arches, was built by John Laws, mason and bridge surveyor for £4150, and was one of the three major Lancashire bridges built in the 1770s and 1780s. Eye Kettleby bridge, also of stone, was much shorter with five arches between eighteen and twenty-four feet span; the contract price was £1287 and the builder was Joseph Vinrace of Ashby de la Zouch. (Lancashire Record Office, QAR/2; and Leicestershire Record Office, QS 30/2/14.)

great cost and with specially careful building of foundations. While Shropshire's outlay was small (just on repairs) before the later 1760s, the county now provided bridges for important Severn crossings. Atcham bridge replaced a flood-damaged structure; Tern bridge had a ninety foot single arch; and the noted Buildwas iron bridge was erected with a 130 foot arch eighteen feet wide following water destruction. Middlesex and Surrey had the precedent of corporation bridges on the Thames, when replacing a wooden structure often needing repair and with weak abutments and banks by a stone bridge at Chertsey; the five arches were forty-two feet, thirty-six feet and thirty feet long, and twenty-five feet wide to allow two footpaths. Growing wheeled traffic explains the other major bridge works in Surrey. Three privately-owned bridges lying on a main road, those at Cobham, Leatherhead and Godalming, were adopted by the county under an act of 1782; they were narrow, incommodious and dangerous for passengers, and shut to carriages except during floods; their rebuilding or repair was obviously, as the act stated, in the public interest. They were all widened when rebuilt in 1782–83. A fourth private wooden bridge at Church Cobham on the Dorking-Leatherhead road was only for pedestrians and horses. It was rebuilt for use by carriages after the principal piles were found to be resting on the river bed instead of having being driven into it, with the result that the wooden framework nearly fell apart. It was rebuilt again in brick in 1786–87. The four Surrey bridges cost about £6600.[6]

In several counties increased expenditure in the 1770s and 1780s involved an outlay on numerous bridges costing a few hundred pounds, but none of outstanding size. This often concerned bridge widening rather than rebuilding. In Devon bridges were being altered or rebuilt to help wheeled traffic for sums up to £300. In the North Riding in the 1770s and 1780s about twenty bridges were widened and rebuilt; they cost between £120 and £1715. During the 1790s at least three other counties began building more. In Staffordshire Strongford bridge was built for £1829 in 1793 and the Wichnor bridges were rebuilt for £1954 in 1796–97. Wolseley bridge of three arches, designed by John Rennie, was began in 1798 at an estimate of £2118 13s. 8d. but it cost much more. These were unprecedented sums for the county to spend on bridges. The West Riding began the most expensive county bridge work yet undertaken when a new Ferrybridge bridge was started in 1797; designed by the York architect John Carr, it had three stone arches of sixty-six, sixty and sixty feet, and was thirty-six feet wide including the parapets.[7]

The increased sums spent on bridges by some counties from the 1770s helped to increase total county expenditure, and meant that a high proportion was being spent on bridges. Shropshire's steep rise in bridge expenditure from the early 1760s to 1782 has already been mentioned. In 1784–85 in Hampshire one of the chief arguments of the opposition organised against the building of a new county gaol was the recent heavy expenditure on bridges (which included Romsey bridge); this and the

---

[6] See below p. 121; West Yorkshire RO, QS 024, fol. 52; North Yorkshire RO, QS minute and order book, 1766–75; *The Works in Architecture of John Carr*, York Georgian Society (York, 1973), pp. 6, 8; Durham RO, Q/F3; Northumberland RO, QS 010, 013, 014 and CS Misc. 1, 2; 18 George 3 c. 44; Ruddock, *Arch Bridges*, pp. 76, 99–100, 240–41; C. Chalklin, 'Bridge Building in Kent, 1700–1830: The Work of the Justices of the Peace', in *Studies in Modern Kentish History*, ed. A. Detsicas and N. Yates (Maidstone, 1983), p. 51; Cheshire RO, QJB 3/16; Warwickshire RO, QS 24/61; Suffolk RO, 105/2/50; Greater London RO, MA/Ci, MF1–2 and MJ/OC 8; Surrey RO, QS 2/1/21, 22, 25, 26 and QS 5/1/1; 22 George 3, c. 17; O. Manning and W. Bray, *History and Antiquities of Surrey*, iii (London, 1814), p. xxxiv, appendix; Derbyshire RO, QAH 1/1; Dorset RO, QS treasurers' accounts, 1739–77 and 1777–1806.

[7] Devon RO, QS 1, 1759–76, 1777–91; *The Works in Architecture of John Carr*, pp. 1–33; R.B. Wragg, 'The Bridges of John Carr', *Transactions of the Hunter Archaeological Society*, 10 (1979), pp. 332–33; Staffordshire RO, Q/FAa 1/4–5; A. Bayliss, *The Life and Works of John Trubshaw, 1777–1853* (Stockport, 1978), p. 6; West Yorkshire RO, QS order book 1794–7, fol. 346, and QS accounts of money estreated for bridges, 1797–1873.

large outlay on militiamen's families on account of the war had led to a great growth in total county expenditure.[8]

In some counties, including Hampshire, Surrey and Northumberland, the jump in expenditure at some point in the period between the 1760s and 1780s was connected with the construction of several important bridges; on their completion expenditure fell to lower levels. In other cases it continued to be high (perhaps after a short break), on account of the rising number of county bridges or of several additional large undertakings. Shropshire's expenditure averaged nearly £2000 a year in the 1790s, on account of many more county bridges (thirty-eight by 1808) and other major works.[9]

During the 1780s and 1790s county bridge work followed a course which was different from other types of building and construction. Several large bridges were erected between 1779 and 1786, but building was less in the later 1780s and at beginning of the 1790s when house erection and later other transport construction were at a peak. Possibly heavy expenditure on prisons explains the drop in bridge work. More likely the major county bridge problems had been largely resolved by the unprecedented volume of construction in the previous twenty years. As prison and shire hall work fell in the later 1790s, bridge construction revived in many counties. Greater bridge charges were accompanied by the continued creation of turnpike trusts; both bridge works and road improvement were a response to rising transport costs, owing to the growing price of horse keep.[10]

Another great increase in expenditure on bridges is noticeable in some counties between about 1808 and 1814. There was a boom in road transport and in building in general at this time. Rising bridge charges are not very noticeable among counties which were already relatively big spenders in the north or the north midlands, such as Cheshire, Staffordshire or the West and North Riding, but there was a marked growth in outlay in some of the counties in the south midlands and in southern England. Several of these counties had previously spent only trifling amounts on bridges. As an extreme case, Berkshire justices spent only £41 5s. 0d. in the nine years between 1792 and 1800; by 1812–20 the figure had risen to £2249 11s. 8d. Wiltshire bridge expenditure totalled

[8] See above p. 54; Hampshire RO QS bridge committee minute book, 1782–1817, fol. 29; *Salisbury and Winchester Journal*, 30 August 1784.

[9] See above p. 54; Rolt, *Telford*, pp. 48–49; M.C. Hill, 'Iron and Steel Bridges in Shropshire 1788–1901', *Transactions of the Shropshire Archaeological Society*, 56 (1959), pp. 106–9; Ruddock, *Arch Bridges*, p. 240.

[10] W. Albert, *The Turnpike Road System in England, 1662–1840* (Cambridge, 1972), pp. 54, 185–86.

£750 5s. 4½d. between 1792 and 1800; in 1812–20 the amount was £9384 15s. 8½d. Despite an increase in building costs of possibly about 70 per cent as much, the rise in outlay is very marked. In other counties, such as Dorset and Suffolk, expenditure had been larger in the last quarter of the eighteenth century, but the rise about 1810 was still sharp. In Suffolk the expenditure on bridges was as follows: 1806–9, £3221; 1810–13, £9098; and 1814–17, £8580. Even Hampshire and Devon, both among the heavier bridge spenders in the eighteenth century, increased their outlay noticeably in 1808–9.[11]

The most important cause of the growth of expenditure was the rise in the number of bridges for which counties were responsible from the 1780s. Hertfordshire, for example, added six bridges between 1786 and 1797, three in 1811, two in 1821, and one each in 1822, 1826, 1828 and 1830. The increase in county bridges was the result of the justices taking over (whether willingly or not) many more bridges for which the liability to repair could not be shown to belong to an individual, corporation or other local authority. It was encouraged by an important legal decision in 1780, when the West Riding was indicted for not repairing a small bridge in Glasburne township, recently built by it. The judges held that the Riding was liable: 'if a man build a bridge, and it becomes useful to the County in general, the County shall repair it'. As the bridge was recently built, the township was not liable by prescription, nor was it liable by tenure. In the words of the Webbs:

> this interpretation of the law, which was adapted in various successive cases, clearly involved Counties in the liability for all bridges, large and small, erected since the beginning of legal memory, which could not be said to be maintained by prescription, if they were not maintained as an incident of the tenure of specific lands, provided that they had come to form part of the common highway, or were of distinct public utility.

The effect was said to have been visible first in Staffordshire, Lancashire and the West Rising. In 1800 both Staffordshire and Lancashire complained of being burdened with the repair of rebuilding of many smaller bridges erected by subscription which the justices were now, as the result of these legal decisions, expected to support.[12] In the 1800s

[11] *Parliamentary Papers* (1825), vi; (1833), xxxii.

[12] *Hertfordshire County Records: Sessions Books, 1752 to 1799*, 8, ed. W. Le Hardy (Hertford, 1931), p. xxviii, and ibid., *Sessions Books, 1799–1833*, 9, ed. W. Le Hardy and G.L. Reckitt (Hertford, 1939), pp. xxviii, 129, 240, 253, 327, 396 and 445; S. and B. Webb, *English Local Government: The Story of the King's Highway* (London, 1920), p. 99; A.L. Thomas, 'Geographical Aspects of the Development of Transport', *Collections for a History of Staffordshire Edited by the William Salt Archaeological Society, 1934* (1935), p. 92.

and 1810s counties in southern England also began to feel the effect of the Glasburne judgement. This was found to be true of Middlesex when a committee of justices held an inquiry in the early 1820s. They reported that, until the 1790s, the county only maintained three bridges on main roads and no one expected it to deal with bridges on the minor roads, normally used by local people. Since then the number of applications from localities to repair or rebuild smaller bridges had grown steadily. Either the justices ordered works to be done without inquiring as to who was liable; or, if indicted, they had judgement passed against them because local witnesses withheld information that a parish was responsible by prescription or an individual *ratione tenurae*.[13] By 1830 there were about 3000 county bridges, two and a half times the number in 1700. Twelve authorities had more than 100 bridges, Devon having the most (254 in 1821, nearly 400 in 1834). Twenty counties had more than fifty bridges, and all except five at least twenty.[14]

Behind the extension of the justices' bridge responsibilities lay the further growth of wheeled traffic, both on main roads and now increasingly on local roads linking villages to market towns. There was a growing feeling that the building and maintenance of bridges was in the public interest, but, particularly in the case of building, the cost often put it beyond the means of a parish or an individual. Legislation supported the view that the counties had a duty to maintain bridges of varying importance. An act of 1803 put in their care bridges erected by subscription, or by individuals, provided the work had been done to the satisfaction of the county surveyor.[15]

Increased county bridge expenditure therefore had several reasons. Naturally the huge growth in numbers contributed. The new county bridges were often the less important ones and most were repaired and altered over the years, but not rebuilt. In six years, 1825–30, Shropshire spent on average on fifty-three bridges a year, most of the payments being under £10, though total outlay was between £1155 and £2442. The changing structure of bridges added to costs. Those with wide arches to improve the passage of water and boats needed stronger abutments. Lower arches to reduce gradients particularly increased the force on the centre. They became still wider. Leicestershire spent between £244 and £1450 on nineteen bridges between sixteen and twenty-seven feet

---

[13] J. Rider, *Report of the Committee of Magistrates Respecting the Public Bridges in the County of Middlesex* (London, 1826), pp. 1, 3–6, 43.

[14] For the growth of expenditure on county bridges, see above, p. 115.

[15] 43 George III, c. 59.

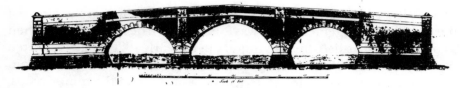

Fig. 6.4. Zouch bridge, erected 1790 for Leicestershire and Nottinghamshire at a cost of £700 by John Cheshire, a builder of Over Whitacre; mainly stone, it was 167 feet long; the span of the middle arch was thirty-five feet and of the two end arches thirty feet. (Leicestershire Record Office, QS 30/2/1.)

wide in 1790–1829, some being of minor significance (Figs 6.4, 6.5). The making of the foundations was more sophisticated: in some cases bearing or sheeting piles were hammered down within caissons or cofferdams from which the water had been removed. Approaches were made more convenient. Dorset illustrates the greater expenditure on individual bridges by counties which had always been active in bridge maintenance. Although rising costs need to be remembered, the pattern is clear. In 1750–75 the most expensive structure cost £330. In 1775–1800 sessions spent more than £1000 on two bridges, and between 1800 and 1825 similar sums on at least seven works.

Large sums were spent particularly on bridges which the justices regarded as important. This is evident when one considers the amounts

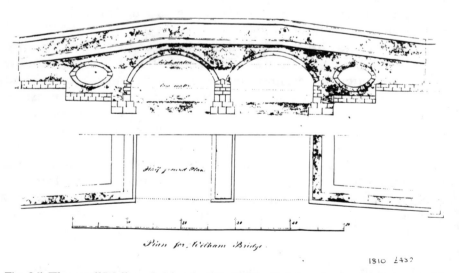

Fig. 6.5. The small Welham bridge, built in 1810 of brick and stone for Leicestershire and Northamptonshire by Joseph Vinrace of Ashby de la Zouch for £482. The span of the arch was only fourteen feet. (Leicestershire Record Office, QS 30/2/6.)

spent on major bridges. Most of the innumerable county bridge works of the period 1800–30 cost well under £1000, despite the doubling of building costs since the 1780s. Some counties, such as Hertfordshire and Northamptonshire, with only small bridges in their care, rarely spent more than £400 or £500 on an undertaking. On the other hand, many counties erected several bridges costing at least £2000 or £3000. Bridges involving such sums were erected in the 1810s and 1820s in Cumberland and Shropshire.[16] In a few counties considerably more was spent on several bridges. In Staffordshire fourteen bridges were built between 1798 and 1832 costing more than £2000; eight of them cost more than £5000 (Table 6.2). The most ambitious undertaking was Wolseley bridge (1798–1802), designed by Rennie. Two others erected later (when prices were higher) cost the county more than £10,000; one of them, High Bridge, being iron. In Devon there was a noticeable jump in expenditure after 1808; between then and 1835 eight bridge undertakings cost more than £2000. Three involved an outlay of between £5000 and £10,000.[17]

In the whole of England eleven bridges erected by counties cost more than £10,000. They were built over important rivers and compared in cost with some of the larger bridges built in provincial England by bridge companies and trusts. On the Thames the old Dorchester bridge, which was regarded as narrow and inconvenient, was replaced in 1813–15 by a new stone structure, with its causeway 1160 yards long. The famous Marlow suspension bridge replaced a decayed and dangerous structure; it and its approaches were built by Buckinghamshire and Berkshire for about £22,000 between 1829 and 1832. It has a span of 217 feet slung between two monumental stone pylons. Gloucestershire and Monmouthshire shared the expense of the new Chepstow bridge, built in 1814–16, an iron structure of five arches; this was thought to be preferable to repairing and widening the old bridge. The most costly bridge erected by a county in southern England before the 1830s was Over bridge in Gloucestershire. Telford proposed either an iron or stone bridge with a span of 175 feet; this was to prevent any impediment to flood waters coming down the Severn which were now faster flowing and higher than formerly. He estimated the expense of the iron bridge at £24,000 and the elliptical stone arch at £40,000. The reasons for building the latter

[16] Shropshire RO, QS accounts, 1768–1883; Leicestershire, RO, QS 30/2, QS 111/1; W.N. Thomas, *The Development of Bridges* (London, 1920), pp. 184–89; Dorset RO, QS treasurers' accounts, 1739–77, 1777–1806, 1806–25; J.B. Bradbury, *A History of Cockermouth* (Chichester, 1981), pp. 233–35; Shropshire RO, bridge book, 1741–1827, fos 115, 122; Hill, 'Iron and Steel Bridges', p. 113.
[17] Staffordshire RO, Q/FAa 1/5–8; Devon RO, CT 137/1.

Table 6.2

County Bridge Works Costing at Least £5000, 1800–30[18]

Date	Place	£
1797–1804	Ferrybridge, West Riding	27,400
1798–1802	Wolseley, Staffordshire	11,884
1800–3	Morton, North Riding	8240
1803–5	Yarm, North Riding and Durham	8980
1804–7	Elvet, Durham	6900
1804–7	Radford, Staffordshire	6375
1805–8	Castleford, West Riding	14,000
1806–9	Caerleon, Monmouthshire	9530
1811–12	Caerleon, Monmouthshire	2030
1808	Finney, Devon	6602
1809–13	Canford, Dorset	6477
1809–13	Hele, Devon	5398
1810–11	Deptford, Kent	6777
1810–15	Melksham, Wiltshire	8404
1811–14	Weston, Staffordshire	6101
1813–14	Hopwas, Staffordshire	11,741*
1813–15	Cowley, Devon	9663
1813–15	Dorchester, Oxfordshire	23,857
1813–15	Howsham, East Riding	5977
1814–16	Chepstow, Monmouthshire and Gloucestershire	22,116
1812–16	Eden, Cumberland	70,000
1815–17	Tutbury, Staffordshire and Derbyshire	5180**
1815–20	Tempsford, Bedfordshire (contract)	9550
1824–26	Llanvihangel, Monmouthshire	*c.* 5000
1824–28	Salters, Staffordshire	9006
1825	Leeds, West Riding	5000
1825	Shincliffe, Durham	5337
1825–26	Fazeley, Warwickshire and Staffordshire (contract)	7000
1826–27	Over, Gloucestershire	43,500
1829–32	Marlow, Buckinghamshire and Berkshire	22,000
1829–32	High, Staffordshire	10,582
1829–30	Harraby, Cumberland	5000***

*   including temporary bridge costing £1116 9s. 9d.
**   Staffordshire share
***   £1000 also from turnpike commissioners

[18] West Yorkshire, RO, QS order book, 1794–97, fol. 346, QS accounts of money estreated for bridges; William Salt Library, Staffordshire treasurers' accounts, 1777–1832; Staffordshire RO, Q/FAa 1/5–8; North Yorkshire RO, book of bridges, p. 71, QS treasurers' accounts, 1802–15; Durham RO, QS OB 16; Devon RO, CT 137/1; Monmouthshire RO, T. Acc. B 0002–4; Chalklin, 'Bridge Building in Kent', p. 62; Wiltshire RO, county treasurers' accounts, 1810–12; *Victoria History of the County of Oxfordshire*, vii, p. 40; Humberside RO, CT 2; Chepstow, Over and Marlow bridges, see note 19 below; Lewis, *Topographical Dictionary*, i, p. 379; Bedfordshire RO, 'Lock Gate', i, pp. 191–94; Durham RO, Q/F4; Warwickshire RO, QS 24/28 p. xix.

are unknown; erected in 1826–27, it cost £43,500.[19] According to a printed contemporary source, Cumberland spent £70,000, £26,500 more than the price of Over bridge, on building Eden bridge, Carlisle of five elliptical arches designed by the architect Robert Smirke in 1812–16.

Greater expenditure was accompanied by more detailed specifications in contracts than before. The few surviving Cheshire building agreements before 1748 are between a few sentences and a page long. Contracts for Devon, Dorset, Leicestershire and other county bridges in the early nineteenth century were, in contrast, long and elaborate. Steps bridge, on the River Teign near Chudleigh, was rebuilt by Devon sessions in 1815 under contract with an Exeter builder for £1970. Among eighteen clauses in the agreement, the first stated that it was to be above the existing bridge on a staked line, of three arches, the centre one being twenty-seven feet and the two side arches twenty-five feet in span, with a roadway eighteen feet wide for the length over the arches, gradually increasing by curved wing walls to twenty-four feet at the extremities; the arches were to form segments of circles, the centre arch rising four feet and the side arches three feet six inches from the springing of the arch, which springing was to be eleven feet above the common summer level of the river. Other clauses dealt in detail with the masonry and the mortar. The construction of the abutments was the subject of the second clause. The third described that of the piers, the fourth the wing walls, the fifth the arches in detail, the sixth the spandril walls and the eighth the haunch backing over the abutments and in the spandrils of the arches. The ninth dealt with the cornices and projections, the tenth the pilasters, the eleventh the parapet walls and the twelfth their coping. The last two clauses described the bridge approaches and sides of the road. In general, piers were narrower on account of sounder foundations and the arches kept to a minimum, allowing freer passage of both water and boats. Illustrations of 130 Devon county bridges in the mid nineteenth century show fifty with one arch, twenty-nine with two and thirty-nine with three arches; of the rest six had four, five had five and one had seven arches. While many were medieval, sixteenth- and seventeenth-century survivals, between one third and a half had been rebuilt since 1750.[20]

These large outlays and the care taken over building reflect the need

[19] *VCH, Oxfordshire*, vii, p. 40; Berkshire RO, QS 014 p. 231; E. Mare, *The Bridges of Britain* (London, 1954), p. 172; Gloucestershire RO, QS 014, fos 19, 38, QS M3/2, M3/3, pp. 179, 186, 194, 198, 204, 216, 231, Q/AB 3/3; *Life of Thomas Telford*, ed. J. Rickman (London, 1838), p. 267; Lewis, *Topographical Dictionary*, i, p. 379.

[20] Cheshire RO, QAR 1–7; Devon RO, QS 88/62 etc., QS 90; Dorset RO, bridge contracts.

for more sizeable and more secure bridges to cope with the growth of wheeled transport. The justices had the example of the great company bridges in London built in the years after 1811, and of smaller provincial bridges erected by companies or trusts such as the stone Bedford bridge completed in 1813, or the iron bridge at Boston finished in 1807. They were spending more money on other types of building, particularly prisons but also (in some counties) courthouses and (after 1808) pauper lunatic asylums. They were thus more ready to accept the expenditure of larger sums on important bridges. As in the 1770s and 1780s, there were surveyors with the skill to advise them. The case of Devon in 1808 highlights the problem and its solution. An amateur surveyor, William White, repeatedly presented the same bridges as in want of repair in the years after 1803. In 1806 'it was decided to build by contract a new bridge to plans drawn up by White, who was to act as supervisor. Apparently all went well, but at the January sessions of 1808 it was reported that the new Finney bridge had been washed away and destroyed. At the subsequent inquiry, White was shown to be to blame for bad plans and insufficient supervision of the materials used by the contractor'. A professional surveyor, James Green, was appointed, 'a civil engineer of approved talents and ability' at a salary of £300 a year, who was to make at least one general inspection of the county bridges each year, prepare plans and estimates and superintend all work. In the following years there was a great increase in expenditure on county bridge works. Finney bridge was rebuilt the same year for £6602 and other major bridge works were carried out in the following years.[21]

Bridge construction made heavy though uneven demands on the temporary increase in the county rate. Gloucestershire's county rates more than doubled in 1827 and 1828, almost entirely on account of the building of Over bridge. In England as a whole during the years 1821–30 bridges absorbed 11 per cent of county expenditure, an annual average of £68,967 out of £640,684. It reached a peak in 1825–27, nearly corresponding with the building cycle boom of 1824–26.

As in the seventeenth and eighteenth centuries, the acreage of a county and the number and size of its rivers obviously helped to decide the amount of its bridge costs. Expenditure for smaller inland counties, such as Buckinghamshire and Hertfordshire, with no major rivers was understandably still relatively modest. Costs for some counties with larger rivers were heavily reduced by the existence of special authorities

[21] Lewis, *Topographical Dictionary*, i, pp. 125, 210; Tucker, 'Quarter Sessions', pp. 184–85, 191, 197; Devon RO, CT 137/1.

Table 6.3

Bridge Expenditure in Three Counties, 1821–30

County	1821	1822	1823	1824	1825	1826	1827	1828	1829	1830
	£	£	£	£	£	£	£	£	£	£
Devon	5019	4390	3310	3584	4039	5307	5387	5385	3134	2780
Cheshire	2893	3049	3586	5764	9975	6196	5402	5631	3856	5578
Cumberland	8096	3829	4492	2398	1511	1718	1953	4243	4057	4169

Table 6.4

Approximate Expenditure on County Bridges, 1640–1830*

Period	Outlay in Current Prices	Outlay in Early Nineteenth Century Prices
1640–1760	£250,000–350,000	£600,000–800,000
1760–1800	c. £600,000	c. £1,200,000
1800–1830	£2,238,430	£2,238,430

*outlay on building and repair, i.e. total expenditure.

established by act of parliament to maintain individual bridges, paid for by the collection of tolls. This was the case in Worcestershire, where all the important bridges were outside the control of the county; in Nottinghamshire bridge expenditure by the county was also limited by the existence of independent bridge authorities on the Trent. In other counties, such as Northumberland and Surrey, expenditure was modest in these years because of the major bridge works undertaken in the 1770s and 1780s. Apart from this, the number of smaller bridges for which quarter sessions were responsible by prescription, in contrast to parishes or private landowners and corporations, necessarily varied considerably. In 1825 Derbyshire had eighty-three county bridges: Dorset, a slightly larger county with some important rivers, only sixty. It has been seen that Devon had 254 bridges in 1821. In this respect the scale of county bridge responsibilities was partly a matter of historical custom. The counties which were the largest bridge spenders in the 1820s were those which had been so since the seventeenth century and earlier.

It is possible to compute very approximately the total outlay by English counties (excluding the hundreds) on bridges in the first three decades of the nineteenth century and compare it with that of the earlier periods (Table 6.4). Expenditure in the 1820s was £689,967. Figures do not exist for all counties in the 1800s and 1810s, but a near-contemporary estimate

Table 6.5

Percentage of County Expenditure Spent on Bridges, 1821–30

County	Total Outlay on Bridges £	Percentage of Total County Expenditure
Westmorland	11,743	36
Monmouthshire	12,951	29
Gloucestershire	45,033	27
Staffordshire	54,452	25
Cumberland	36,466	25
Dorset	20,030	23
Durham	22,320	22
Devon	42,335	21
Shropshire	17,914	20
Yorkshire, West Riding	80,054	18
Yorkshire, North Riding	23,910	17
Cheshire	51,930	14
Herefordshire	9216	14
Bedfordshire	11,038	14
Northumberland	15,686	12
Oxfordshire	8529	12
Derbyshire	17,019	11
Northamptonshire	5939	10
Hampshire	9314	8
Berkshire	6579	8
Warwickshire	15,437	8
Wiltshire	12,324	8
Somerset	14,577	8
Suffolk	11,376	7
Middlesex	29,743	7
Cornwall	5782	7
Buckinghamshire	5005	6
Essex	12,680	6
Leicestershire	12,046	6
Hertfordshire	2715	6
Cambridgeshire	3051	4
Sussex	3953	4
Norfolk	6991	4
Rutland	488	4
Kent	6086	3
Lancashire (county)	13,632	3
Lincolnshire	8317	3
Nottinghamshire	3310	3
Surrey	7940	3
Yorkshire, East Riding	2788	3
Worcestershire	1430	2
Huntingdonshire	576	1

was £1,006,669 in the 1810s; much less, £541,794 in the 1800s. The estimated total for 1801–30 was £2,238,430. This represents more than a doubling of annual real expenditure since the years 1760–1800, and a growth of at least ten times compared to annual outlay before 1760. While some of the increase was about 1810, most of it was in the later 1760s and 1770s. These years witnessed the beginning of an important phase in English bridge work.[22]

The growth of expenditure on individual bridges is symbolised by the cost of the most expensive undertaking in each of the three periods. These were (in current prices) Brentford (£3350), Lancaster (up to £17,000) and Eden bridge, Carlisle (£70,000). Outlay on the main bridges in each period also reveals the significance of the years between the 1760s and 1820s in the history of bridge building. The long age of bridge maintenance was replaced by one of construction.[23]

[22] *Parliamentary Papers* (1825), vi; (1833), xxxii.
[23] *Parliamentary Papers* (1839), xliv.

Fig. 7.1. The Shirehall, Chelmsford, Essex, 1789–91, designed by the Essex county surveyor John Johnson, with an imposing decorated façade. (Essex Record Office, SCN 3076; reproduced by permission).

7

Courthouses and Judges' Lodgings, 1650–1830

County halls were intended to provide suitable accommodation for quarter sessions, assizes and county courts. They symbolised the community spirit of the county and the self-esteem of its rulers. This was reflected in dear materials, a splendid facade or palatial rooms, or all of them, similar to larger contemporary country houses. This was true especially from the 1770s, when county meetings discussing political radicalism or costly new buildings were common. The desired combination of convenience and splendour is illustrated by the comments of the architect Daniel Alexander on existing shire halls to West Kent sessions in January 1811:

> The best are Stafford, York, Lancaster, and Chester. In the first less accommodation is given to the courts, and more to a county meeting room, and other rooms, than is proper. York is a fine pile of building, well arranged, but the parts are too small and these have been perpetually amending by repeated enlargements, and some parts must be taken down in order to compleat it. Lancaster and Chester are very magnificent and beautiful structures (the former Gothic, the latter Greek) far surpassing any building we have in the south of England; but, sad to say, very bad to hear in.[1]

In the later seventeenth and eighteenth centuries the twice-yearly assizes and the sessions held quarterly sometimes used county premises, sometimes borough or privately-owned rooms. Assizes were held in one or more towns in the county, often in a guildhall or local court room. The floor of the court hall at East Grinstead, Sussex, collapsed when the judges were there in 1684. Bedfordshire assizes always met in Bedford: the old chapel of St Mary in the Herne was used until 1705; then the upper room of a new market house in the High Street was converted for assize meetings. Surrey assizes were at Southwark, Kingston, Guildford, Croydon and Reigate at various times in the seventeenth and eighteenth centuries. The little Kingston and Croydon town halls were used. The

---

[1] *New Maidstone Gaol Order Book, 1805–1823*, ed. C.W. Chalklin, Kent Records, 23 (Maidstone, 1984), p. 40.

Kingston premises about 1800 typified the conditions with which assize judges had had to cope during the previous 200 years: markets were held in the lower part of the building, the section at the south end being closed during assizes for the crown court; 'the room over it upstairs is appropriated to the Judge who sits at Nisi prius . . .'[2] Alternatively assizes were held only in the county town at a shire hall, as in Lincolnshire and Warwickshire.

Some quarter sessions were held in the county town, often in a shire hall or town hall which the local corporation also used; thus at Gloucester the Booth Hall was shared with the city. After the more formal business with juries or counsel, sessions were often adjourned to an inn to deal with administrative matters such as the passing of accounts, the making of orders and the appointment of officials. In other counties the four quarterly meetings were held in different towns because of poor communications. Each sessions might meet several times in various places, by adjournment, to handle business of particular districts. In the 1720s, for example, the North Riding justices held sessions at least once a year in Thirsk, Stokesley, Helmsley, Guisbrough, Northallerton, Malton, Easingwold and Richmond.[3] In these cases the buildings were seldom county property, although an occasional grant might be made to the owner to improve the suitability for meetings. West Riding adjourned sessions used court houses or large rooms owned by the corporation or an individual. In the 1780s Skipton sessions occupied a room in Lord Thanet's castle; at the same time Knaresborough and Wetherby sessions used court houses owned by Sir Thomas Slingsby and the duke of Norfolk respectively. Pontefract corporation made their town hall available, and the trustees of the Bradford New Cloth Hall agreed in 1777 to give the room over the hall. Leeds Moot Hall was used in the eighteenth century, and Halifax made available its court house until the 1720s.[4]

Several shire halls were erected in the later sixteenth and early seventeenth centuries. Essex probably paid for the Chelmsford building in 1569, though it remained the property of the Mildmay family. It

[2] A. Fletcher, *Reform in the Provinces: The Government of Stuart England* (New Haven and London, 1986), p. 106; J. Godber, *History of Bedfordshire, 1066–1888* (Bedford, 1969), p. 323; O. Manning and W. Bray, *History and Antiquities of the County of Surrey*, i (London, 1804), pp. 32, 279, 343, ii (London, 1809), p. 535.

[3] I.E. Gray and A.T. Gaydon, *Gloucestershire Quarter Sessions Archives, 1660–1889* (Gloucester, 1958), p. 14; S. and B. Webb, *The Parish and the County* (London, 1963), pp. 425, 438; *North Riding Record Society Publications*, 8, *Quarter Sessions Records*, ed. J.C. Atkinson (1890), pp. 165–88; see above, pp. 28–29.

[4] West Yorkshire RO, QS general index, court houses.

was also used for marketing. It was a free-standing structure resting on eight columns. The courts occupied the colonnaded area on the ground floor. At the west end was the nisi prius court; the crown court was in the east. Apart from the protection of private buildings on two sides, the courts were open to the weather in the seventeenth century, except when canvas was hung.[5] A shire hall was built in Cambridge in 1572, and an assize hall in Taunton castle in 1577. Staffordshire county hall was erected between 1587 and 1607 by subscriptions and gifts. In 1612 a wealthy mercer and justice built Hicks Hall for the Middlesex justices.[6] In this period private donations were probably more important than rates in paying for sessions houses.

Expenditure on accommodation for assizes and sessions remained occasional for more than a century after 1650. Only fourteen or fifteen buildings erected independently of prisons were rebuilt or newly constructed between 1650 and the early 1760s (see Table 7.1). The largest were the Norfolk shire hall rebuilt in 1749–51 and the Warwickshire shire hall erected between 1757 and 1763. The latter was of one story with a main room ninety-three by thirty-four feet for county meetings and with two octagonal court rooms.[7] The others were much smaller: the Cambridgeshire shire hall erected on pillars above an open market had two courts and rooms for the grand and petty juries, despite its relatively modest cost.[8] The Monmouthshire shire hall of 1724 and the Bedfordshire town and county sessions house (1753) were used jointly by the county and corporation. The Bedfordshire shire hall, although smaller than that of Warwickshire, also had two courts and a county room and jury rooms. This was to be the normal requirement for court houses intended for assizes later. Several halls were repaired and improved or altered. Substantial repairs were done by Cheshire sessions to the shire hall in Chester Castle in 1668 for £100 and in 1682–83 for £171. At Lincoln the Bench raised £100 in 1669 for work on the middle part of the shire hall, and an attempt was made to build a shire hall in the castle in 1688. Subscriptions paid for the Bedfordshire house, county

---

[5] *Essex Quarter Sessions Order Book, 1652–1661*, ed. D.H. Allen (Chelmsford, 1974), pp. xv–xvi.

[6] *Victoria County History of Cambridgeshire*, iii, ed. J.C.P. Roach, (London, 1959), p. 118; S. Lewis, *A Topographical Dictionary of England*, iv (London, 1831), p. 271; *Victoria County History of Staffordshire*, vi, ed. M.W. Greenslade and D.A. Johnson (Oxford, 1979), p. 201; C. Radcliffe, *Middlesex* (2nd edn, London, n.d.), p. 72.

[7] *Warwick County Records*, 7, ed S.C. Ratcliff and H.C. Johnson, *Quarter Sessions Records, Easter 1674 to Easter 1682* (Warwick, 1946), p. cxxv.

[8] *VCH, Cambridgeshire*, iii, p. 118.

rates for the other buildings. Occasional sums given by quarter sessions for the rebuilding of town halls on account of county use included the vote of £30 by North Riding on 30 January 1730 for rebuilding Easingwold courthouse.[9]

Norfolk shire hall was rebuilt after a fire made replacement essential. Probably extreme decay of an old structure meant that repairs were impossible on three buildings. Otherwise more room was the object of the judges and justices. The Bury St Edmunds shire hall was enlarged after the assizes had noted the 'want of room . . . and narrowness', and the need to help the grand jury, petty jury and witnesses. Attractive buildings were being erected. The Warwickshire shire hall of 1676, which had a grand jury chamber and a nisi prius and crown court for assizes, had a stone classical front with huge Ionic pilasters and a Corinthian centrepiece. The front of the Leicestershire hall was built in newly fashionable brick, Leicester houses still being timbered.[10] There was clearly no general move to add to the size of the facilities (Table 7.1).

From the 1770s new works became more numerous; the motive to provide larger and more commodious accommodation became more important; the need for a more convenient situation in the town was also occasionally cited as a reason for a new building. Pressure for improvements of shire halls or replacement of town hall accommodation by a shire hall often came from the judges. At the summer assizes of 1782, Baron Hotham laid a fine of £2000 on Shropshire in order to compel the justices to provide a new shire hall for holding the courts.[11] The justices were also periodically interested in expenditure to provide themselves with better facilities. In the 1770s and 1780s the justices of the West Riding tried to improve the accommodation in the various courthouses they used. For example, when in April 1781 the courthouse at Knaresborough was said to be in decay, the court decided that it was willing to pay for its repair and enlargement. In October 1783, the room used by the justices having been condemned as incommodious, a group of justices were asked to look out for a better room. This led to the building of a new courthouse by

[9] K. Kissack, *Monmouth: The Making of a County Town* (Chichester, 1975), p. 295; Bedfordshire RO, box 770; Staffordshire RO, QS O 12; Dorset RO, QS treasurers' accounts, 1739–77; Cheshire RO, QJB 3/1,3; Lincolnshire RO, Lindsey QS minutes, 1665–79; J.W.F. Hill, *Georgian Lincoln* (Cambridge, 1966), p. 4; *North Riding Record Society Publications*, 8, *Quarter Sessions Records*, ed. J.C. Atkinson (1890), p.186.

[10] A.C. Wood, *The Shire Hall, Warwick: Its Rebuilding in the Mid Eighteenth Century* (Warwick, 1983), p.5.

[11] H. Owen and J.B. Blakeway, *A History of Shrewsbury*, i (Shrewsbury, 1825), p. 584.

Table 7.1

The Building of County Court Houses, 1650–1765[12]
(a new building unless otherwise stated)*

Date	County and Location	Cost
1654–55	Devon, Exeter	£688
1661	Derbyshire, Derby	not known
c. 1663	Suffolk, Bury St Edmunds	£300
1673–74	Yorkshire, York	£650 or £690
1676–78	Northamptonshire, Northampton	c. £1800
c. 1676–81	Warwickshire, Warwick (walls etc. rebuilt)	c. £1500
c. 1695	Leicestershire, Leicester (refronted)	not known
1698–c. 1701	Suffolk, Ipswich	£300
1709, 1714	Essex, Chelmsford, c. £100 (1710) + £355 (1714)	£455
1721	Lincolnshire, Lincoln (repairs)	£300
1722–24	Staffordshire, Stafford (repairs and alterations)	£389
1724	Monmouthshire, Monmouth	£1700
1732–35	Suffolk, Bury (repairs and enlargement)	up to £500
1747	Cambridgeshire, Cambridge	c. £800
1749–51	Norfolk, Norwich	at least £3082
1750–51	Dorset, Dorchester	£709
1753	Bedfordshire, Bedford (subscribed; site £500)	£2771
1757–63	Warwickshire, Warwick	c. £4200
1761–63	Sussex, Lewes	£1677

*excluding buildings erected primarily as town halls, but used also by the county and to which it made a financial contribution.

Sir Thomas Slingsby, towards which the justices contributed £200.[13]

While pressure from judges or the wishes of the justices provided the immediate reason for acting, the timing of the decision to build may have been in part influenced by one or two other factors. It is noticeable that decisions to alter, extend or rebuild this official accommodation were mostly made at times when other forms of building and construction had been buoyant for several years. There were seven or eight building extensions or new courthouses in the 1770s, when other forms of construction were at a

[12] *Sources:* Devon RO, Q51/9, 24 April 1655; J.C. Cox, *Three Centuries of Derbyshire Annals*, i (London, 1890), p. 13; East Suffolk RO, 105/2/13, fol. 69; West Yorkshire RO, Q51/13/9–10; W. Hargrove, *History and Description of the Ancient City of York* (York, 1818), p. 230; C.A. Markham, *History of the County Buildings of Northamptonshire* (Northampton, 1885), pp. 40–41; *Warwick County Records*, eds S.C. Ratcliff and H.C. Johnson, 7, *Quarter Sessions Records, Easter 1674 to Easter 1682* (Warwick 1946), pp. cxix-cxx; ed. C. Morris, *The Illustrated Journeys of Celia Fiennes* (1984), p. 146; East Suffolk RO, 105/2/13, fos 71, 87; R.E. Negus, *A Short History of the Shire Houses of Essex* (1937), p. 2; Essex RO, QS 04, pp. 194, 252, 268; Lincolnshire RO, Holland QS, 1715–32; East Suffolk RO, 105/2/19, fos 74, 89, 92, 112, 120; East Sussex RO, QAF2/1/Æ1.

[13] West Yorkshire RO, QS general index, courthouses, and QS O, 1781–85.

peak; the early and mid 1790s also witnessed some new buildings. Then there was almost a complete absence of interest in new construction until about 1804, corresponding with a trough in building in general about 1799–1800. The justices may have been influenced in their decision to build by the existence of the flourishing state of other types of building and construction locally. Newspapers and local sources contain references to signs of the 'spirit of improvement' being visible in the shape of the construction of new terraces of houses or new urban roads. Other types of public building, such as market developments or commercial buildings, may have also encouraged the justices in a decision to improve their own accommodation. Another influence was the 'demonstration effect', the tendency for knowledge of the erection of one building to encourage the building of other courthouses, perhaps within the same county or in a neighbouring one. A factor affecting timing was expenditure on other types of construction by the justices. Thus the building of the Staffordshire shire hall between 1795 and 1797 followed the completion of the county gaol begun in 1786. There is no direct evidence that factors on the supply side, such as the price of materials or the availability of loans, influenced the decision to build shire halls.

The greater interest both in putting existing premises into proper repair and in rebuilding from about the later 1760s is to be seen in the legislation coming before parliament. An act of 1769 (9 George III c. 20) confirmed the power of quarter sessions to repair shire halls used for meetings of assizes and sessions, 'doubts [having] arisen in several counties . . . whether there be any lawful authority', for their repair. But this led to doubts 'in several counties' whether this gave the power to pull down and rebuild. A bill was prepared in 1774 to provide such authority specifically, but did not become law.[14] Between 1768 and 1782 seven county hall buildings were begun (see Table 7.2) and there were alterations to at least three others. The Devon assize hall and sessions house was not only 'ruinous' but 'very incommodious' before new buildings were erected in 1771–74, while the alterations to the Cambridgeshire shire hall in 1777 were intended to add 'greater decorum and ease'. The altered buildings only involved the expenditure of some hundred pounds; thus Hampshire in 1773–74 spent £704 9s. 6d. on rebuilding and altering the grand jury chamber, measuring thirty-two by twenty feet.[15]

The seven new county halls were all substantial buildings with crown and civil courts, and rooms for grand juries, judges and magistrates.

[14] Coventry RO, bill to explain, amend and enlarge 12 George 2 and 9 George III, so far as relates to public bridges and county halls and shire halls, 1774.
[15] Devon RO, QS 1/1759–76, 1777–91; LSE, Webb Collection, Cambridgeshire; Hampshire RO, QO 18, fos 101, 106, 108, 157.

The largest in provincial England were the assize courts built for Yorkshire between 1772 and 1777 at a contract price of £5500, and the Hertfordshire shire hall erected in 1768–70 for about £7000.[16] The latter building, in the fashionable white brick, comprised courts, a council chamber for the use of the corporation of Hertford, an assembly room, and rooms for the juries and justices. Both buildings were intended to provide additional accommodation in the face of existing cramped conditions. By far the biggest courthouse for England as a whole to be erected in these years was the Middlesex sessions house, which cost about £16,000, including the site purchase for £2036. Practically everything possible had been wrong with the former building: its structure was precarious, approach inconvenient, situation noisy, accommodation unsuitable. The growth of business made a more extensive building essential.[17]

Although the decade after about 1785 saw a high level of building of most types, and the counties themselves spent unprecedented sums on prisons, building on courthouses by quarter sessions was limited to almost a dozen benches. New gaols and bridewells were regarded as more necessary. Four shire halls were erected independent of accompanying prisons, at Shrewsbury, Chelmsford, Stafford and Dorchester, the cost of the last two showing the rising price of materials and wages by the mid 1790s. The Shropshire and Staffordshire halls were used by the corporations of Shrewsbury and Stafford, who paid a small part of the expenditure.[18]

The buildings differed in plan and size. That at Shrewsbury had the two courts separated by a grand lobby and staircase on the ground floor, and shire and guild hall, grand jury room, exchequer and offices above, all covering about a hundred and fifty feet. In the Stafford hall of about a hundred by eighty feet, the ground floor was a market-place with offices and prisoners' rooms; the first floor had a big hall in front and the two courts in the rear, with grand jury and judges' room and two petty jury rooms.[19] The Essex shire hall, about eighty by 110 feet, had a market-place with the two courts behind on the ground; above were the county room and the smaller grand jury room (in the rear). The whole design was influenced by the Hertford building.[20] The Dorchester hall was the

[16] K.T. Meaby, *Nottinghamshire; Extracts from the County Records of the Eighteenth Century* (Nottingham, undated), pp. 54–56; Lewis, *Topographical Dictionary*, iii, p. 430; see Table 7.2.

[17] Greater London RO, MJ/OC 11, pp. 8–12.

[18] See Table 7.2; Shropshire RO, minutes of commissioners to build shire hall and gaol, fol 14.

[19] Shropshire RO, plans of Shrewsbury shire hall; Staffordshire RO, Q/AS 1.

[20] N. Briggs, *John Johnson, 1732–1814: Georgian Architect and County Surveyor of Essex* (Chelmsford, 1991), pp. 91–104.

smallest and was built without elaborate decoration, perhaps because wartime taxation discouraged lavish county expenditure.

Four courthouses were erected with new prisons. On a small scale were the two little groups of rooms at Northallerton for the North Riding (1784–88), and the Surrey sessions house (1792–99), with one court room and no county room or shire hall. The Lancashire and Cheshire buildings were much more extensive. A great civil court or shire hall, designed as seven sides of a polygon arranged in semi-circular formation and jury room, about 1792–99, and a slightly later crown court were erected at Lancaster Castle (Fig. 7.2). Although in both counties expenditure was at least several thousand pounds, it is impossible to

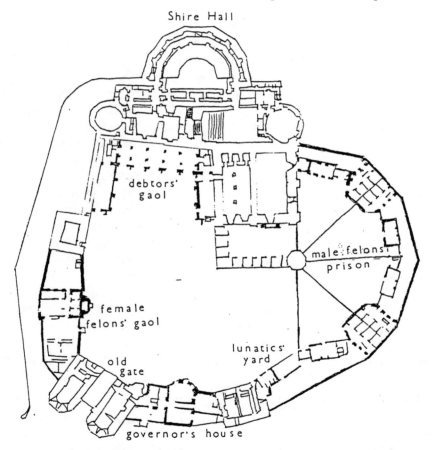

Fig. 7.2. Lancaster Castle, *c.* 1800, showing the prisons and courts built in the 1790s, designed by Thomas Harrison and placed beside the older castle buildings. (R. Evans, *The Fabrication of Virtue: Prison Architecture, 1750–1840*, Cambridge, 1982, p. 152).

separate it from the outlay on the prisons. In sum, a minority of counties received better facilities in this period (Table 7.2).

Table 7.2

The Building of County Court Houses, 1765–1800[21]

Date	County and Location	Cost
1768–70	Hertfordshire, Hertford	c. £7000
1770–71	Lincolnshire, Lincoln	£944
		or
		£1202
1770	Nottinghamshire, Nottingham	at least
		£3000
1772–77	Yorkshire, York (assize courts)	c. £5500
1773–76	Devon, Exeter	c. £4800
1774	Westmorland, Appleby	not known
1779–82	Middlesex, Clerkenwell	c. £16,000
1784–85	Shropshire, Shrewsbury	c. £11,000
1789–91	Essex, Chelmsford	£13,790
1790–1801	Cheshire, Chester (with new gaol)	not known
1792–99	Lancashire, Lancaster (with new gaol)	not known
1795–97	Staffordshire, Stafford	£14,650
1796–97	Dorset, Dorchester	£7162

*excluding sessions houses attached to prison buildings (except Lancashire and Cheshire courthouses)

For nearly ten years after the start of the building of the Dorset shire hall in 1796 no large new courthouse was begun; nor were there any improvements to existing buildings around 1800. Construction in general was at a low level in these years; a scheme for a Gloucestershire shire hall in 1802, because the corporation Booth Hall was insecure, was postponed indefinitely in July 1803 on account of 'the unexpected political events . . . in the defence of the country and other movements of great magnitude', that is, the outbreak of war and presumably its expected financial demands. Interest in more spacious court accommodation began to revive in about 1804–5. In Suffolk the small shire halls at Bury and Woodbridge were altered and

[21] *Sources: Hertfordshire County Records: Calendar to the Sessions Books, 8, 1752–99,* ed. W. Le Hardy (Hertford, 1935), pp. 250–51, 280; Lincolnshire RO, Holland QS, minutes, 1765–71, p. 549; Lincolnshire RO, Kesteven QS, minutes, 1760–71, p. 655; West Yorkshire RO, QS 027, fol. 144; North Yorkshire RO, county treasurers' accounts, book A; Cumbria RO, Kendal WQ/09; H. Owen, *Some Account of the Ancient and Present State of Shrewsbury* (Shrewsbury, 1808), p. 410; Negus, *A Short History of Shire Houses of Essex,* p. 4; Essex RO, Q/AS 2/4/6; Cheshire RO, QAB 1/1/1–2; J.M. Crook, 'A Reluctant Goth: The Architecture of Thomas Harrison – I', *Country Life,* 15 April 1971; Staffordshire RO, QS Q/AS 1; Dorset RO, QS treasurers' accounts, 1806–25.

improved in succession between 1805 and 1808 at the relatively small cost of £1440 and £1206 respectively.[22] More ambitiously, the West Riding justices initiated new courthouses at some of the eleven towns where quarter sessions were held. The existing buildings were the property of individuals or corporations, and not therefore under the control of the justices, and were 'mostly very ancient, out of repair and inconvenient' for holding sessions. The first and largest project was the Wakefield court house. This was accompanied by a smaller building at Pontefract. In the following years smaller sums were voted towards the construction of courthouses by the respective town authorities at Sheffield, Leeds and Barnsley, with whom the use of the buildings was to be shared; the Sheffield and Barnsley courthouses were relatively small and the Leeds courthouse was combined with a prison. The quarter sessions contributed £2700 towards Sheffield town hall, erected between 1808 and 1811 at a total cost of £5600.[23]

Between 1808 and 1815 five substantial courthouses were begun. Presumably their construction was encouraged by a boom in building in these years. The largest were the Cumberland courts at Carlisle built between 1808 and 1822 for about £100,000. In 1810 the Northumberland county courts (which included a gaol for the custody of prisoners on trial) were begun, the total cost being £52,000. The building was 144 feet long and seventy-two feet deep; in the middle was a grand entrance hall with the nisi prius court on the left and the crown court on the right; beyond was a grand jury room; in the wings were rooms for the judge, petty juries and witnesses; above were rooms for the gaoler and other court officers; below were cells for the prisoners on trial.[24] Sussex built a new assize hall in 1810–12 at Lewes, partly on account of the impractical position of the town hall or sessions house in the middle of the high street; a smaller building than that erected for Northumberland, it cost about £16,500, including £4228 10s. 3d. for the property purchased on the site.[25] Gloucestershire and Herefordshire erected large court buildings between 1814 and 1816 and 1815 and 1818 respectively, both existing buildings being 'inconvenient and ill-adapted for the administration of justice'; the former cost £47,064 18s. 6d. excluding the site but with the furnishing, and the latter cost £36,360, of which a little more than £7000 was spent on the purchase of property to include a judges' lodging. The Hereford building was much more extensive

---

[22] Gloucestershire RO, Q/AS 1; East Suffolk RO, 105/2/53.

[23] K. Grady, 'The Provision of Public Buildings in the West Riding of Yorkshire, c. 1600–1840' (unpublished Ph.D. thesis, University of Leeds, 1980), p. 446.

[24] Lewis, *Topographical Dictionary*, iii, p. 357.

[25] R.F. Dell, 'The Building of the County Hall, Lewes, 1808–12', *Sussex Archaeological Collections*, 100 (1962), p. 11.

and spaciously laid out than the Lewes assize hall. In front was a portico placed some fifty feet back from the street; behind it was an oblong vestibule twenty-four feet deep, to the rear of which lay the two courts, each about forty-five by sixty feet; behind again were the grand jury and counsels' rooms. Finally, at the back of the building, was the shire hall, seventy-two feet by forty-eight feet; prisoners' and witnesses' rooms were at basement level, and a county depot for arms, clothing and accoutrements under the shire hall. The county left open an area of about forty feet around the building.[26] In addition, in the period between 1805 and 1817 at least four court buildings were erected in conjunction with prisons, as in the case of County Durham, and several court buildings were extended, such as the enlargement of the Northamptonshire county hall between 1812 and 1813.

Several more substantial projects were begun between 1822 and 1824, especially the Lincolnshire county hall (1822–26), the Norfolk shire hall (1822–23), and the Kent court house (1824–27) (Fig. 7.3). The

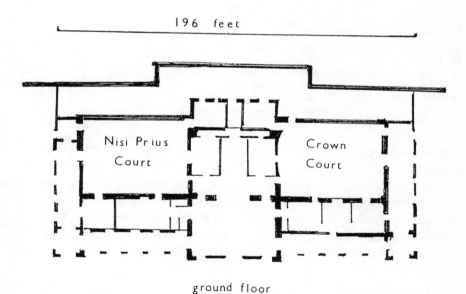

ground floor

Fig. 7.3. Kent courthouse, Maidstone, erected 1825–26. A typical county sessions building with its Nisi Prius and Crown Courts and rooms for the juries, judges and magistrates, designed by Robert Smirke, an enormously prolific architect. (*Guide to Kent County Archives Office*, ed. F. Hull, Maidstone, 1958, pl. 4.)

[26] Herefordshire RO, shire hall minutes and plans, 1814–19.

Derbyshire courts were extended in 1828–29. There were also smaller buildings: in Lincolnshire courthouses were built as part of town halls at Bourn and Sleaford.

Table 7.3

The Building of County Courthouses, 1800–1830[27]
(a new building unless otherwise stated)

Date	County and Location	Cost
1806–11	Yorkshire, West Riding, Wakefield	£15,100
1807–11	Yorkshire, West Riding, Pontefract	£7000
1808–10	Kent, Canterbury	£5491
1808–22	Cumberland, Carlisle	c. £100,000
1810–15	Northumberland, Newcastle (including gaol)	£52,000
1810–12	Sussex, Lewes	£16,500
1812–13	Northamptonshire, Northampton (enlarged)	c. £4200
1812–14	Yorkshire, York	c. £5000
1814–16	Gloucestershire, Gloucester	£47,065
1815–18	Herefordshire, Hereford	£36,360
1821–22	Lincolnshire, Kesteven	£2500
1822–23	Norfolk, Norwich	c. £20,000
1822–26	Lincolnshire, Lincoln	£24,240
1824–27	Kent, Maidstone	£29,106
1825–28	Lancashire, Preston	c. £10,000
1828–29	Derbyshire, Derby	£18,939
1829–31	Monmouthshire, Monmouth	£7300
1830	Lincolnshire, Kesteven, Sleaford	£7000

Altogether the twenty-five years after 1805 saw seventeen undertakings in the form of complete new buildings or improvements to existing courthouses, apart from the numerous small sessions houses attached to prisons (Table 7.3). One reason for this prolonged activity was the increasing amount of administrative and judicial business which faced the justices of the peace, and their growing consciousness of the cramped nature and inconvenience of their existing premises. The Lancashire

[27] *Sources*: West Yorkshire RO, QS 0 1805–6, 1807–9, 1809–11; Centre for Kentish Studies, Q/AGe5, QS Oell; J. Hughes, 'The Building of the Courts, Carlisle, 1807–22', *Transactions of the Cumberland and Westmorland Antiquarian and Archaeological Society*, 70 (1971), p. 219; *Parliamentary Papers* (1825), vi; North Yorkshire RO, QS treasurers' accounts, 1802–15; Gloucestershire RO, Q/AS 4; W. White, *History, Gazetteer and Directory of Lincolnshire* (Sheffield, 1856), p. 707; estimated from R.W. Liscombe, *William Wilkins, 1778–1839* (Cambridge, 1980), p. 267, and G.K. Blyth, *The Norwich Guide* (Norwich, 1843), p. 202; Lincolnshire RO, Co.C.2/3; Lancashire RO, QSV 9; S. Glover, *History of the County of Derby*, ii (Derby, 1833), p. 449; *Parliamentary Papers* (1835), xiv (*Report from the Select Committee on the County Rates, 1834–35*, p. 17); White, *Lincolnshire*, p. 433.

court house at Preston was rebuilt between 1825 and 1828 because the justices found it inconveniently situated (in the middle of the house of correction) and too small. At the holding of the Lancashire general sessions in September 1824 'the Chairman rose, and made some pointed observations on the state of the Preston Court-House, and the smallness of the Sessions-room they were sitting in, which in hot weather (crowded, too, as it generally is) was most intolerable . . .' £10,000 was voted immediately towards the work. According to a contemporary historian, the Lincolnshire brick county hall of 1770 was 'mean' and the collapse of the foundations made it unsafe.[28] It is also likely that the assize judges brought sustained pressure to bear on the magistrates to provide more suitable courts in the case of those buildings where assizes were held. The old Hereford court house had been 'continuously objected to by the Judges for many years past'.[29] As has been seen, in these years improvements were in the air in connection with the law courts centred on Westminster Hall. In the 1780s and 1790s the court of Common Pleas was extensively altered, and in 1805 it was decided that the courts of Chancery and King's Bench should be removed and rebuilt 'in the same manner as the Common Pleas'; more new courts were built between 1822 and 1827.[30] Changes at Westminster, or at least the prospect of them, may have made the judges more importunate in seeking improvements in the frequently tiny and sometimes dilapidated provincial courthouses in which they were compelled to hold the assizes.

The growing importance of the assizes and the need to provide suitable premises for the judges is also seen in the provision of judges' lodgings in several counties in the fifteen years after 1806. Renting gave the benches insufficient control of a building, which needed now to be larger and more sumptuously furnished. The great county of Yorkshire with its three Ridings was the first, about £6000 being spent. The 'demonstration effect' is visible in the case of six other counties, all in the midlands. Benches were influenced by action in adjoining shires, where in some cases the judges were the same. Lincolnshire followed its neighbour by building a judges' house in 1809–13 for £9090. Warwickshire's lodgings cost £8000 in 1814. Leicestershire's house with a record room and offices £7220 (1818), and the smaller Northamptonshire and Shropshire rooms about £3700 in 1818 and £4000 in 1821 respectively. Herefordshire's

---

[28] *Lancaster Gazette*, 18 September 1824; T. Allen, *The History of the County of Lincoln*, i (London and Lincoln, 1834), p. 200.

[29] Herefordshire RO, shire hall minutes, 11 January 1814.

[30] J.M. Crook and M.H. Port, *The History of the King's Works*, vi, *1782–1851* (London, 1973), pp. 499, 504–11.

tiny lodgings were built, at the same time as the new county hall, for £2500 in 1818–19. Leicestershire's, Northamptonshire's, and Shropshire's premises were bought and altered, those at Warwick were built. Both the Lincolnshire and Leicestershire expenditure, and probably that for Yorkshire and Northamptonshire, included substantial sums for furnishing. The Lincolnshire total of £9090 not only included £2444 for the purchase of property in a central location, and £550 for the act, but also £1681 for furnishing and fitting up the rooms.

To reduce immediate pressure on the rates, the money was usually borrowed. As a variation, the Surrey bench obtained an act for £234 in 1815 to provide a record room, clerk's offices and official residence, estimated to cost £3600 for the property and £2365 for the new buildings, including £530 on the record room. It reflected the growing work and status of the county's chief official.[31] Expenditure on judges' lodgings by a few counties and on clerk's accommodation by Surrey are significant examples of the extension of building work by the justices in the early nineteenth century. The revival of house construction generally in the 1800s was presumably an encouragement.

Many of the courthouses built from the 1770s were more expensive in real terms than those erected in the early and mid eighteenth century. They were larger, two-story buildings with ampler rooms. Among the factors adding to the cost of construction, the site was sometimes expensive because a central location was chosen. In some cases the existing place was used, as at Nottingham when the shire hall was rebuilt in 1770. In other instances the position chosen and the need to buy sizeable properties increased the cost. Out of nearly £16,000 spent on Middlesex shire hall in 1779–82, £2036 paid for the site. The cost of the new Essex courthouse in 1789–91 (£13,790) included £3782 on buying properties. The decoration of the facade also added to the cost, although it is not usually possible to calculate the amount from the accounts. The Essex shire hall, of white and red brick, had a Portland stone frontage which cost, in the purchase of stone, freight and stonemasonry, about £900. Porticos were sometimes added, as at Gloucester and Chester. At Chester the twelve Doric columns of the massive portico were of single stones

---

[31] North Yorkshire RO, county treasurers' accounts E, 1802–15; Lincolnshire RO, Lindsey QS minutes of meeting about the judges' house, 1809–13; *Warwick County Records*, 7, p. cxxviii; J. Simmons, 'Notes on a Leicester Architect, John Johnson (1722–1814)', *Transactions of the Leicestershire Archaeological Society*, 25 (1949), p. 156; *Parliamentary Papers* (1825), vi; Surrey RO, QS 2/6, Midsummer 15, nos 22, 23a; Leicestershire RO, QS 6/2/1, 25/1/1, 3,6.

twenty-three feet high and three feet two inches broad. The architect Daniel Alexander's abortive proposal for a courthouse for West Kent in 1811 estimated the cost at £46,110; the extra charge for a Portland stone front would have been £11,177 and for a portico £7100. Nor were the cheapest materials always used for the main structure. Sandstone was obtained from nearby quarries for the building of the Warwickshire shire hall in 1757–63, while in the case of the Lincolnshire shire hall in the 1820s both the ordinary stone and ashlar for facing came from neighbouring quarries. There were thus no freight costs. In other cases, even when brick was the normal local building material, stone was brought from some miles. The Gloucestershire shire hall in 1814 was built principally of Bath and Beckhampton stone, the first being brought by water down the Avon navigation and up the Severn, the second by a railroad from quarries about seven miles east of Gloucester. The Cheshire county buildings were faced with stone from the Manley quarries, seven or eight miles away; other stone came from Runcorn by canal. The cost of the courthouses reflected not only the need for ample accommodation for assizes and courts, it also sometimes involved the requirement of a central position. There was also always the desire for an architecturally imposing building that would reflect credit on the county.[32]

---

[32] See sources in Tables 7. 1–3; also F. Simpson, 'Chester Castle, AD 907–1925', *Journal of the Chester and North Wales Archaeological and Historic Society*, new series, 26 (1925), pp. 103, 110; Lincolnshire RO, Co. C. 2/3; Lewis, *Topographical Dictionary*, ii, p. 231, for the Gloucestershire shire hall; *New Maidstone Gaol Order Book*, ed. Chalklin, p. 49.

8

Gaols and Bridewells, 1650–1765

The building of gaols and bridewells between 1650 and 1830 was in three stages. Before the 1770s there was the occasional new prison. Building grew gradually, especially after 1700, yet less than half the counties erected a gaol; the rest did spasmodic repairs and a few made alterations. Gaols were not purpose-built. They just separated men and women, at least at night; and often debtors and felons. New buildings cost between £1000 and £10,000. The majority of benches replaced one or more of the much smaller bridewells. In contrast to the later period, justices had relatively little interest in prisons.

During the second phase, between about 1770 and the mid 1790s, most counties erected a prison and some two or three. This surge of construction was the product of the general growth of English population from the 1750s, and of the greater use of imprisonment as a punishment. More particularly, the prison reform movement, which began in the mid 1770s under the inspiration of John Howard, and gathered pace in the 1780s, led to the erection of gaols with wards for each type of prisoner, and with cells for solitary night occupation. These might cost up to £40,000. Houses of correction were also planned in a more intricate way; with three exceptions the price was under £10,000. From 1784 money was raised by loans.

After a short relative pause in construction in the later 1790s, a third, continuous phase of building lasted from the early 1800s until the 1830s, reflecting further population growth, especially in urban areas, and the developing reform movement. The Gaol Act (1823) took planning further by classifying prisoners uniformly in the buildings.

County gaols before the 1770s were used for debtors and those awaiting trial rather than for felons. Debtors were often poor retailers and craftsmen imprisoned by creditors to try to force payment. Some gaols lay in part of a medieval castle, as at Chester, Gloucester, York and Lancaster. Others consisted of converted houses, as at Bedford, Reading (Berkshire) and Southwark (Surrey). Several gaols had been built as prisons by the sheriff in the middle ages. These prisons were run by the gaolers as a business based on fees, apart from a small allowance for each inmate. The first comprehensive description of most gaols is that by John Howard in 1773, after a century of changes that had included some improvements. The larger medieval county prisons had had several 'chambers' and 'pits' or dungeons. Typically there were chambers for debtors who could pay and a ward for the majority who could not; a day room for inmates awaiting trial and any felons, sometimes a 'dungeon' below ground, with separate night rooms for the men and women, were the other quarters; there was probably a court. The sexes were inadequately kept apart, while overcrowding before assizes or sessions led to outbreaks of smallpox and typhus. The buildings were dirty, without a water supply and ill-ventilated. The gaoler sold drink and allowed visitors (and family residents of debtors) to those inmates who paid. As buildings were often insecure, escapes happened and prisoners were sometimes shackled. Others were let out for a fee if there was no risk of flight. The Wiltshire prison (erected 1568–78) had by 1672 a 'common gaol', 'upper gaol' (both probably for criminals); 'upper cabin', 'the Whitehall', 'Whitehall chamber', 'Rosechamber', and 'Forest chamber', (rooms presumably for debtors); and a tap house. The building measured fifty-three by twenty-eight feet with twenty-three feet high walls, and there was probably a keeper's house as had existed originally. The stone Staffordshire gaol erected in the 1620s had two dungeons, presumably for men and women, probably with wooden partitions for sleeping, and a wooden house for the gaoler. Worcestershire had at least thirty prisoners before trial in 1619 and twenty-eight in 1638, but how typical these figures were is not known. The sheriff, who claimed repayment from the Exchequer for some repairs until the 1730s, was charged with safe custody of prisoners and appointed the gaoler. In the seventeenth century sessions became responsible for providing gaol buildings, probably with reluctance as they had no legal responsibility and were often pressed to act by the assize judges. The Wiltshire and Staffordshire prisons are the first known to have been built by the justices.[1]

Counties also had one or more small prisons known as 'bridewells' and

[1] R. Evans, *The Fabrication of Virtue: English Prison Architecture, 1750–1840* (Cambridge, 1982), pp. 12–46; S. McConville, *A History of English Prison Administration*, i, *1750–1877* (London, 1981), pp. 49–54; J.R.S. Whiting, *Prison Reform in Gloucestershire, 1776–1820* (Chichester, 1975), pp. 1–2; J. Howard, *The State of the Prisons in England and Wales* (2nd edn, Warrington, 1780); R.B. Pugh, *Imprisonment in Medieval England* (Cambridge, 1970), pp. 349–56; *Victoria County History of Wiltshire*, v, ed. R.B. Pugh and E. Crittall (London, 1957), p. 94, vi, ed. E. Crittall (London, 1962), p. 182; *Victoria County History of Staffordshire*, vi, ed. M.W. Greenslade and D.A. Johnson (Oxford, 1979), p. 204; *Quarter Sessions Records for the County of Somerset*, ed. E.H. Bates, Somerset Record Series, 23 (1907), p. 349, for reference to 'new gaol' in 1624; J.W. Willis Bund, *Worcestershire County Records Calendar, 1591–1643*, (Worcester, 1900), pp. clvi, clvii, clx, clxii.

'houses of correction'. Set up by the justices under statute from 1576, there were over seventy by 1650. They were tenements of two or three rooms, one for men, one for women, with sometimes a workroom. They punished vagabonds, idle and disorderly persons, and the mothers of bastards with short terms of imprisonment and with work, intermittently provided. In short, they were to discipline the poor. Sometimes they were combined with parish workhouses. Criminals were also often sent there by the justices.[2]

The Dorset gaol erected by its sessions cost £1000 in 1624. The bridewells converted from tenements or built between the 1610s and the 1630s cost about £150 or several hundred pounds; unusually £1000 had been spent on the bridewell at Exeter in the 1630s. Prison building almost ended in the 1640s. Particularly between 1643 and 1646, the collapse of normal authority or respect for it during the Civil War made rates difficult to collect.[3]

Three gaols were rebuilt or converted by the justices between the 1650s and the 1670s. At Horsham in Sussex a prison had been built on a new site in 1640; its full cost is unknown but there were problems raising the money over the following years. In 1649 it was said to be too weak to stop escapes and repairs were ordered in 1651. The craftsmen were forced 'to build it from the ground'. It cost £420 spread over two and a half years; £50 was needed for repairs in 1658, after which further defects were found (Fig. 8.1). Essex spent a substantial sum buying a Chelmsford house and converting it into a combined gaol and bridewell. Until the 1650s the gaol was in Colchester Castle, owned by the crown. By 1659 it was so ruinous that 'the prisoners therein cannot lye dry'. The location was unsatisfactory because prisoners had to be taken twenty-two miles to Chelmsford for sessions and the assizes. The county's title to the gaol was also doubtful, rest-

---

[2] J. Innes, 'Prisons for the Poor: English Bridewells, 1555–1800', ed. F. Snyder and D. Hey, *Labour, Law and Crime: An Historical Perspective* (London, 1987), pp. 42, 62–77.

[3] J. Hutchins, *The History and Antiquities of the County of Dorset*, ii (3rd edn, London, 1863), p. 371; and *Acts of the Privy Council 1629–30*, p. 260; *Quarter Sessions Records*, ed. Bates, p. 344; *North Riding Quarter Sessions Records*, ed. J.C. Atkinson, ii (1884), pp. 183, 229, 240, iii (1885), p. 134; B. Osborne, *Justices of the Peace, 1361–1948* (Shaftesbury, 1960), pp. 68–69. The East Riding house of correction was leased: G.C.F. Foster, *The East Riding Justices of the Peace in the Seventeenth Century* (York, 1973), p. 40. For Petworth: McConville, *History*, p. 93; Wiltshire RO A1/160/1; S.S. Tollit, 'The First House of Correction for the County of Lancashire', *Transactions of the Historic Society of Lancashire and Cheshire for 1953*, 105 (1954), pp. 73–85; Devon RO, QS 1/7 Easter 1633, Michaelmas 1637, Epiphany 1637/38, Easter 1639; W. Albery, *A Millenium of Facts in the History of Horsham and Sussex, 947–1947* (Horsham, 1947), p. 340; *Victoria County History of Northamptonshire*, iii, ed. W. Page (London, 1930), p. 35; C.A. Markham, *The History of the County Buildings of Northamptonshire* (Northampton, 1885), p. 11; J.S. Furley, *Quarter Sessions Government in Hampshire in the Seventeenth Century* (Winchester, n.d.), pp. 37–38.

Fig. 8.1. Sussex gaol, Horsham, built 1640, 1651–53, from a rough sketch *c.* 1700. (W. Albery *A Millennium of Facts in the History of Horsham, 1947.*)

ing merely on custom. For these reasons, and the high cost of more repairs, in January 1659 the bench decided to buy the Cross Keys messuage in Moulsham, Chelmsford, for £400, using money it held. Next sessions £500 rates were ordered to convert it. At Canterbury the gaol and bridewell used by the eastern division of Kent were rebuilt between 1669 and 1676 following a fire. Consisting of two 'strongholds', or divisions, for men and women, it cost £1123, rated on this part of the county. Records do not survive for some counties and there may have been other similar work. Destruction by fire, the condition of the prisoners and the need for greater security appear in these three cases as important reasons.[4]

A few houses of correction were built, bought or extended, and a similar number closed during these thirty years. Occasionally the location was changed. The district which was to use them sometimes paid.

---

[4] Albery, *Millenium*, pp. 340–41; *Essex Quarter Sessions Order Book 1652–1661*, ed. D.H. Allen (Chelmsford, 1974), pp. xxi, 129–30, 134; Centre for Kentish Studies, QS Oe 1, fos 123, 128, 131, 134, and QS Oe 2, fol. 24.

At least a few were also workhouses, as rising poor rates for outrelief and the near identity of vagrants and paupers encouraged parish overseers and the justices supervising them to put paupers in them. Devon spent £40 on materials for the Exeter bridewell 'that the house bee repaired . . . and all weake places strengthened' in July 1668. Later it was found to be convenient, and presumably cheaper, to keep vagabonds and other bridewell prisoners together there; the Honiton house was sold for £130 in 1674 and that at Newton Abbot fetched £85 in 1679. Other benches set up bridewells to save charges. £110 may have been raised by Lindsey sessions in 1669 to build or buy a house at Gainsborough because of the cost of moving prisoners to Louth. In Suffolk two small bridewells cost £150 at Mildenhall in 1661 and £76 6s. 3d. at Clare in 1662, paid for by the individual hundreds. £600 was spent on a bridewell at Beccles, Suffolk, in 1679–80, the premises being used partly as a workhouse. At midsummer 1677 Nantwich petitioned Cheshire sessions to raise £494 18s. 6d. for a house of correction and workhouse there, because it was 'much infested with rogues, vagabonds and sturdy beggars' and the 'poor are grown very numerous and necessitous', being unemployed and driven to theft. The town agreed to maintain and repair it. Two years later it had a stock of £200. As population was stationary, the stock of bridewells was probably accepted normally as sufficient.[5]

In the 1680s and 1690s concern about crime increased and prison work grew a little. Fear of social disorder fed by memories of the Interregnum and the Popish Plot and Exclusion Crisis was related especially to concern for property. Government, parliament and the upper classes reacted harshly. After the Bloody Assizes Judge Jeffreys was lord chancellor (1685–88). (As examples of the public outlook, a pamphlet of 1700 urged more suffering on the scaffold, such as breaking on the wheel; another in 1701 was called *Hanging Not Punishment Enough for Murtherers, High-way Men, and House-breakers*.) Corn prices were low in the 1680s; the 1690s included seven lean years, interrupted trade, war taxes, clipping and coining. A moral reform movement was encouraged by the monarchy and the archbishop of Canterbury, and supported by many justices from 1691. It attacked drinking, prostitution, gambling and profanity. There was a short surge of prosecutions under the game laws in the 1680s and a growth of indictments linked to

[5] Innes, 'Prisons', p. 77; Devon RO, QS 1/10, Baptist 1668, QS 1/11, Baptist 1674, QS 1/12, Michaelmas 1679; East Suffolk RO, 105/2/5, fos 61, 91, and 105/2/10, fos 51, 74; Lincolnshire RO, Lindsey QS minutes, 1665–79 p. 621; Cheshire RO, QJB 3/3.

moral crimes in the 1690s. Prosecutions for the other reasons already mentioned grew in the 1690s.[6]

The revival of royal authority at the end of Charles II's reign and under James II and pliant justices led to three successful attempts by assize judges to improve gaols in the 1680s. Leicestershire spent over £1000 in 1686 on its prison, erecting a building with at least fourteen or fifteen rooms of varying sizes; there was also space for a court. Staffordshire enlarged its gaol in 1687. In the same year the grand jury at Herefordshire assizes presented its gaol as so much unrepaired that it was not only unsafe for the custody of prisoners but also dangerous, being about to fall. The court threatened sessions with a fine of £1000 unless a prison was built. The bench decided to build it in Hereford, using part of the house of correction so that 'no more shall be spent but what is absolutely necessary'. A little work was done in brick and stone in the next years for about £66, but not until 1694 was the gaol erected for £700, probably in addition. All three gaol works involved new buildings only in part.

There were at least two other changes in the 1690s. Northamptonshire spent about £450 in 1691 on buying a house next to the county hall which had been used as a gaol since its building after the town fire of 1675. The Hampshire justices spent £200 for their gaol in Winchester about 1675, and in 1692 they ordered two new rooms, a cellar and the enlargement of the court, 'believing the place to be infectious by reason of the smallness of the court and the want of roome in the house'.[7]

Bridewell work was restricted in the 1680s and 1690s, despite the poverty of the second decade. At Warwick a new building erected by county sessions cost several hundred pounds in the 1680s. After its destruction in the town fire of 1694, about £1060 was spent on another bridewell; it had at least six ground floor rooms, with chambers above them, and adjacent buildings. In 1685 the Warwickshire bench ordered the expenditure of £400 on the erection of a house of correction in Birmingham, where population was growing rapidly; in fact Birmingham

[6] G. Holmes, *The Making of a Great Power, 1660–1722* (Harlow, 1993), pp. 279, 418; P.B. Munsche, *Gentlemen and Poachers: The English Game Laws, 1671–1831* (Cambridge, 1981), pp. 71, 85–86; J.M. Beattie, *Crime and the Courts in England, 1660–1800* (Oxford, 1986), pp. 292, 482, 487–90; Innes 'Prisons', p. 81; D.W.R. Bahlman, *The Moral Revolution of 1688* (New Haven, 1957), pp. 1–63.

[7] Leicestershire RO, QS 32/3/2; Staffordshire RO, QS 010, Easter 1692; Herefordshire RO, QS 02, fos 222, 244 and QS 03, fos 10, 60, 82, 86, 101; Hampshire RO, Q07, fol. 57; *Victoria County History of Northamptonshire*, iii (London, 1930), p. 35; C.A. Markham, *The History of the County Buildings of Northamptonshire* (Northampton, 1885), p. 11; J.S. Farley, *Quarter Sessions Government in Hampshire in the Seventeenth Century* (Winchester, n.d.), pp. 37–38; Hampshire RO, Q07, fol. 57.

paid for a house for its own use. A fourth Gloucestershire house of cor-rection was set up at Winchcomb in 1692, providing a building in a part of the county previously without one.[8]

Several factors perhaps explain why building did not react immediately and more considerably to the growth of crime and poverty in the 1690s. The war taxes may have been a deterrent for the gentry, although they did not hinder benches ten years later. In 1693 Surrey decided not to erect a new gaol, 'having considered the great charge . . . and how dif-ficult it would be to raise and charge the county with so great a sum'. There was overcrowding in Surrey prisons. In 1696 public concern about imprisonment led to the judges being asked to meet to 'consider what regulations may be proper to be made in relation to prisons and their keepers in order to oblige those keepers to look better to their prison-ers and to prevent escapes . . .' Royal authority under William III was weaker and parliament had still not given the counties statutory power to build gaols. The greater crime which accompanied the demobilisa-tion on the return to peace in 1697 began a long wave of cruel acts making offences against property punishable by death. This culminated in the notorious Black Act of 1723 which created fifty new capital crimes. Sessions were given power to build by a 1699 act (11 and 12 William III c. 19). On being 'prejudicial to the health of prisoners and insufficient for the safe custody of them' and after the presentment by the grand jury of 'the insufficiency and inconveniency' of the gaol, sessions might appoint a receiver and raise rates to rebuild or enlarge.[9]

Despite the fall in the numbers of prisoners after the outbreak of war in 1702, continued harshness is shown by an interest in imprisonment at hard labour as a penal weapon, even for minor crimes. It led to an act in 1706 allowing assizes and sessions to imprison felons granted benefit of clergy (that is, branded) for up to two years in bridewells or workhouses. The act 12 Anne c. 23 concerning vagrants encouraged the building of more bridewells to limit the cost of moving them. A statute in 1720 provided for the detention in bridewells as well as gaols of those accused of lesser felonies. Transportation was brought in for non-capital offences in 1718: the usual postwar release of servicemen and rise of prosecuted

---

[8] *Warwick County Records*, 7, ed. S.C. Ratcliff and H.C. Johnson, *Quarter Sessions Records Easter 1674 to Easter 1682* (Warwick, 1946), pp. cxii-cxvii, cxx-cxxi, cxxxiv-cxxxv, 124, 137: although property was bought in 1676 for a new gaol and house of correction, it does not seem to have been built and the existing house was used; *Gloucestershire Quarter Sessions Archives, 1660–1889* (Gloucester, 1958), pp. 21–22.

[9] Beattie, *Crime and the Courts*, pp. 292–93; Holmes, *Making of a Great Power*, pp. 279–80.

crimes encouraged opinion that imprisonment was insufficiently harsh. While it increased the temporary use of gaols for convicts awaiting shipment, sentences to hard labour in bridewells fell. Pressure on the bridewells was also reduced by the workhouse act of 1723, encouraging parishes to save money on outrelief by building a workhouse. Bridewells were kept now for their traditional inmates and those awaiting trial for felonies.[10]

Continued public anger about crime and poverty, more prosecutions especially in postwar years, and the consequent legislation, led to major, building works between 1700 and 1725. Another influence may have been greater financial and administrative efficiency by the justices. The government was raising and spending more effectively from the 1670s and 1680s. This was paralleled by sessions, with outlay being restricted more carefully to those bridges known to be county responsibilities. Sessions chairmen were controlling meetings which were often spread over two or three days to handle growing business. Attention was given to improving court accommodation. This was linked to enthusiasm on the part of the justices, among whom county families were well represented. Party conflicts between 1680 and 1714 made the office of justice seem electorally and politically valuable, encouraging attendance at session and an interest in its work.[11]

Four gaols were erected in five years after the 1700 act and there were eleven major gaol works before 1725 (Table 8.1). The same number of bridewell works costing more than about £200 (Table 8.2) followed the 1706 act and there were other smaller foundations. Altogether these years may be seen as a first if inadequate period of prison reform. There were fewer improvements between the later 1720s and about 1765. Six major gaol works and seven sizeable new bridewell buildings have been traced. Other houses of correction were closed. There were several possible reasons for the diminished activity. The previous burst of building had filled some obvious deficiencies. There was a continued pause in population growth in most areas until the 1750s. The long period of peace and the war in the 1740s prevented any outbursts of crime before 1748. The incomes of landowners were held down by bountiful harvests in most of the 1730s and 1740s, often referred to as a period of the agricultural depression. Tory landlords, often among the wealthiest, were kept off the bench by Whig governments. Justices were usually lesser

---

[10] Beattie, *Crime and the Courts*, pp. 293, 300; Innes, 'Prisons', pp. 88–94.

[11] A. Fletcher, *Reform in the Provinces: The Government of Stuart England* (New Haven and London, 1986), p. 187; P. Langford, *Public Life and the Propertied Englishman, 1689–1798* (Oxford, 1991), p. 395. See above, Chapters 2 and 5, for the responsibilities and attitudes of the justices.

Table 8.1

The Building of County Gaols, 1700–65[12]
(new buildings, major enlargements and alterations)

Date	County and Location	Cost
1701–4	Hertfordshire, Hertford (new building)	£1600
1701–5	Yorkshire, York (new building)	c. £8000
1703–4	Northumberland, Morpeth (rebuilding of old gaol bought for £144)	£1368
1704–5	Shropshire, Shrewsbury (new building)	not available
1707–8	Norfolk, Norwich ('repairs', presumably major alterations)	c. £1350
1713–15	Norfolk, Norwich ('repairs', presumably major alterations)	£600
1714–15	Staffordshire, Stafford (rebuilding, and building house of correction)	£600
1718–19	Suffolk, Ipswich (purchase of town gaol and enlargements)	c. £700–£750
1720	Sussex, Horsham (rebuilding)	£822
1721–23	Surrey, Southwark (new building)	£2800
1721–24, 1737–40	Buckinghamshire, Aylesbury (new building, with county hall)	c. £9000
1733–34	Suffolk, Ipswich (purchase of house for £500 to extend gaol, and repairs)	£700
1746–47	Kent, west division, Maidstone (new building)	£2538
1752	Middlesex, Clerkenwell (extension and repairs)	c. £500
1753	Devon, Exeter (purchase of house for debtors' prison; including £200 for act of parliament)	c. £500
1754–56	Derbyshire, Derby (new building)	£1550

gentry and professional men, and there were still few clergy. In the absence of party conflict keenness to attend and be active on sessions waned. There was a postwar crime wave about 1750 and public concern about prisons revived. The major London prison, Newgate, suffered from periodic gaol

[12] *Sources: Hertfordshire County Records: Calendar to the Sessions Books 1700 to 1752*, ed. W. Le Hardy, 7 (Hertford, 1931), p. 17; Humberside County RO, QAY 1/1; Northumberland RO, QS 04 (treasurers' accounts at end); *Orders of the Shropshire Quarter Sessions*, ed. O. Wakeman, i, *1638–1708*, p. 220; Norfolk RO, C/S2/6 (15 July 1707, 13 April 1708), C/S2/6, C/S2/7 (6 October 1713, 26 July 1715); Staffordshire RO, QS 011 (Easter 1714–Epiphany 1715/16); East Suffolk RO, 105/2/14, fos 141, 142, 144, 147, 158, 175, 177; East Sussex RO, QO/EW 16, QM/EW 6; Surrey RO, QS 2/1/12, p. 96; *Records of Buckinghamshire* 12, (1927), supplement, pp. i-xi; East Suffolk RO, 105/2/19, fos 98, 107; Centre for Kentish Studies, QS B 1746; Greater London RO, MF/1 April 1752, January 1753; Devon RO, QS 1/19 Michaelmas 1753; J.C. Cox, *Three Centuries of Derbyshire Annals* (London, 1890) ii, p. 10; Derbyshire RO, QSM R4, fol. 180.

Table 8.2

The Building of County Houses of Correction, 1700–65[13]
(new buildings, purchase of houses etc. costing more than £200)

Date	County and Location	Cost
1706–7	Kent, Deptford (new building)	£560
1708	Oxfordshire, Thame (new building)	not available
1713–14	Northumberland, Morpeth (purchase and conversion of house; including £130 for house)	c. £300
1714	Staffordshire (see Table 8.1)	
1716–18	Worcestershire, Worcester	c. £250
1716	Gloucestershire, Bristol, Lawford's Gate (new building)	£500
1719	Surrey, Southwark (new building)	£550
1720–21	Kent, Dartford (new building)	£745
1721	Sussex, Lewes (rebuilding)	c. £260
1723–24	Kent, Maidstone (rebuilding)	£255
1725	Somerset, Bedminster (new building of bridewell and workhouse)	£196
1733	Lincolnshire, Gainsborough (rebuilding)	£275
1737–38	Somerset, Bedminster (new building)	£600
1743	Hampshire, Odiham (new building)	£348
1746	Hampshire, Gosport (purchase of house)	£200
1754–55	Somerset, Wilton, Taunton (new building)	£1850
1757	Middlesex, Westminster ('work and repairs')	c. £550
1763	Hertfordshire, Berkhamsted (purchase of three tenements, £112, and alterations)	£233

distemper and deaths. In 1750 a bad outbreak infected the sessions, killing the lord mayor and two judges. The City did not rebuild its gaols, despite making considering improvements; its failure to act may have deterred some of the benches also threatened by overcrowding and disease. Three counties did gaol work, while others considered alterations without acting or introduced ventilators to improve air flows.[14]

[13] *Sources:* Centre for Kentish Studies, QS Ow6; Oxfordshire RO, QS minute book 2, p. 36; Northumberland RO, QS 05, pp. 133, 145, 339, and treasurers' accounts at end; Worcestershire RO, QS order book 2 (1714–31), fos 30, 36, 47, 54; Gloucestershire RO, QS 04, p. 77; Whiting, *Prison Reform*, p. 100; Surrey RO, QS 2/1/11, p. 564; Centre for Kentish Studies, QS B 1721; East Sussex RO, QO/EW 16; Centre for Kentish Studies, QS B 1721, QS OW 7, pp. 194, 201, 239, 248; Somerset RO, QS 09, fol. 378; Lincolnshire RO, Lindsey QS order book, 1729–38, 12 July 1733; Somerset RO, Q/FAe 1; Hampshire RO, QO 13 pp. 419–20; Hampshire RO, QO 14, pp. 86–95; Somerset RO, Q/F, box 6; Greater London RO, MF/1, 10 March 1758; *Hertfordshire County Records*, 8 (1935), pp. 96–97.
[14] C.W. Chalklin, 'The Reconstruction of London's Prisons, 1770–1799: An Aspect of Georgian London', *London Journal,* 9 (1983), p. 22; Beattie, *Crime and the Courts,* p. 304; Evans, *Fabrication of Virtue,* p. 100.

As earlier, county gaols were built or altered primarily when the problem of security in the existing prison became critical, either on account of structural weaknesses or because of the intermingling and close confinement of prisoners of different types. Repairs were therefore an inadequate remedy. The prelude to the rebuilding of the Sussex county gaol at Horsham in 1720 was the complaint that it was ruinous and irreparable. Another prominent motive for rebuilding was overcrowding in a prison in a town centre which led periodically to outbreaks of disease, killing some of the prisoners. Apart from being a matter of concern in itself, there was the fear of the infection spreading among the townspeople. In January 1752 the Berkshire court was told that 'the county Gaol is too small to contain commodiously the number of prisoners frequently committed there, whereby as well the debtors as felons therein are when the Gaol is full in great danger of infectious diseases'. Sessions considered enlarging the prison, but nothing was done at the time.[15]

The safe custody of prisoners and structural defects were also principal reasons for the rebuilding of several houses of correction. The Surrey bridewell at Southwark was built after 1719 because the old one was ruinous and insufficient to hold the prisoners safely and 'also prejudiciall and destructive to their healths by the dampness and coldness of it'. Bridewells were set up for the first time or rebuilt in areas where the population had grown rapidly. This was the case with the Kent and Surrey bridewells near London, the Bristol building (1716), the later structure at nearby Bedminster, and the Gosport house of correction. The last was built at a time when war was expanding Portsmouth in 1746 (see Table 8.2). The building of the bridewell at Lawford's Gate, Bristol, in 1716 shows the influence of the legislation from 1706. The Gloucestershire order book records that the court decided to erect it because under the recent vagrancy act of 12 Anne 'the County has been at great charges conveying vagrants from the western part about Bristol to the northern part'. The new bridewell meant that 'vagrants and such disorderly persons being sent to it at little charge and there well corrected may be deterred from that profligate way of life and the county eased thereby'.[16] Less often they were built in rural areas without one, as at Odiham, the Winchester house being thought insufficient for north Hampshire.

The two largest new prison buildings in this period were in Buckinghamshire and Yorkshire. The Surrey county gaol and the west

---

[15] East Sussex RO, QO/EW 15, 13 November 1719; Berkshire RO, QS Mo 2 Epiphany 1752.
[16] Surrey RO, QS 2/1/11 p. 564; Gloucestershire RO, QS O4 p.77.

Kent building were also sizeable (see Table 8.1). The Northumberland and Hertfordshire prisons were smaller gaols. Structurally these prisons were little more than a substantial house or group of two or three houses, with the various rooms leading off one another or off corridors, with the court or courts taking the place of a yard or garden. Sometimes, as at Maidstone, they adjoined other houses in the street. When brick was cheaper they were built of it, as at Derby and Hertford. Several were little or no improvement as regards rooms on the older prisons still in use. They were sometimes inadequate in that male and female felons shared a day room, and there was no separation of prisoners of different ages, or those awaiting trial from those convicted. Only two are known to have had architectural pretensions, perhaps to symbolise county prestige. The York gaol, designed probably by William Wakefield, a country house architect, had a baroque facade and central corridor with sole access to the wards. The following is a brief description of Derby gaol (1754–56), planned by William Hiorns, with a Palladian front.

> The area of the prison, including the gaoler's [house] in the front, the back rooms of which commanded a view of the several courtyards, was 126 by 121 feet. The ground behind the prison was divided into three yards, one for male felons, another for male debtors and house of correction prisoners, and a third, much smaller one, for women. There were only seven separate cells, and a common day-room for the felons, so that young and old, untried and convicted, capital and petty offenders, all herded together . . . Irons were used on all committed before trial.[17]

The larger new bridewells were the equivalent of substantial houses, particularly the new Somerset building in 1754–55 and the Dartford bridewell (see Table 8.2). Howard noticed the improvement of this house at Taunton, with its 'convenient apartments' over the Shepton Mallet building with a common day room and two close night rooms. The Lawford's Gate house had four rooms, each eighteen by sixteen feet. Several were converted tenements, as at Morpeth in 1713–14. Though often intended for very few inmates, some of them lacked a court for exercising. Like the county gaols, most were no improvement on the surviving older bridewells.[18]

The majority of buildings were maintained by periodic repairs. Thus between 1679 and 1775 twenty-two sums of between 9s. 9d. and £24 3s. 1d. were spent on the bridewell at Battle, Sussex, including £8 10s. 7d.

[17] J.C. Cox, *Three Centuries of Derbyshire Annals*, iii (London, 1890), p. 10.
[18] Howard, *State of the Prisons*, pp. 325, 337–38.

for flooring (1745) and £6 7s. 1d. for a new chimney (1745); also there were major repairs costing £108 8s. 6d. in 1708. Occasional minor improvements were done, as at Bedford in the early 1750s by installing a ventilator and adding five new cells. If consideration was being given to a new building or improvement, work might be delayed several years or never done. Schemes to enlarge the Wiltshire county prison in 1713 and 1730 were abandoned. Several reasons may be suggested for the small amount of prison building before the 1770s. The justices had never spent much money on county prisoners and, in view of the dislike by the squirearchy of the national and parish (poor rate) taxes, their reluctance to take on extra financial burdens is understandable. When the Essex justices decided to provide an additional but very small house of correction at Halstead in 1714 they agreed 'after long consideration and debate' to appoint a keeper at £20 a year and £5 for rent, and to provide £10 for materials, implements and furniture, 'but that no other or further summe or summes of money shall be ever hereafter given upon account of the said house of correction on any pretence'. Prison numbers were in fact normally small. Gaols had up to thirty or forty prisoners usually, with occasional overcrowding. Surrey with its London population had between forty and eighty gaol inmates between 1703 and 1713, then up to 170 for a year or two when peace returned. Gloucestershire gaol held forty or fifty in the 1770s. Bridewells often had no more than five or six prisoners. Gaols were intended to confine debtors and those awaiting trial; convicted prisoners were whipped, transported or hanged, not given prison sentences. Commitments to bridewells were for short periods. Before the 1750s rising numbers affected only a minority of counties, such as those adjoining London or with growing naval dockyards. Thus it was easy to ignore the condition of prison inmates. There was no penal philosophy and (apart from providing a meagre subsistence allowance for some types of prisoners) justices did not feel that their obligations extended beyond safe custody (often achieved by chaining) and sometimes disease prevention. Parliament voted money for the transportation of felons in 1718 and for the rebuilding of the King's Bench prison in the 1750s. While there was the rare parliamentary inquiry or book about prisons, in general public concern was small.[19]

[19] East Sussex RO, QAP/3/E5; Bedfordshire RO, QS M 11; *Victoria County History of Wiltshire*, vi, ed. E. Crittall (London, 1962), p. 182; Essex RO, QS 04, pp. 227, 260, although next year the bench paid £97 12s 0d. to fit up a prison; Beattie *Crime and the Courts*, p. 293; Whiting, *Prison Reform*, p. 2; J. Innes, 'The King's Bench Prison in the Later Eighteenth Century', ed. J. Brewer and J. Styles, *An Ungovernable People: The English and their Law in the Seventeenth and Eighteenth Centuries* (London, 1980), p. 376.

9

Gaols and Bridewells, 1765–1800

The first major wave of prison building was in the 1770s. Altogether between 1766 and 1780 at least twelve county gaols and eight bridewells were erected or substantially enlarged (Tables 9.1, 9.2). Newgate Prison was being rebuilt throughout the 1770s and there were also at least two new provincial city prisons. The initial impetus came probably from the

Table 9.1

The Building of County Gaols, 1765–80[1]
(a new building unless otherwise stated)

Date	County and Location	Cost
1768–69	Berkshire, Reading (enlargement)	£1199
1770–71 and 1774–76	Westmorland, Appleby	not available
1771	Surrey, Southwark (enlarged)	£689/13
1773	Northamptonshire, Northampton (new rooms)	£716
1773–75	Middlesex, Clerkenwell (extension)	at least £3500
1773–77	Essex, Chelmsford	£18,042
1775	Norfolk, Norwich (improved)	£1030
1775–79	Sussex, Horsham	c. £4850
1776–80	Hertfordshire, Hertford	c. £7000
1778–79	Cornwall, Bodmin	c. £6850
1779–83	Warwickshire, Warwick (enlargement; contract price)	£3000
1779–82	Essex, Chelmsford (alterations)	c. £2650
1780–83	Yorkshire, York (addition of female prison; contract price)	£1850

[1] *Sources*: Berkshire RO, QS 04, QS Rm5, QS Mo4; Cumbria RO, Kendal WQ/09; Surrey RO, QS 2/1/22, pp. 561–63, 2/1/23, p. 13; Northamptonshire RO, QS record book, 1754–82; Greater London RO, MA/G/GEN 1; Essex RO, Q/FAa 4/2; Norfolk RO, C/Sb 1/8, pp. 102–38; West Sussex RO, QAP4/WE 1; *Hertfordshire County Records*, 8 (1935), pp. 250–51, 280; *Sessions Books, 1752–99*, ed. W. Le Hardy; Cornwall RO, QSM 4; *Warwickshire County Records*, 7 (Warwick, 1946), p. cxxvii; *Quarter Sessions Records Easter 1674 to Easter 1682*, ed. S.C. Ratcliff and H.C. Johnson; Essex RO, Q/FAa 4/2, QS 0 13; NorthYorkshire RO, QS order book, 11 January 1780.

Table 9.2

The Building of County Houses of Correction, 1765–80[2]
(a new building unless otherwise stated)

Date	County	£
1765	Lincolnshire, Spalding (rebuilding)	800
1766–71	Yorkshire, West Riding, Wakefield	3108
1766	Essex, Chelmsford (repairs and new rooms)	*c*. 640
1767	Surrey, Guildford	853
1768	Lincolnshire, Folkingham	200
1772	Surrey, Southwark	2816
1774–77	Kent, Maidstone	2311
1775	Surrey, Kingston	1037
1775	Essex, Newport	1060
1774–75	Lancashire, Manchester	1671

growing pressure of numbers on existing prison room. Several houses of correction were erected in counties adjoining London, which had a renewed period of population growth, and Lancashire, the West Riding of Yorkshire, Warwickshire and Bath each provided a new prison and underwent considerable urban expansion. The rebuilding of the huge Newgate prison had been discussed intermittently by the City since 1750 and its beginning in 1770 probably encouraged hesitant sessions in the provinces.

A possible influence on the county justices may have been the general surge of building and construction which started in the mid 1760s and lasted until about 1778. These years saw the first boom in canal construction; harbour and bridge building were also active. In the towns there was an unprecedented growth of house building and street improvement, such as paving and the removal of nuisances. In London an act of 1767 for Newgate also raised money to repair the Royal Exchange and finish the building of Blackfriars bridge. The prevailing optimistic mood which all this construction reflected may have encouraged the justices to be more ready to undertake building works than in earlier years. Certainly in bridge building they followed the example of the trusts and companies set up by statute to reconstruct bridges over major rivers. A case of the greater willingness of the justices to spend money on building was the work on the Mid-

---

[2] *Sources:* Lincolnshire RO, Holland QS minutes, 1750–65, pp. 499–528, 1765–71, pp. 7–36, 109–112; West Yorkshire RO, QSO 24, 25; Essex RO, Q/FAa 4/2; Surrey RO, QS 2/1/21 p. 387; Lincolnshire RO, Holland QS minutes, 1765–71, p. 497; Surrey RO, 2/1/23 p. 337; Centre for Kentish Studies, QS B 1774, 1775; QS Ow 11, pp. 68–158; Surrey RO, QS 5/1/1, pp. 233–34, 250; Essex RO, QS 012, pp. 374, 397, 414; M. De Lacy, *Prison Reform in Lancashire, 1700–1850: A Study in Local Administration* (Manchester, 1986), pp. 25, 74.

dlesex New Prison, Clerkenwell, between 1773 and 1775. Although it was justified on the ground of the need to repair its ruinous condition, at least £3500 seems to have been spent on extending it with more room for felons, a public taproom and keeper's apartments. John Howard on his visit in 1779 described the prison as more commodious than formerly.[3]

As has been seen, there was a modest growth of interest in county business generally among justices from the 1760s. Tories were no longer kept off the commission, clergy justices began to be numerous and more wealthy landowners were at sessions. Readiness to spend was increased by growing landed incomes now corn prices were rising.[4]

The publicity given to prison abuses, and the proposals of the prison reformer John Howard in 1773–77, thus fell on fruitful soil. Howard first became fully aware of the horror of prison conditions while he was sheriff of Bedfordshire in 1772. In 1774 he testified before a Commons committee against the practice of gaolers' fees. Next he visited every prison in England and Wales, publishing his findings (and proposals for reform) in *The State of the Prisons* (1777). Howard's influence made occupation needs more comprehensive and detailed. His aim was not only the security and physical wellbeing of prisoners but also their reform – based on work during the day in the company only of prisoners of the same type, solitary confinement at night and religious services. Among his specific recommendations were the building of blocks of night cells, of arcades giving access to courtyards for work and exercise for the different classes of prisoners, the installation of baths, of ovens to disinfect clothing, of infirmaries and a chapel. Some of the most eminent lawyers of the time were also thinking in terms of prisons both as a deterrent and as a means of reforming criminals through the combination of solitary confinement, well-regulated labour and religious instruction.

Parliament's interest in improved prisons was seen in an act of 1774 requiring, among other things, separate rooms for sick prisoners. Its concern was increased by the ending of transportation to America in 1776, which with the death penalty had provided previously the main form of punishment for more serious offences. Dissatisfaction with transporting felons had been growing in the 1750s and 1760s, as disorder continued in London; a short imprisonment began to be regarded as more suitable for the minor offender. The reforming spirit is best shown by the act of 1779, drafted by the lawyers Blackstone and Eden, which

---

[3] Greater London RO, MA/G/GEN 1, 22 and 28 April 1773, 12 May 1773, 13 March 1775; J. Howard, *The State of the Prisons in England and Wales* (2nd edn, Warrington, 1780), p. 193.
[4] See above, pp. 36.

proposed the erection of two national penitentiaries and urged the counties to build large prisons.[5] The influence of Howard was immediate. In 1774 the West Kent justices took his advice in building a bridewell. The Sussex bench rebuilt the county gaol at Horsham following Howard's first visit, with a separate cell for each felon.[6]

By far the largest prison building undertaking in the 1770s was Newgate, on which about £70,000 had been spent by 1780.[7] The most substantial new county gaol was in Essex. This was regarded by Howard as an exceptional prison project; while the old gaol had been 'a close prison, frequently infected with the gaol-distemper', the new one 'exceeds the old one in strength almost as much as in splendour. The county, to their honour, have spared no cost . . . The prison was finished and occupied at the time of my last visit'.[8] Hertfordshire, Cornwall and Sussex gaols were all substantial buildings.[9] Both the Bodmin and Horsham structures reveal strongly the influence of Howard with not only separate wards and courts for the different types of prisoners, but individual cells, a gaoler's house, chapel and infirmary. The houses of correction of the 1770s, which varied in cost between £1037 and £2816, contained separate wards for men and women with workshops and a number of rooms.[10]

Some new prison work was begun during the height of the American War between 1778 and 1783. Bodmin gaol was built in 1778–79, the enlargement of Warwickshire county gaol was made between 1779 and 1783 and there was work on the female prison at York between 1780 and 1783.[11] A second and much greater surge of county gaol building occurred between the mid 1780s and mid 1790s. In these years over fifty county gaols, houses of correction and town prisons in England were rebuilt or considerably extended. Nearly every county undertook at least one prison building work, involving the erection of a new gaol or house of correction or the enlargement of an existing one. Ten county prisons cost more than £20,000, the largest being the new Middlesex house of correction at Coldbath Fields on which about £70,000 was spent (including

[5] M. Ignatieff, *A Just Measure of Pain* (London, 1978), p. 52; R. Morgan, 'Divine Philanthropy: John Howard Reconsidered', *History,* 62 (1977), pp. 398, 403–5.

[6] Centre for Kentish Studies, QS B 1774, 1775; Howard, *The State of the Prisons*, p. 230.

[7] City of London RO, Journal of the Newgate Committee, 1767–85, pp. 356–61.

[8] Essex RO, Q/FAa 4/2; Howard, *The State of the Prisons*, p. 220.

[9] *Hertfordshire County Records*, 8, ed. Le Hardy (1935), pp. 250–51, 280; Cornwall RO, QS M4; West Sussex RO, QAP 4/WE 1.

[10] Surrey RO, QS 2/1/23, 5/1/1.

[11] *Warwick County Records*, 7, ed. Ratcliff and Johnson (Warwick, 1946). p. cxxvi; Howard Colvin, *A Biographical Dictionary of British Architects, 1600–1840* (3rd edn. New Haven and London, 1995), p. 191; North Yorkshire RO, North Riding QS order book, 1766–82 (11 January 1780).

the land).[12] Not only were far more new gaols and houses of correction erected than in the 1770s but the outlay on the larger ones greatly exceeded the expenditure on the large prisons in the 1770s (Tables 9.3, 9.4). There

Table 9.3

The Building of County Houses of Correction, 1781–1800[13]
(costing at least £200)

Date	County and Location	Cost
1782–84	Essex (Halstead)	£2004
1783–86	Dorset (Sherborne)	£1541
1784–85	Norfolk (Walsingham)	£730
1784–88	Norfolk (Wymondham)	£2395
1784–85	Buckinghamshire (Aylesbury)	£1030
1784–88	North Riding (Northallerton) (with court house)	£5544
1784–87	Warwickshire (Warwick)	£15,000
1785–87	Suffolk (Beccles)	*c.* £600
1785–86	Berkshire (Reading)	£3280
1785–91	Lancashire (Preston)	£12,040
1785–88	Sussex (Petworth)	*c.* £7000
1786–88	Suffolk (Bury)	£2000+
1786–87	Hampshire (Winchester)	£8393
1786	Westmorland (Kendal)	*c.* £400
1787	Norfolk (Swaffham)	not available
1787–90	Gloucestershire (Littledean)	£3309
1787–90	Gloucestershire (Lawford's Gate)	£4991
1787–90	Gloucestershire (Northleach)	£5111
1787–90	Gloucestershire (Horsley)	£6181
1787–90	Lancashire (Salford)	*c.* £23,000
1787	Nottinghamshire (Southwell) (enlarged)	£677
1788–95	Middlesex (Clerkenwell)	£65,656
1789–90	Lincolnshire (Folkingham) (enlarged and altered)	£370
1789–93	Sussex (Lewes)	£9528
1790–92	Hertfordshire (Hertford)	£3999
1790–94	Lincolnshire (Kirton)	£8387
1791–93	Northumberland (North Shields)	£525
1791–92	Essex (Barking)	£1337
1792	East Riding (Beverley) (altered and repaired)	£748
1793–94	Northumberland (Morpeth)	£496
1794, 1797	Northumberland (Hexham) (bought and altered)	£385
1798–1800	Staffordshire (Wolverhampton) (altered)	£803
1799–1800	Suffolk (Botesdale)	£900 or £1300
1799–1801	Lincolnshire (Kirton) (new wall)	£509

[12] H. Mayhew and J. Binny, *The Criminal Prisons of London* (London, 1868), p. 280.
[13] *Sources:* Essex RO, Q/FAa 4/2; Dorset RO, county treasurers' accounts; Norfolk RO, C/S2/12, pp. 15–24, C/S2/12, pp. 15–49; Bucks RO, QS O21 Easter 1784, Midsummer 1785; North Yorkshire RO, North Riding, QS orders, 1782–87, pp. 105, 342, and accounts 1783–99; *Warwickshire County Records*, 7, p. cxxvii; East Suffolk RO, 105/2/47,

Table 9.4

The Building of County Gaols, 1781–1800[14]
(new buildings, except where stated)

Date	County and Location	Cost
1783–84	Wiltshire, Fisherton Anger (additions and alterations)	£1707
1784–85	Dorset, Dorchester	£3000
1784–89	Kent, west division, Maidstone (extension; including site £570)	£4179
1785–91	Gloucestershire, Gloucester (including site £1422)	£25,892
1785–95	Worcestershire, Worcester (extension)	£4283
1785–88	Oxfordshire, Oxford	£10,000
1786–89 and 1790–91	Lincolnshire, Lincoln	£13,062
1786–91	Suffolk, Ipswich (with house of correction; site £600)	c. £20,000
1786–89	Somerset, Ilchester (extension)	c. £2500
1787–93	Shropshire, Shrewsbury	c. £30,000
1787–98	Lancashire, Lancaster	c. £21,000
1788–93 and 1796–98	Warwickshire, Warwick (additions)	c. £6000
1788	Monmouthshire, Monmouth	c. £5000
1788–92	Hampshire, Winchester	£14,032
1788–93	Staffordshire, Stafford (including land £287 4s. and act £368)	£25,133
1789–95	Dorset, Dorchester	£16,180
1789–97	Devon, Exeter (estimate)	£20,000
1790–93	Norfolk, Norwich	c. £15,000
1790–92	Leicestershire, Leicester	£6000
1791–99	Surrey, Newington	£39,020
1791	Buckinghamshire, Aylesbury (improved)	c. £1110
1791–94	Northamptonshire, Northampton (with house of correction)	£15,000–£16,000
1791–94	Wiltshire, Fisherton Anger (addition)	£2415
1791–98	Somerset, Ilchester (addition)	c. £9000
1792–1820	Cheshire, Chester (with courthouses)	c. £85,000
1792–95	Berkshire, Reading (contract)	£3000
1793–95	Yorkshire, York (alterations)	c. £1350
1793–98	Herefordshire, Hereford (with house of correction)	£22,461
1798–1801	Bedfordshire, Bedford (with house of correction; contract)	£6850

continued

fol. 98, and 105/2/48, fos 1, 7, 22, 29; C.W. Chalklin, 'Prison Building by the County of Berks, 1766–1820', *Berkshire Archaeological Journal*, 69 (1979), p. 66; Lancashire RO, QS O 2/152–63; West Sussex RO, QAP/5/W1; East Suffolk RO, 105/2/47, fos 124, 125; Hampshire RO, QT2; Cumbria RO (Kendal), WQ/O 8, Easter 1785, Michaelmas 1785; Norfolk RO, C/S2/12, p. 80; J.R.S. Whiting, *Prison Reform in Gloucestershire, 1776–1820* (Chichester, 1975), pp. 14, 138, 145, 160; Lancashire RO, QS O 2/152–63; Nottinghamshire RO, CT1/1; C.W. Chalklin, 'The Reconstruction of London's Prisons, 1770–1799', *The London Journal*, 9 (1983), p. 27; Lincolnshire RO, Kesteven QS proceedings, 1789–95, pp. 41, 105; East Sussex RO, 'Proceedings on Replacing Cliffe House of Correction'; *Hertfordshire County Records*, 8, pp. 396, 424; Lincolnshire RO, Lindsey, QS

was particular activity in Gloucestershire, where the justices rebuilt the county gaol and four houses of correction, and in Lancashire, where the houses of correction at Manchester and Preston were rebuilt. Before their completion work began on the reconstruction of the county gaol in Lancaster Castle.

It was in this period that a distinct form of prison plan emerged under the influence of William Blackburn which embodied the principal recommendations of Howard. The extended layout (particularly radiating cells, which was the crux of the architect's scheme) explains, together with the increased accommodation, the greater charge. Necessarily the financial outlay during the years of building increased the burden on the county rates substantially. Counties involved in more than one large undertaking sometimes spread the cost by completing one structure before beginning another. This was the case in Sussex. The county gaol at Horsham had been built between 1775 and 1779; now the two principal houses of correction were reconstructed in succession, that at Petworth between 1785 and 1788 and that at Lewes between 1789 and 1793. In these decades it also became common (though not universal) to borrow part or all of the necessary money for building, and to repay it over a period of years.

In the mid 1780s part of the pressure for building resulted from the

abstract of accounts for building Kirton bridewell, 1794; Northumberland RO, QS O 13, p. 374; Essex RO, Q/FAa 4/3; Humberside RO, CT2; Northumberland RO, QS O 13, p. 508, 14 pp. 26, 27, 59, 109–11; Northumberland RO, QS O 14, pp. 157, 388; *Parliamentary Papers* (1825), vi; East Suffolk RO, 105/2/51, fos 37, 38, 86; Lincolnshire RO, Lindsey, QS minutes, 1797–1800, 1800–2.

[14] *Sources*: Wiltshire RO, county treasurers' accounts; Dorset RO, county treasurers' accounts; see below, p. 186; J.R.S. Whiting, *Prison Reform*, p. 15; V. Green, *History and Antiquities of the City and Suburbs of Worcester*, ii (1796), pp. 28–30; Oxfordshire RO, QS minutes 4, 5; *Chester Chronicle*, 7 September 1792; Lincolnshire RO, Kesteven QS minutes, 1775–89, 1789–95; East Suffolk RO, 105/2/47, fol. 117; Somerset RO, Q/FAe2; H. Owen, *Some Account of the Ancient and Present State of Shrewsbury* (Shrewsbury, 1808), p. 430; *Warwick County Records*, 7, pp. cxxvi–cxxvii; Lancashire RO, QS 0/2, 1787–98; K. Kissack, *Monmouth: The Making of a County Town* (Chichester, 1975), p. 216; Hampshire RO, QT2, William Salt Library M605; S. Lewis, *A Topographical Dictionary of England*, ii (1831), p. 57; Devon RO, Q5/1/101; G.K. Blyth, *The Norwich Guide* (Norwich, 1843), p. 43; J. Nichols, *The History and Antiquities of the County of Leicester*, i, pt 2 (1815), p. 530; O. Manning and W. Bray, *History and Antiquities of the County of Surrey*, iii (1814), pp. xiv, xv; Buckinghamshire RO, QS 0 23; S. Dugdale, *British Traveller*, iii (1820) p. 678; Wiltshire RO, county treasurers' accounts; Somerset RO, Q/FAe 2; *Parliamentary Papers* (1825), vi; Chalklin, 'Prison Building by Berks', p. 66; North Yorkshire RO, treasurers' accounts D, 1792–1802; Lewis, *Topographical Dictionary*, ii, p. 366; E. Stockdale, 'Bedford Prison', *Bedfordshire Historical Record Society*, 56, p. 87.

ending of transportation to the American colonies in 1776, and the effect of the act of 1779 which enabled judges to use prison sentences as an alternative punishment to transportation.

Heavy taxation during the war years deterred justices from new building undertakings or alterations. In April 1781 the Middlesex justices decided not to alter the New Prison at a cost of at least £1300 on the recommendation of a committee that 'in the present state of this county labouring under the heavy burthens which have lately been theron imposed it will not be expedient to carry into execution the erections and alterations proposed'.[15]

In the words of the prison reformer Sir G. O. Paul, 'the judges proceeded to sentence convicts as directed, whilst the Justices on their part have neglected to provide the "proper places" to receive them as also directed; and of course the ordinary wards of county gaols became . . . dangerously overcrowded'. Overcrowding affected the health of prisoners and in 1783 there were outbreaks of gaol fever in some prisons, spreading outside the walls. County authorities not affected by these outbreaks feared that there would be similar attacks in their prisons. In 1783 there were petitions to the House of Commons from Berkshire, Flint, Gloucestershire and Oxfordshire about the overcrowding of gaols, the result both of the award of long prison sentences and the difficulty of removing those sentenced to transportation.[16]

As late as 1787 some prisons were full of convicts awaiting transportation. There were fifty in Surrey county gaol sentenced in 1783 and the following years. Nevertheless, following the 1784 act for the transportation of felons and with the decision to transport to New South Wales in 1786, the problem of the removal of convicts eventually lessened and the pressure to rebuild simply for this reason eased. In October 1788 the Berkshire quarter sessions decided to defer the rebuilding of the county gaol not only for financial reasons but 'from the removal of convicts having of late become more frequent'.[17] On the other hand, the numbers of criminals given prison sentences continued to increase, partly because of the general growth of population, particularly in the urban and industrial areas, and partly because imprisonment was taking the place of transportation as the punishment of first resort for petty felonies,

[15] Greater London RO, MA/G/GEN 1, 1773–81.

[16] S. and B. Webb, *English Local Government*, vi, *English Prisons under Local Government* (London, 1963), pp. 50–51; *Journals of the House of Commons, 1782–84*, 39, pp. 731, 733, 744.

[17] J. Howard, *Account of the Principal Lazarettos in England* (London, 1787) p. 147; Berkshire RO, QS O 6, p. 215.

that is, minor property offences.[18] Those awaiting trial and convicted felons began far to outnumber debtors, whose number did not grow.

In addition to the pressure of growing numbers, the building of new prisons was the result of the desire to improve accommodation not only for the proper security but also for the health, reform and labour of prisoners. Following Howard's *The State of the Prisons*, in the 1770s publicists continued to try to influence opinion in favour of prison reform and the building improvements which were its inevitable corollary. In 1786 Dr John Webb wrote *Thoughts on the Construction and Policy of Prisons* for the benefit of the Suffolk justices considering the building of a county gaol at Ipswich and a house of correction at Bury St Edmunds. Howard was still writing and investigating, publishing his *Account of the Principal Lazarettos in England* in 1787, while Alexander Wedderburn published his *Observations on the State of the English Prisons* in 1793. The Proclamation Society, founded in 1787, to lead and support moral reform, included prison improvement among its concerns. It circulated pamphlets on prisons referring to Howard's *The State of the Prisons* for distribution to grand juries at assizes, and sent circular letters to sessions. Cells for solitary confinement in new prisons were a special interest of the society. The reformers thus had various ways of spreading their views.[19]

The continued concern of parliament for prison reform may be seen in further laws relating to local prisons and houses of correction. This was the result partly of a House of Commons committee inquiry in 1776, which obtained statistical data about houses of correction, and partly of the 1779 prison act proposing the establishment of national penitentiaries with an elaborate code of prison discipline. The act 22 George III c. 64 related to houses of correction and was drafted by Thomas Gilbert as part of a wider scheme for dealing with poverty and vagrancy. Gilbert had published the previous year *A Plan for the Better Relief and Employment of the Poor; for Enforcing and Amending the Laws Respecting Houses of Correction and Vagrants; and for Improving the Police of this Country*. The act stressed the need for accommodation to separate the different types of prisoners, and also to provide work 'having regard to the classing of the several persons who shall be kept there, according to the nature of their crimes

---

[18] Ignatieff, *Just Measure*, pp. 92–93; V. Markham Lester, *Victorian Insolvency: Bankruptcy, Imprisonment for Debt, and Company Winding Up in Nineteenth-Century England* (Oxford, 1995), p. 97.

[19] S. and B. Webb, *English Prisons*, pp. 39–40; J. Innes, 'Politics and Morals: The Reformation of Manners Movement in Later Eighteenth-Century England', *The Transformation of Political Culture: England and Germany in the Late Eighteenth Century*, ed. E. Hellmuth (Oxford, 1990), pp. 57–59, 87–97.

and punishments, and to the providing proper places for the employment of such persons who are committed to hard labour, and to the keeping every part of such prisons clean and wholesome'. In each county justices were to inspect and report to quarter sessions on the state of the existing houses of correction, and to settle plans for alterations and building; they were to provide separate apartments for all persons committed for felony, and to hard labour, and for women. Two years later there was an amending act (24 George III c. 55), allowing quarter sessions which had omitted to inspect or to introduce changes under the previous act to proceed as before. There had been doubt as to whether the 1782 law was still in force. As an additional power the justices were given the authority to borrow on the security of the rates to defray the capital costs, if the amount of the estimate exceeded one half of the ordinary annual assessment for the county rate, the money to be repaid within fourteen years. In cases where new buildings were erected, the justices were also given the right to sell the old houses of correction. This act was accompanied by another, to speed up the construction of county gaols (24 George III c. 54), which contained similar provisions regarding the borrowing of money; in the words of one of the act's promoters (a Middlesex justice) 'to ease Countys of the great hardship of levying the whole charge of building gaols upon the present inhabitants according to the present law'. All three acts reflected some of the ideals of the 1779 act requiring divisions for the different types of prisoners. The majority of larger prisons were built with the help of borrowed funds, and the availability of borrowing powers was clearly one factor in the great wave of building in the years after 1785. In 1791 the prison reformers in parliament passed a general prison act, laying down a general code of suggested rules for all prisons, though most of the clauses were permissive not mandatory.[20]

In addition to this legislative encouragement there were considerable signs of reforming zeal among the magistrates of the counties. In some cases individual justices took the initiative. In Sussex, where Horsham gaol was erected between 1775 and 1779, 'the duke of Richmond, in concurrence with other gentlemen of the county, interested himself much in this affair'; in the 1780s the duke was active in organising the building of the Petworth bridewell.[21] In the case of the Salford house of correction the leading spirit was T. B. Bayley, a Lancashire country gentleman who later became chairman of quarter sessions. He carried through the

---

[20] Greater London RO, MA/G/CBF, 5 August 1784; S. and B. Webb, *English Prisons*, pp. 40–41.

[21] Howard, *The State of the Prisons*, p. 230; S. and B. Webb, *English Prisons*, p. 54.

project against much initial opposition. On completion the premises were named after him. He was also active in directing the rebuilding at Lancaster Castle in the 1790s. In the words of his biographer, the building of Salford prison

> was afterwards so highly approved, even by those justices who were at first strenuous against it, that the premises were styled the NEW BAYLEY in honour of the projector, by the unanimous vote of the whole bench of magistrates ... For the improvement in the courts of Assize, and the County Gaol at Lancaster, the like praise is due to Mr Bayley. Such indeed was the general sense of his skill in the construction of places of confinement, that he was consulted about most of the prisons, which of late have been enlarged or erected in this kingdom.

In Norfolk the 'new bridewell erected at Wymondham [was constructed] under the direction of the public-spirited magistrate, Sir Thomas Beever, Bart'. When he wrote an account of its administration in the *Annual Register* in 1786, gentlemen in eight counties and Wales and Scotland wrote for more information. The most energetic and persevering justice was Sir George Paul of Gloucestershire, whose campaign for prison reform, begun in 1783, was to last more than thirty years, during which it had produced in Gloucestershire by 1791 a county gaol and four houses of correction. If in other counties no one magistrate dominated the proceedings as Paul did in Gloucestershire, the succession of committees to examine and select sites, to consider and alter plans submitted by architects and surveyors, and to supervise and inspect construction, and the willingness to levy additional rates, bear witness to the widespread interest of groups of justices in the initiation and completion of local public building schemes on an unprecedented scale. Only in a few instances (Leicestershire, Norfolk and Bedfordshire) were benches who created new prisons apathetic to the reforming spirit (Fig 9.1, 9.2).[22]

A final factor which may explain the wave of building between the mid 1780s and the early 1790s is the general spirit of optimism which affected all types of building. These years saw an unprecedented surge in house building, urban improvement and canal construction (often based partly on borrowed money), which probably stimulated the justices

[22] T. Percival, *Biographical Memoirs of the Late Thomas Butterworth Bayley* (Manchester, 1802), p. 4; S. and B. Webb, *English Prisons*, p. 55; Innes, 'Politics and Morals', p. 12; Whiting, *Prison Reform in Gloucestershire, 1776–1820* (Chichester, 1975), pp. iii, viii-xi; R. Evans, *The Fabrication of Virtue: English Prison Architecture, 1750–1840* (Cambridge, 1982), p. 187.

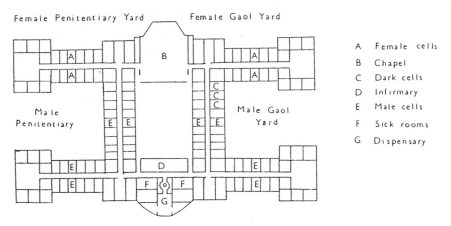

Fig. 9.1. Gloucestershire gaol, built 1785–91, one of the earliest carefully planned purpose-built prisons of the 1780s, designed by William Blackburn. (J.R.S. Whiting, *Prison Reform in Gloucestershire, 1776–1820*, Chichester, 1975, p. xviii.)

to greater expenditure on building. Turning first to the new bridewells, although most were smaller than the new gaols, they were much more numerous, and their rebuilding began a year or two earlier. The response to the 1782 act was widespread to the extent of the dispatch of visiting justices to inspect existing facilities in bridewells and to make recommendations for improvements. Thus in County Durham on 17 July 1782 a justice was ordered to view the house of correction and report on its condition, and on the alterations and additions needed to classify the prisoners and employ them; the two surveyors of the county bridges were to make plans and estimates. No further action was recorded. Halstead, Essex, bridewell was erected between 1782 and 1784, and that at Sherborne, Dorset, between 1783 and 1786, but the other bridewells were not begun before 1784 or 1785 at the earliest.[23] Presumably the first House of Correction Act of 1782 was premature in that war was still continuing, with its additional taxation, and justices were hesitant to spend money on a new undertaking. The 1784 act also provided an additional inducement in giving counties borrowing powers. By 1785 and 1786 about twelve houses of correction were in process of construction. While these were being finished in two or three years, at least twelve others were begun in the years 1787 to 1793, in several counties in conjunction with a county gaol; and at least six more were considerably extended.

Basic to the layout of all the more substantial bridewells was at least

[23] Durham RO, QS OB 14; Essex RO, Q/FAa 4/2; Dorset RO, county treasurers' accounts.

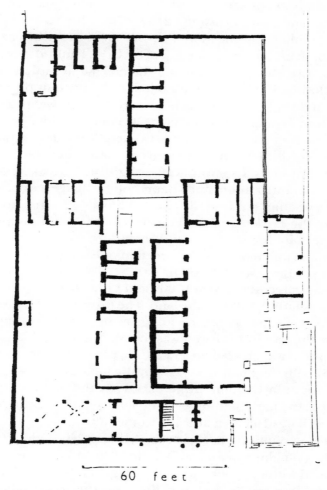

Fig. 9.2. Leicestershire gaol plan, 1789. Costing a little over £6000, it was a cheap prison, using existing buildings partly, with less cell accommodation than planned originally and a relatively cramped layout. The architect and contractor, George Moneypenny, designed other prisons later. (R. Evans, *The Fabrication of Virtue: Prison Architecture, 1750–1840*, Cambridge, 1982, p. 186).

one long row of cells of one or two stories with adjoining exercise yards, sometimes with chapel, infirmary and keeper's and other rooms in the centre. Some of the larger ones had several wings laid out to provide access and supervision from a central building comprising keeper's quarters, chapel, etc. As an example of a smaller house of correction, that built at Barking, Essex in 1791–92, with separate accommodation for different types of prisoners, workrooms and solitary cells, was erected on a site with two houses costing £210.[24] About twelve bridewells were substantial buildings costing more than £3000. The four Gloucestershire bridewells built under the leadership of Sir G. O. Paul, all model prisons designed by Blackburn, were among them. That at Littledean (£3308 16s. 6d. including £50 for land) intended for twenty-four prisoners, had a day cell and night cell for each prisoner in two wings, day rooms underneath at ground level, a chapel, keeper's parlour, kitchen and infirmary and four yards (for felons, women, fines and vagrants). The bridewell at Northleach, on a site given by a landowner, was built to hold thirty-seven prisoners. Its layout was hexagonal, with a keeper's house (including committee room and chapel) on the longest side, and seven courtyards radiating out from it. The cell blocks, of three stories, were built round the far ends of the courtyards. They had twenty-five day rooms, especially for working, and including storerooms, kitchens, washrooms and infirmaries, with women in one wing; above were thirty-six cells for sleeping, seven by six feet.[25]

Four bridewells cost between £7000 and £10,000, the price of the Kirton project including £500 for the land. The three largest houses outside London were in areas with a rapidly-growing manufacturing population. By far the largest bridewell was the Middlesex building. Like the Salford prison it was erected on a radiating plan. This three-story building with 232 cells was made necessary by the huge and growing demand for prison room in London: in January 1784 the building committee reported that the highest number of prisoners in the existing bridewell at Clerkenwell was 103 men and 131 women.[26]

Over half the counties of England rebuilt their gaols or added extensively to the existing buildings between 1785 and 1800. In a few cases a bridewell was combined with the gaol; more often a gaol was erected on its own. In the mid 1780s much work was done on the Kent, Wiltshire and Worcestershire gaols, and new prisons were begun for Gloucestershire, Oxfordshire, Shropshire and Suffolk. By 1789 and 1790 similar new building was also being done for Devon, Dorset, Hampshire, Lancashire, Leicestershire, Norfolk, Staffordshire and Warwickshire. In the early 1790s prisons were begun for Northamptonshire, Herefordshire, Surrey and Berkshire, and work started on the long-drawn out reconstruc-

[24] Essex RO, QS O 14, pp. 545, 583; QS O 15 p. 39.

[25] Whiting, *Prison Reform*, pp. 112, 146–147; Gloucestershire RO, Q/AG 7 p. 141.

[26] Lincolnshire RO, Lindsey QS abstract of accounts for building Kirton bridewell, 1784; Greater London RO, MA/G/CBF 5 March 1784, 5 August 1784.

tion of Cheshire gaol. No gaol was started in the mid and later 1790s, apart from the combined Bedfordshire gaol and house of correction between 1798 and 1801.

The sites of gaols and bridewells erected from the 1780s represented often only a small item in the total expenditure because a location was chosen on or beyond the edge of the town, which was both cheap and healthy. Most prisons were built largely of the cheaper material, brick (or stone in some areas), but an imposing or ornamental facade in stone added slightly to the cost. The brick Shropshire gaol had an ornamental stone entry lodge; the Norfolk gaol was faced with Aberdeen granite; the Chelmsford, Essex, bridewell (1802–7) had a Portland stone front; and the Kent gaol (1812–19) was faced with Kentish ragstone. Portland stone was often chosen because of its hardness and attractive appearance. For the building of Chelmsford prison the mason received about £880 and the bricklayer around £2500 out of a total expenditure of approximately £7400. Otherwise the justices kept costs of materials as low as possible. One assumes that the labour to materials ratio in building prisons and courthouses was similar to that in house construction, with the cost of labour being roughly similar to that of materials in carpentry and joinery, and wages being more expensive than bricks on account of the labour content in brickmaking.

There is relatively little evidence about the cost of the contribution of the trades. Near the end of the eighteenth century, three building accounts reveal the varying content of woodwork in comparison with masonry and brickwork. The input of ironwork, plastering, plumbing, glazing and roof slating was least. The abstract of accounts of building Kirton, Lindsey, bridewell in July 1794 were:

Thomas Berry, carpenter and joiner	£1269	11s.	8d.
William Hargrave, mason and plasterer	£4871	0s.	2d.
Edward Mossom, smith	£598	9s.	4d.
Christopher Fairweather, plumber and glazier	£321	3s.	7d.
John Blow, ditto	£94	2s.	4d.
John Richardson, slater	£432	10s.	9d.
William Pudsey, painter	£57	10s.	9d.
William Lumby, surveyor	£238	18s.	11d.
Thomas Wass, Kirton	£3	17s.	3d.
	£7887	4s.	9d.

The masonry was the principal charge, costing with plaster work 60 per cent of the whole, and four times that of the woodwork, presumably floors, ceilings and rafters alone. The ironwork, and especially the plumbing and glazing, and roofing were each much less than 10 per cent of the total charge. The accounts of the Essex Halstead and Chelmsford bridewells (1782–84 and 1802–7) have also survived. For the first (totalling about £2000), the brickwork and masonry was charged at £916 10s. 0d. and the carpentry £593, suggesting that the interior walls were also wooden; the ironwork was £106 12s. 0d., glazing and plumbing £52. A wooden interior is also suggested at the bigger Chelmsford bridewell where the carpenter and bricklayer were the major payees. In contrast the great Maidstone gaol (1812–19) was built with iron pillars (beginning to be widely used in the 1810s) and brick and stone walls; woodwork was at a minimum. The Leicestershire gaol, erected in 1826–28, seems to have been similarly built: out of £48,685 spent on the building, stonework cost £19,683, brickwork £14,120, wood and carpentry only £4924 and ironwork £5265.[27]

Occasionally a wing or sets of cells were added to an existing prison, as in Kent, Wiltshire and Worcestershire. Thus at Worcester improvements to the gaol and house of correction included eight cells, a reception centre and separate apartments for women and debtors. Among small prisons, the Bedfordshire gaol and bridewell intended for only forty prisoners was built in the form of a cross with the governor's house in front. Most new prisons comprised several blocks of building laid out in an articulate form to provide for inspection and for intervening exercise yards. The relatively large Shropshire gaol had most of its buildings arranged in a square with a chapel in the centre divided into four courts. They included a keeper's house and two rows of cloisters with sleeping cells for prisoners above; the males were separated from the females, felons from debtors. The inmates were subdivided into classes, and to each class was assigned a court, with day rooms. The most expensive buildings were the Surrey gaol and prison blocks at Chester Castle. But account should be taken of the rising wage level and higher material costs in the later 1790s.[28]

The decline in prison building after about 1794 was marked. Schemes already begun were continued, particularly the improvements to the Chester and Lancaster castle gaols, the new Surrey prison, and the partial

[27] Essex RO, QS O 18, p. 71, Q/FAc 6/3/1, Q/FAa 4/2; *New Maidstone Gaol Order Book, 1805–23*, ed. C.W. Chalklin, Kent Records, 23 (Maidstone, 1984), pp. 24, 27; Leicestershire RO, QS 6/2/1.

[28] H. Owen, *Some Account of the Ancient and Present State of Shrewsbury* (Shrewsbury, 1808), pp 432–33; *Victoria History of the County of Shropshire*, iii, ed. G.C. Baugh (Oxford, 1959), p.113; O. Manning and W. Bray, *History and Antiquities of the County of Surrey* (London, 1814), pp. xiv, xv; F. Simpson, 'Chester Castle, AD 907–1925', *Journal of the Chester and North Wales Archaeological and Historic Society*, new series, 26 (1925), pp. 103–5; *Parliamentary Papers* (1825), vi.

rebuilding of the Somerset gaol. Only two prisons were started, the Bedfordshire gaol and house of correction in 1798; and the small Botesdale, Suffolk, bridewell in 1799. Several projects for rebuilding or enlarging prisons were considered but not implemented. The Essex court discussed the inadequacy of the Chelmsford bridewell in regard to repairs needed, the want of separate apartments and lack of room for employment as early as October 1792; a site was bought in 1795, but building did not begin until 1802.[29]

Several reasons can be suggested for the reduction in building. One may have been the greater difficulty in borrowing money. Normally counties found raising money no problem because of the quality of the security. The mid 1790s was a period, however, when cash for all kinds of business transactions was often in short supply. Cheshire continued to borrow money for the castle improvements each year, especially in 1796 when £6200 was obtained. On the other hand, several counties, including Surrey and Herefordshire, found borrowing less easy than before the outbreak of war. This problem may have deterred other counties from beginning building. Another factor may have been rising costs: not only was the price of loans higher (5 per cent instead of the 4 per cent which had been the most common rate at the beginning of the 1790s), but wages and the price of building materials were increasing more sharply through the mid and later 1790s than had been the case in the previous decade. Other county expenditure was also rising in the later 1790s, though general prices were also increasing in the same period.[30] Probably of more importance were rising national taxes and parish rates. On account of the war assessed taxes trebled in 1797, preceded by new taxes on the use of hair powder, dogs, clocks and watches. At the same time poor rates continues to rise inexorably. Interest in prison improvement waned along with that in all kinds of reform, due to the fear of political radicalism among the propertied classes. Several counties were also still paying off the debts incurred during the building of previous years, such as Berkshire and Hampshire. All types of building work slumped, and the relative absence of general activity may have influenced courts in deciding whether or not to start a new prison or extend an existing one. The government was equally deterred from building projects. In 1795 George III approved a scheme for rebuilding Westminster Palace costing £124,000, but 'Lord Grenville regretted that in the present state of

---

[29] Essex RO, QS O 15, pp. 152, 426–427; QS O 16, p. 15; QS O 18, pp. 302, 316, 375.
[30] See above, Chapter 3.

the country it would be inexpedient to commence the works'.[31] The sharp decline of county prison building for various reasons was part of a general collapse of public building which the failure to reconstruct the palace symbolised.

Fig. 9.3. Kent County Gaol, Maidstone, built 1811–23 for about £200,000 and designed by Daniel Alexander, the most sophisticated county prison to this date. This view shows a long three-storey wing, principally of cells, and the keeper's house with the chapel over it.

[31] W. R. Ward, *The English Land Tax in the Eighteenth Century* (Oxford, 1953), p. 133; *Parliamentary Papers* (1825), vi, relating to Hampshire; C. W. Chalklin, 'Prison Building by the County of Berks, 1766–1820', *Berkshire Archaeological Journal*, 69 (1979), p. 62; J. M. Crook and M. H. Port, *The History of the King's Works*, vi, *1782–1851* (London, 1973), p. 514.

10

Gaols and Bridewells, 1800–1830

In contrast to the absence of new building projects during the later 1790s, the first years of the nineteenth century saw a general revival of interest in prison construction. A stream of works continued through the following decades. This may have been encouraged by the general recovery of other forms of building, especially housing, and urban improvement in the early 1800s, which were accompanied by a return to easier credit conditions. More basically it reflected the pressure on prison accommodation which had continued to grow during the 1790s. The sustained building of the next decades was partly the result of a further rise in the number of criminals, caused by continued population growth. Especially from about 1816, there was another, even greater rise of crime on account of demobilised servicemen and the greater intensity of chronic unemployment, including among juveniles, particularly in the countryside and London. For example, the combined Bedfordshire prison of 1798–1801 was intended for about forty prisoners on the assumption that transportation would continue and that there would be no increase in crime. By 1818 there were often one hundred prisoners, partly the result of the rise in population in Bedfordshire (1801: 63,393; 1821: 83,716), and partly because of the growth of the crime rate, which necessitated the erection of a separate bridewell between 1818 and 1820. Bedfordshire was still largely a rural county. In Warwickshire, which included the large towns of Birmingham and Coventry, as well as several lesser country towns, there was a noticeable jump in the number of larceny cases and of juvenile offenders about 1816.[1]

In the two areas where urban expansion was greatest, London and south Lancashire, prison construction in the form of new buildings or extensions may be seen to be linked closely to a dramatic rise in the

---

[1] E. Stockdale, 'Bedford Prison', *Bedfordshire Historical Record Society*, 56, pp. 88, 106–97; P. Styles, *The Development of County Administration in the Late Eighteenth and Early Nineteenth Century, Illustrated by the Warwickshire Court of Quarter Sessions, 1773–1837*, Dugdale Society Occasional Papers, 4 (Oxford, 1934), pp. 22–23.

Table 10.1

Number of Middlesex Prisoners, 1804–17

Date	New Prison	House of Correction
1804	2444	1250
1805	2129	1150
1806	2254	1180
1807	2345	1462
1808	2215	1271
1809	2483	1131
1810	2726	1138
1811	2830	1348
1812	2830	1461
1813	2414	1671
1814	2708	1691
1815	3291	2106
1816	3847	2875
1817	4046	3667

numbers of prisoners. In 1818 the Middlesex prison surgeon gave the figures of numbers confined in the New Prison and Coldbath Fields house of correction (Table 10.1). In response to the rapid growth of numbers from about 1810 the New Prison was extended in 1816. There was a similar response over ten years later, when the rapid increase of crime rates and petty police arrests after 1828 led to a huge expansion of the Westminster and Coldbath Fields bridewells.[2] The growth in the number of prisoners in the whole country, particularly after the end of the Napoleonic wars, is perhaps most clearly illustrated by the following numbers of persons committed for trial at assizes in England and Wales:

1805–09	23,462
1810–14	30,163
1815–19	58,662
1820–24	65,227

In the later 1820s committals for summary offences, particularly vagrancy, rose sharply: the number of vagrants in custody grew by 34 per cent between 1826 and 1829, and by 65 per cent between 1829 and 1832.[3]

The prison reform movement was also active, placing more pressure on justices to increase space (Table 10.2). As in the 1780s, the aims were

[2] Greater London RO, MJ/OC 18, pp. 2–4, 286; M. Ignatieff, *A Just Measure of Pain* (London, 1978), p. 185.
[3] Ibid., pp. 154, 179.

Table 10.2

Number of Gaols and Bridewells Built or Substantially Enlarged, 1801–30

1801–1805	10	1816–1820	21
1806–1810	14	1821–1825	18
1811–1815	8	1826–1830	15

security, healthy conditions and reformation. Emphasis was now placed on the last, improving morals, and it was to be done through classification, inspection and employment. Classification of prisoners into groups was furthered, inspection became a fetish and a task popular with the justices. To allow surveillance, radial plans were particularly important; polygonal designs were also used. After about 1812 parliamentary interest in prisons was reawakened, as select committee reports and acts of parliament show. Peel's act of 1823, largely the culmination of many years of growing public (especially evangelical) interest in prison reform and particularly of the demand of the Society for the Improvement of Prison Discipline for uniform standards in prison treatment and discipline, 'for the first time made it peremptorily the duty of the justices to organise their prisons on a prescribed plan, and to furnish quarterly reports to the Home Secretary upon every department of their prison administration'. Many prisons were extended and altered as a result of this act.

The S.I.P.D. (led by T.F. Buxton, and with Wilberforce and Samuel Hoare as members) published books with details on prison rules and building in 1820 and 1826, and benches used its opinions to alter their architect's plans. Another influence was the fear of social disorder provoked by more unemployment, the new labour-saving machinery and falling wages, as well as by the decline of apprenticeship and a dwindling of boarding by labourers in farmhouses. Harsh prison conditions seemed the best deterrent for crime. In the 1820s the hardening of attitudes among justices towards prisoners led to the use of bread and water diets and the erection of buildings to house treadmills, intended to encourage dread and terror. In some cases, too, the development of professional standards among prison governors resulted in prison alterations.[4] Two keepers, John Orridge of Bury and Thomas le Breton of Canterbury, wrote a book together; Orridge helped George Byfield design the Bury gaol (1803), contributed to the Carlisle gaol design (1822), and planned a prison for the emperor of Russia.

[4] S. and B. Webb, *English Local Government*, vi, *English Prisons under Local Government* (London, 1963), p. 74; Ignatieff, *Just Measure*, pp. 168, 176–184; R. Evans, *The Fabrication of Virtue: English Prison Architecture, 1750–1840* (Cambridge, 1982), ch. 6.

Turning to the chronology of prison building in the three decades after 1800, the Bury St Edmunds division of Suffolk began a county gaol in 1801 on a radial plan, Cambridgeshire gaol was started in 1803, and additions to the county gaol at York were begun in the same year (see Table 10.3). A new debtors' prison for the Hampshire gaol was started in 1804. All were substantial projects costing over £10,000. Essex and the Ipswich division of Suffolk began houses of correction in 1802, while the East Riding and Woodbridge division of Suffolk started additional buildings in 1804. New projects appeared at much the same rate during the next five years. The prisons included the Kent county gaol at Canterbury and the Worcestershire gaol. By far the largest scheme was the Durham county gaol and bridewell in 1809, built in conjunction with the county courts. At least eight new houses of correction were begun, including the large bridewells built at Exeter for Devon (1808–11).

The number of prisons begun fell between 1811 and 1815, the last years of the war, perhaps in part on account of the difficulty in borrowing large sums for building. On the other hand, they included the most ambitious county prison project yet undertaken, that of the Kent county gaol at Maidstone, begun in 1811. From about 1817 the number of new works grew. Particularly notable were five large houses of correction. Between 1817 and 1823 Cheshire constructed a large house of correction at Knutsford. Lancashire started an extensive enlargement of its house of correction at Salford and began a new one at Kirkdale near Liverpool. Surrey built two substantial houses of correction, at Brixton and Guildford. Building continued uninterruptedly throughout the 1820s. In 1822 and 1823 four large new county prisons were begun, for Cumberland, Northumberland, Essex and Derbyshire. Later in the 1820s massive alterations were begun to the York Castle gaol. A large Leicestershire gaol and smaller Huntingdonshire prison were erected between 1826 and 1828. Work went on in the early 1830s in the form of additions and alterations, but there was a lull in the construction of new prisons, apart from the great Westminster bridewell which had cost £183,906 by 1834; as at Maidstone, the nucleus had to be split to handle the number of classes (twenty-four) needed, and the architect Robert Abraham finally devised three five-wing radials round a huge entrance court. Several other gaols and houses of correction were altered and enlarged. The most sizeable was the Middlesex Clerkenwell bridewell on which £77,793 was spent between 1801 and March 1831 inclusive; after the erection of a large treadmill in the early 1820s, its 600 cells were increased to 1150 between 1825 and 1832 by adding two five-wing radials within the old walls, 'the Steel' became the largest English prison, with more than 10,000 vagrants, beggars, disorderlies, drunks and petty thieves in it each year. The Kent county gaol erected between 1811 and 1819 was the most ambitious county prison building in England before the late 1820s. Laid out in the form of four nearly identical radials, it divided its prisoners into twenty-seven classes and provided 452 night cells. The Durham county gaol and house of correction for thirteen classes of prisoners included forty-eight wards, three workrooms and eighteen dayrooms; it also had county courts. Eight prisons cost between £50,000 and £100,000. For example, £78,000 was spent on the Cheshire house of correction at Knutsford, which was provided with a governor's house, infirmary, eight day rooms and 150 cells. Lancashire's enlarged bridewell at Salford cost about £80,000 by 1828, its new one at Kirkdale £85,204; the Brixton (Surrey) house of correction (£54,974) was the other bridewell in this price range. Thirty other prisons (including thirteen bridewells) involved an outlay of between £10,000 and £50,000 each.[5]

The majority of prisons, nevertheless, cost under £10,000. Many of them were substantial buildings, such as the Nottinghamshire bridewell at Southwell (1807–9) an influential building designed by V.T. Becher, the poor law reformer, which comprised a central house and three wings for six classes of prisoners with separate night cells. Others were smaller prisons, such as the Folkingham house of correction in Kesteven (1808), comprising a gaoler's house and two buildings, each with two cells and a workroom.[6] Altogether there were nine gaol and twenty-one bridewell undertakings, either new prisons or enlargements, costing between £2500 and £10,000.

The cost of the treadmills (with the buildings) erected by most counties in the 1820s was typically between £1000 and £2000. The treadmill and buildings erected at the house of correction in Reading for Berkshire in 1822 cost £1700; Nottinghamshire spent £1570 at the Southwell bridewell in 1822, the main items being the machinery (£768) and the building (£596).[7]

The number of new building projects had grown enormously since the early and mid eighteenth century. Between 1700 and 1760 there were about fifteen gaols and fourteen houses of correction built, greatly

[5] *Parliamentary Papers* (1831), xv, (1835), xii; Ignatieff, *Just Measure*, p. 185; Evans, *Fabrication of Virtue*, pp. 310–11, 389–90.

[6] Nottinghamshire RO, CT 1/3; Lincolnshire RO, Kesteven QS minutes, 1802–8.

[7] Berkshire RO, QS O 12, p. 509; Nottinghamshire RO, QAG 5/68/17.

enlarged or set up in existing houses. Between 1800 and 1830 eighty-six were built or substantially improved. The cost of prisons naturally grew many times in real terms. The two largest gaols built in the early eighteenth century were the Yorkshire prison for about £8000 and the Buckinghamshire gaol with a county hall for about £9000. The two largest prisons erected between 1800 and 1825 were the Kent gaol (about £200,000) and the Durham gaol and courthouse (£134,685). The cost of smaller new bridewells such as that at Odiham in 1743 (£348) and Lawford's Gate may be compared with the bridewells at Southwell and Folkingham in the 1800s. Despite the rise in building prices, increasing about twice between 1780 and 1810, there was a real increase of five times or more in the outlay on prison undertakings.

There was a correspondingly huge increase in total outlay on new prisons. Some tentative estimates may be made of total expenditure on prison building between the 1760s and about 1830. The figures draw attention to the minimal expenditure on building before the 1770s, and to the fact that outlay in the 1770s was small compared with succeeding decades. The material suggests the importance of the outlay of the 1780s and the 1790s, and then again of the 1810s and particularly the 1820s; building in the 1800s representing a fall in real terms compared with the expenditure of the 1780s and 1790s. Altogether nearly £600,000 was spent on prison building in the 1780s and 1790s, and almost £2,000,000 between 1700 and 1830 (Table 10.5).

These figures exclude expenditure on repairs and minor alterations. According to an official contemporary estimate, building and maintenance on prisons between 1801 and 1830 cost £2,485,931; therefore outlay on repairs and small changes was at least one-fifth of total expenditure.[8] As a result of the prison reform campaign and the Gaol Act of 1823 a major phase of prison building and improvement was completed, or was in process of being completed, by 1830. The amount of work in the previous thirty years differed greatly among the counties, for a variety of reasons. A few sessions in mainly rural counties with relatively slow population growth did little on account of earlier building, while others were forced into unprecedented activity because of rapid industrialisation and urbanisation, too little work in the 1780s and early 1790s, greater reforming zeal among justices or the Gaol Act. The varying scale of activity may be illustrated by sessions work in Dorset, Kent, Leicestershire and Lancashire.

While the Dorset bench had built an inadequate gaol in the 1780s, it was replaced immediately by a large, well-planned building of six blocks,

[8] *Parliamentary Papers* (1839), xliv.

Table 10.3

The Building of County Gaols, 1801–30[9]

Date	County and Location	Cost
1798–1815	Warwickshire, Warwick (with house of correction)	c. £11,000
1801–6	Suffolk, Bury St Edmunds	over £15,000
1803–9	Cambridgeshire, Cambridge	£17,379
1803–7	Yorkshire, York (additions)	£10,350
1804–7	Hampshire, Winchester (debtors' prison)	£22,500
1806–9	Kent, east division, Canterbury	£15,333
1807–9	Norfolk, Norwich (improvements)	c. £7000
1808–11	Rutland, Oakham	£9352
1809–14	Worcestershire, Worcester (with house of correction)	£19,000
1809–19	Durham (with county courts etc.)	£134,685
1810–11	Somerset, Ilchester (improvements)	£3869
1811–23	Kent, Maidstone	£200,000
1817	Buckinghamshire, Aylesbury (debtors' prison)	c. £11,000
1818–22	Wiltshire, Fisherton Anger	£28,556
1818–20	Devon, Exeter (debtors' prison)	£8562
1819–23	Lancashire, Lancaster Castle	c. £8000–£10,000
1819–21	Sussex, Horsham (extension)	£3200
1819–21	Suffolk, Bury St Edmunds	at least £10,500
1821	Suffolk, Ipswich (additions)	£4021
1822–28	Northumberland, Morpeth (with sessions house)	c. £70,000
1822–25	Dorset, Dorchester (alterations)	c. £7000
1822–28	Cumberland, Carlisle (with house of correction)	£42,000
1822–28	Essex, Chelmsford	c. £57,000

[9] *Sources: Warwickshire County Records*, 7 (Warwick, 1946), p. cxxvii; *Parliamentary Papers* (1825), vi; Cambridgeshire RO, QS 0 11; North Yorkshire RO, treasurers' accounts, 1802–15; *Parliamentary Papers* (1825), vi; Centre for Kentish Studies, Q/AGe 1, 4, 5; *Parliamentary Papers* (1825), vi; *Rutland Magazine*, 4 (1909–10) pp. 215–16; D. Whitehead, 'Georgian Worcester' (unpublished University of Birmingham M.A. thesis, 1976), p. 123; W. Fordyce, *The History and Antiquities of the County Palatine of Durham*, i (Newcastle, 1857), p. 293; Somerset RO, CQ2. 2/6(1); *New Maidstone Gaol Order Book, 1805–1823*, ed. C.W. Chalklin, Kent Records, 23 (Maidstone, 1984) p. 2; *Parliamentary Papers* (1825), vi; Wiltshire RO, A4/2/5/7/2; Devon RO, QS 1/25; Lancashire RO, CTA 2, 4; *Parliamentary Papers* (1831), xv; West Sussex RO, QAP/4/WE3(1); *Parliamentary Papers* (1825), vi; East Suffolk RO, 50/19/4.4(3); *Parliamentary Papers* (1831), xv (1833), xxxii; Lewis, *Topographical Dictionary*, i, p. 380; J. White, 'Chelmsford Gaol in the Nineteenth Century', *Essex Journal*, 11 (1976–77), p. 86; J.C. Cox, *Three Centuries of Derbyshire Annals* (London, 1890), p. 13; D.R. Tucker, 'Quarter Sessions and County Council Government in Devon in the Nineteenth Century', *Report and Transactions of the Devonshire Association*, 89 (1952) p. 199; G.K. Blyth, *The Norwich Guide* (Norwich, 1843), p. 202; Gloucestershire RO, QAG/9, QS M3/3; R.W. Liscombe, *William Wilkins, 1778–1839* (Cambridge, 1980), p. 267; *Victoria County History of Yorkshire: The City of York* (London, 1961) p. 527; Leicestershire RO, QS 6/2/1; M.H. Tomlinson, 'Victorian Prisons: Administration and Architecture, 1835–1877' (unpublished Ph.D. thesis, University of London, 1975), p. 546; *Parliamentary Papers* (1833), xxxii.

Table 10.4

The Building of County Bridewells Costing under £50,000, 1801–30[10]

Date	County and Location	Cost
1799–1807	Yorkshire, West Riding, Wakefield	£13,430
1802–4	Suffolk, Ipswich	at least £1500
1802–7	Essex, Chelmsford (and property £1282 10s.)	*c.* £7500
1804–7	Suffolk, Woodbridge	£4386 19s.
1804–8	Suffolk, Beccles	£5046 11s.
1804–12	Yorkshire, East Riding, Beverley	*c.* £22,000
1805–6	Berkshire, Abingdon (with courthouse)	*c.* £21,000
1806–7	Northumberland, Alnwick	*c.* £1000
1807	Hertfordshire, Hitchin	£527 13s.
1807–9	Nottinghamshire, Southwell	£5882 2s.
1808–9	Lincolnshire (Kesteven), Folkingham	£3308
1808–11	Devon, Exeter	*c.* £32,000
1809	Lincolnshire, Skirbeck Quarter, Boston	under £2500
1810	Hampshire, Gosport	£3956 4s.
1811	Cambridgeshire, Wisbech (with courthouse)	£2803 2s.
1811–12	Norfolk, Wymondham	*c.* £1670
1813–14	Derbyshire, Ashbourne (+£270 site)	£2252 16s.
1814–15	Staffordshire, Wolverhampton (additions)	£482 9s.
1814–16	North Riding, Northallerton (female prison)	£5348 7s.
1814–16	Somerset, Wilton	£6697
1814–19	Leicestershire, Leicester	*c.* £12,800
1817	Sussex, Lewes	£3128 10s.
1817–25	Somerset, Shepton Mallet	£2490
1817–32	Westmorland, Kendal (additions)	£5500
1818	Wiltshire, Marlborough (contract)	£469
1818–19	Nottinghamshire, Southwell (enlargement)	*c.* £13,200
1819–22	Yorkshire, East Riding, Beverley (additions)	*c.* £11,000
1819–22	Yorkshire, North Riding, Northallerton (additions)	£4630 6s.
1819–23	Bedfordshire, Bedford	£4022 9s. + £2238 5s.
1820–23	Surrey, Guildford	£24,770 9s.
1820–23	Norfolk, Swaffham and Walsingham	*c.* £6800
1820–23	Cambridgeshire, Ely (with shire hall)	£10,980 16s.
1821	Monmouthshire, Usk	*c.* £800
1821–24	Yorkshire, West Riding, Wakefield	£28,300
1822	Nottinghamshire, Southwell (treadmill)	*c.* £1570
1823	Surrey, Kingston	£5208 19s.
1823–28	Lincolnshire (Kesteven), Folkingham	£8299
c. 1823	Essex, Halstead (contract)	£580
1824–26	Lincolnshire (Lindsey), Spilsby (with courthouse)	£15,350
1825–28	Yorkshire, North Riding, Northallerton (additions)	£5074 16s.
1826	Cumberland, Penrith	£400
1826	Lincolnshire (Holland), Spalding	*c.* £15,000
1826–27	Lincolnshire (Lindsey), Louth	£12,027 12s.
1827–28	Nottinghamshire, Southwell (enlargement)	£3000
1828	Lancashire, Preston	*c.* £10,000
1828–31	Essex, Ilford	£6500–£7000

with ten courtyards to separate the types of prisoners and eighty-eight cells, keeper's office, committee rooms, prisoners' rooms, bath house, water closets, infirmary and chapel, all the rooms being limewashed and with water laid on, designed by the leading prison architect Blackburn (Fig. 10.1). A bridewell was attached in 1793, when the Sherborne building was closed as superfluous to needs. The population of Dorset grew more slowly than in England as a whole, from 119,000 in 1801 to 161,026 by 1831. Apart from minor improvements for about £2000 in 1806, only repairs costing several hundred pounds annually were done in the 1800s and 1810s. Following general practice, a treadmill was added in 1822 and the Gaol Act led to alterations to make the classification of prisoners more detailed, all at a cost of about £7000 between 1822 and 1825.[11]

Kent's population grew faster than that of Dorset, from 317,442 to 484,492 between 1801 and 1831. Maidstone, the dockyard town of Chatham, and towns near London in the far north west developed quickly. More prison work needed doing in 1800 than in Dorset. East Kent had its own sessions and prisons at Canterbury. Its small gaol was altered and enlarged in 1787 for about £730; and there were extensive repairs, especially to the roof, for about £200 in 1794–96. In 1804 a committee of justices recommended rebuilding on a new site. Early next year the leading prison architect George Byfield

[10] *Sources:* West Yorkshire RO, QSO; East Suffolk RO, 105/2/52; Essex RO, Q/FAc 6/3/1, QS O 18 pp. 2, 24; East Suffolk RO, 105/2/53; *Parliamentary Papers* (1825), vi; Northumberland RO, QS O 16, pp. 85, 89; H.M. Tomlinson, 'Victorian Prisons: Administration and Architecture, 1835–1877' (unpublished University of London Ph.D. thesis, 1975), p. 505; Nottinghamshire RO, CT1/3; Lincolnshire RO, Kesteven, QS; *Parliamentary Papers* (1825) vi; Hampshire RO, QM13, fos 116, 134, 153; *Parliamentary Papers* (1836), xxxv; Norfolk RO, C/S4/1, p. 195; J.C. Cox, *Three Centuries of Derbyshire Annals* (London, 1890), pp. 11, 33; Staffordshire RO, FAa1/7; North Yorkshire RO, QS treasurers' accounts, 1802–15, 1815–24; Somerset RO, CQ2 2/6 (1); *Parliamentary Papers* (1831), xv; East Sussex RO, QAF2/1/E8; Tomlinson, 'Victorian Prisons', p. 563; C. Nicholson, *The Annals of Kendal* (Kendal, 1832), p. 118; Wiltshire RO, A4/2/5/8/2; Nottinghamshire RO, QAG5/37; *Parliamentary Papers* (1825), vi; North Yorkshire RO, QS treasurers' accounts, 1815–24; *Bedfordshire County Records: Notes and Extracts from the County Records, 1714 to 1832*, pp. 196, 200, 215; *Parliamentary Papers* (1825), vi (1831), xv (1833) xxxii; Norfolk RO, C/S4/2; Cambridgeshire RO, Isle of Ely sessions minutes, 1820–23; *Parliamentary Papers* (1831), xv; Tomlinson, 'Victorian Prisons', p. 533; K. Grady, *The Georgian Public Buildings of Leeds and the West Riding* (1987), p. 179; Nottinghamshire RO, QAG5/68/17; *Parliamentary Papers* (1831), xv; Essex RO, Q/AGb 6; *Parliamentary Papers* (1831), xv; North Yorkshire RO, QS treasurers' accounts, 1824–32; QAG; S. Lewis, *Topographical Dictionary of England*, iii, p. 519; *Parliamentary Papers* (1831), xv; Nottinghamshire RO, QAG5/78; *Parliamentary Papers* (1831), xv; Tomlinson, 'Victorian Prisons', p. 482.

[11] M.B. Weinstock, 'Dorchester Model Prison, 1791–1816', *Proceedings of the Dorset Natural History and Archaeological Society*, 78 (1957), pp. 94–97; *Parliamentary Papers* (1825), vi; (1833), xxxii; Dorset RO, QS orders, 1819–27.

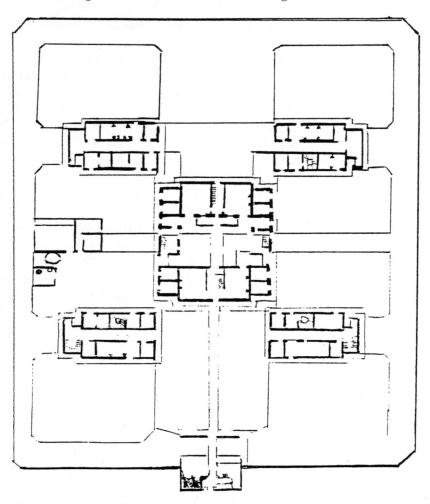

Fig. 10.1. Dorset gaol, Dorchester, finished 1795. It shows the influence of the prison reformers: the centre block had keeper's quarters with chapel above, debtors' rooms and various cells; four smaller blocks with cells were linked to it by iron bridges and the courtyards divided the prisoners; the eighty-eight cells were six by eight feet. (R. Evans, *The Fabrication of Virtue: Prison Architecture, 1750–1840*, Cambridge, 1982, p. 152).

was asked to prepare plans and estimates for a gaol and bridewell. The court decided that a modest prison for forty-eight (later forty) inmates would be sufficient because accommodation was needed only for the relatively few East Kent quarter sessions prisoners; the more numerous bridewell inmates, debtors and assize prisoners being sent to Maidstone gaol. In May the plan of the proposed building was agreed by a select committee. Based on Byfield's scheme with some changes, it had a central keeper's house and three wings. In June the site was fixed and the work advertised, using particulars prepared by Byfield. Charles Hedge, a London builder, won the contract in August 1805 for £12,380. The building was completed by April 1808 when Hedge had received £12,369 7s.7d., including a few extra charges. The land cost about £1750. With Byfield's commission as surveyor, payments to the clerk of the works, legal charges and minor payments to craftsmen, the total cost was between £15,000 and £16,000.[12] There were alterations, including the addition of the usual treadmill, in the 1820s.[13] This East Kent work was typical of procedure for smaller prisons.

The more important West Kent gaol at Maidstone had originally been built in the form of a substantial house in 1746 and 1747 (Fig. 10.2). There were additions in 1775 when the gaoler's house was added to the prison and in 1784 when a debtor's wing and infirmary cost more than £4000. The prison was still outdated compared with the gaols designed by Blackburn, and repairs costing several hundred pounds were made in many years until it was vacated when the new gaol was occupied in 1819. The Dartford bridewell had been enlarged in 1735–36 and 1778. Another had been built in East Lane, Maidstone, in 1774–77 reflecting the early influence of John Howard's ideas, for £2311 6s.10d. in addition to the cost of the land. In 1792–93 the West Kent Justices considered their condition and decided in favour of one new prison designed in part like Blackburn's new gaol at Ipswich. They refused, however, to take on this further financial commitment until they had ceased to be saddled with the sole cost of the Maidstone gaol (which was used in some respects for prisoners from the whole county). With the decline of interest in prison building all over England after 1793, the financial dispute with East Kent deferred the provision of a new gaol. Acts were needed in 1803 (43 George III c. 58), 1807 (47 George III c. 34), and 1809 (49 George III c. 111) to fix the liability of the east division for paying towards costs of prisons in the west, and to base parochial contributions to the rates on existing rentals. Work was stopped until 1811, despite the revival of county building elsewhere.[14]

The shortcomings of the gaol in comparison with newer prisons in other counties was marked. Among them were the cramped site, which restricted the size of the yards and an organised arrangement of the

[12] LSE, Webb Collection, vol. 136, 2 January 1787; Centre for Kentish Studies, Q/FAe 14, Q/AGe 1, 4, 5.
[13] Centre for Kentish Studies, Q/GO 2–3.
[14] *New Maidstone Gaol Order Book, 1805–1823*, ed. C.W. Chalklin, Kent Records, 23 (Maidstone, 1984), pp. 10–14.

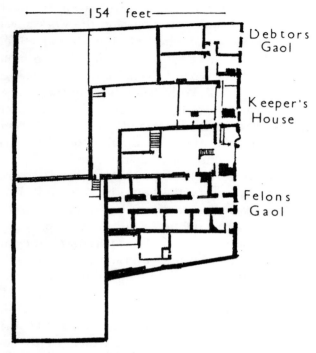

Fig. 10.2. Kent gaol, Maidstone, 1780–1820. Built in 1746 and extended later, the buildings were in the form of three houses with rooms off corridors, lacking a distinctive prison plan of the kind devised elsewhere in the 1780s. It was replaced by the gaol built between 1811 and 1823. (*Crime and Punishment*, ed. E. Melling, Maidstone, 1969, pl. vi.)

various rooms, the lack of a chapel, the inability to separate 'young novices in transgression' from 'notorious offenders' among the felons, the absence of separate sleeping cells, and the use of two totally dark dungeons for condemned prisoners. In the summer of 1805 the west Kent Justices

Table 10.5

Approximate Expenditure on Building Gaols and Bridewells in England, 1761–1830

	current prices	constant prices of 1821–30		current prices	constant prices of 1821–30
1761–70	£6000	£12,900	1801–10	£225,000	£212,000
1771–80	£55,000	£112,000	1811–20	£730,000	£640,000
1781–90	£290,000	£560,000	1821–30	£990,000	£990,000
1791–1800	£305,000	£457,500			

decided that only the house of correction at Maidstone was needed, and that both the Maidstone county gaol and bridewell should be presented formally by the grand jury as insufficient and inconvenient, to allow them to spend on improvements.[15]

A committee met in 1806 to discuss alterations and new building. They consulted George Byfield, who had designed the prisons at Cambridge and Bury St Edmunds, made plans for Worcester gaol, and was advising the East Kent justices about the new Canterbury gaol. At first they decided on a new bridewell and additions to the gaol; then, at Byfield's suggestion, drawing on his experience at Worcester, they considered and finally recommended in August a combined gaol and bridewell for 200 inmates. The need to make the rates fair delayed matters for four years.[16]

When an adjourned quarter sessions met at the Bell inn on 12 May 1810 to decide the principles of the new works, it used Daniel Alexander, who had designed Dartmoor prison and a series of London dock buildings and warehouses, and had acted as surveyor for several county bridge works. His experience was wide and he had handled large projects. While none of the justices appears to have had a predominating influence. the leading group chaired by the earl of Romney probably aimed at perfection in prison reform. The work was planned at a time when general building activity was at a peak. The chosen site was one of four suggested, fulfilling Alexander's desire that it should be near to the town centre and free of building, in a sloping position to help drainage, with rock and brick earth on the ground, and access to the River Medway for the transport of materials from a distance. The huge gaol had its wings arranged in the form of Latin crosses, of which the feet were tied to the keeper's house and the chapel in the middle. Inspection was based on the keeper's and three turnkeys' houses and a triangular grid of passages. The distinctly grouped three prisons were to take the separation of classes 'to the utmost practicable extent', the felons having fourteen classes, the debtors' gaol five and bridewell prisoners eight (Fig. 10.3). Each class was to have a day room, working room and airing yard, an arcade for wet weather and a cell for each of the 452 inmates. The building was erected in brick with a shell of local ragstone, with stone for special purposes coming from suppliers in Scotland and London. The financial difficulties of the Maidstone carpenter delayed work in 1818. The next year Alexander discovered that his clerk had been defraud-

---

[15] Ibid., p. 14.
[16] Ibid., p. 14.

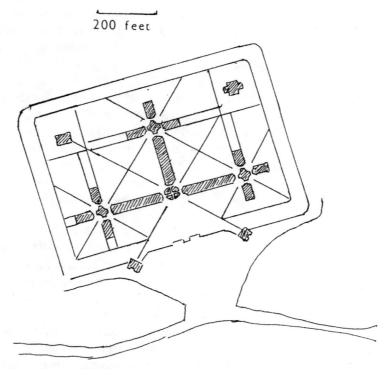

200 feet

Fig. 10.3. Kent gaol, Maidstone, built 1811–23. Designed by a prominent architect, Daniel Alexander, it was the most elaborate county prison erected by this date. It was intended for 452 inmates accommodated in rooms and cells in three long and nine short wings; the lines represent inspection passages linking the keeper's house and turnkeys' buildings. (*Crime and Punishment*, ed. E. Melling, Maidstone, 1969, pl. 6.)

ing the bench for about four years. It was, not withstanding, probably his best architectural work.[17]

Instead of trying to borrow, the bench decided to spread building over about twelve years. Between 1811 and 1820 construction costs varied between £11,932 in 1814–15 and £30,151 in 1815–16. From 1811 total county expenditure was about three times the amount of earlier years.[18]

Leicestershire's population also rose rapidly between 1801 and 1831, due to the growth of the hosiery industry. By 1800 its prison buildings were too small on account of inadequate work in the 1780s and 1790s.

[17] Ibid., p. 15–26.
[18] Ibid., p. 19, 27.

The Leicester house of correction is not recorded to have changed since minor improvements in 1778–81. In 1789 the bench rejected a proposal for a new gaol costing up to £15,000 applying fully the principles of the reformers. Instead they erected a smaller cramped prison for sixteen felons and thirty debtors costing £1700 for property and £4150 for building. The exceptionally poor and outdated bridewell accommodation led finally to two attempts between 1803 and 1818 to create suitable structures. Following a committee's report that the house did not conform to statute regulations such as those of 1782, that it was insecure and insufficient, and that it failed to separate men and women in daytime or provide compulsory work, the bench spent £1430 on a two-story building with men and women's courts, day rooms, workshops, sickrooms and thirteen cells, adding three cells and a large workroom for £640 in 1809. Its small size and its many more prisoners made it unsatisfactory almost immediately. In 1815–18 the justices erected a prison on a fresh site consisting of a building with two wings for eighty inmates costing about £10,000. Treadmills were added in the early 1820s. Even this prison was crowded at times by 1825.[19]

There was abortive discussion of a new gaol in 1818 when the bridewell was finished, with only small improvements to the debtors' part. The justices were forced to proceed by the requirements of the Gaol Act. After delays for much of 1824, a committee open to all the county justices met between October 1824 and January 1825, deciding against extending the existing gaol because of the cost of buying the adjoining property (at least £15,513) and the inadequacy of its space (7435 square yards), and in favour of a revised plan of the county surveyor, William Parsons, using a new site of over three acres. Finished in 1828 for £59,574, the gaol had eight wards round a central governor's house, with a chapel over it linked by bridges to the upper stories of the wards. These included day rooms, workrooms, airing yards and cells. The front was in castellated Gothic style.[20]

The population of Lancashire grew faster than that of any other county between 1781 and 1831, almost doubling from 1801 – on account of the rapid emergence of cotton manufacturing as the largest English industry. Consequently prison building was almost continuous, concentrated in the decade after 1785 and the years after 1816. Despite the building of

[19] Leicestershire RO, QS 5/1/7,9, QS 6/2/1, QS 30/2/19, QS 32/1/1, QS 32/3/3, 4, 5, 7, 9, 10, 12; *Leicester Journal*, 17 July 1789, 16 October 1789, 16 April 1790; J. Neild, *The General State of the Prisons* (London, 1812), p. 337.
[20] Leicestershire RO, QS 6/2/1, 32/2/1, 32/3/14, 15; *Leicester Journal*, 2 April, 7 May, 16 July, 10 September, 22 October 1824, 22 April 1825.

a small Manchester bridewell for Salford hundred in 1774–75, all three county prisons were renewed after 1785. An extensive three-story bridewell designed by Blackburn was built in the northern outskirts of Preston in 1785–91. Blackburn was also responsible for the larger Salford building, a three-story octagonal structure with four wings, including one hundred cells and numerous working rooms to handle the huge growth of prisoners, in 1787–91. From 1787 to 1796 the gaol at Lancaster Castle was extended, Thomas Harrison planning and superintending a gaoler's house, men and women felons' wards and rooms for debtors, all in hewn stone. Works in the 1780s and 1790s therefore corresponded with the growth of prisoners.[21]

While there was a lull in bridewell building, gaol works carried on beside county court building at the castle without a break until 1824, including a female penitentiary in the 1810s. By 1814 cells intended to be occupied singly in the Salford bridewell had risen to 140, occupied by 319 prisoners on account of the huge population growth in the Manchester area. At the Manchester adjournment of the Epiphany sessions 1815, a committee recommended a plan of more buildings, probably by the Salford architect Thomas Wright, and land adjoining the existing prison was bought. The new work comprised two parallel crescents each in nine parts. It included day rooms and ranges of sleeping cells, totalling 232, and workshops. After completion in November 1817 the prison was presented as needing further enlargement. Alterations appear to have been almost continuous during the following decade, with numbers of prisoners growing steadily. On 24 October 1825 the visiting justices appointed a committee to discuss the best way of enlarging the prison to house at least 150 more prisoners according to the terms of the Gaol Act; and how to improve the female part to allow inspection and classification. The works were done in 1827–28, after which there was a pause in alterations. By far the most ambitious work was the erection of the Kirkdale bridewell between 1818 and 1823. The procedure was begun at September and November 1816 sessions with the decision to enlarge Preston bridewell, which was too small for all the prisoners now sent to it from the five other Lancashire hundreds. Preston sessions the following February had resolutions from Liverpool corporation, a committee of borough justices and a meeting of county justices near Liverpool. These were apparently about the need to house prisoners in West Derby hundred, that is, the Liverpool area, which had also had a huge popula-

---

[21] Lancashire RO, QSO2/152–63; *Manchester Mercury*, 26 April 1796; Neild, *General State*, pp. 327, 382, 491–93.

tion growth. The annual sessions at Preston on 26 June hired three wings of the Liverpool gaol for three years and decided to build a bridewell in the Liverpool area. The five-year building of two three-story detached semi-circular wings, designed by Wright, was marred by a collapse in November 1818 and a complaint about the mortar in January 1819. About £4000 was spent in 1825–26 on a chapel, chaplain's house, watch house, laundry and drying-house. More prisoners in the Preston house led to the erection of a treadmill, the classifying of inmates during labour and a bigger chapel costing about £15,000 between 1824 and 1828. Altogether Lancashire had probably caught up temporarily with its number of prisoners by 1830.[22]

The contrast in expenditure among the four sessions seems great, despite the difference of county population. Dorset spent about £7000 in the three decades, Kent around £220,000, Leicestershire £80,000 and Lancashire £250,000. Outlay in terms of population growth per head was broadly similar in Kent and Leicestershire, where prisons were outdated in 1800, but lower in Lancashire which had done much more building in the 1780s and 1790s.

When counties were not spending on prisons they were better able to afford courthouses and lunatic asylums. While shire halls have been treated already, pauper lunatic asylums remain to be discussed.

[22] Lancashire RO, QS O 1/1, QS G 1/1, QS O 2/183–8, 194.

Fig. 11.1. Pauper lunatic asylum, Thorpe, near Norwich, built in 1811–14 for £35,221. Designed by the county surveyor, Francis Stone, it had a three-storey seven-bay centre and two lower wings, all of grey brick; it is shown before the extensions of 1830–32.

11

Pauper Lunatic Asylums, 1810–1830

The final field of quarter sessions building work lay in the construction of pauper lunatic asylums under an act of 1808. During the later eighteenth century there was growing medical interest in insanity as part of the philosophical movement of enlightenment. The mad began to be viewed as human beings who were possibly curable, not as beasts to be cowed by whipping or permanently chained. As the number of private madhouses run for profit grew, the emergence of public concern for their treatment is shown by an act of 1774 requiring them to be licensed and inspected by quarter sessions. Periodic licensing helped to make justices at sessions aware that lunacy was a matter with which they were concerned. There were also charity asylums supported by subscription in some towns. Although public hospitals for paupers erected in the later eighteenth century were their models, the insane were excluded from these. Most pauper lunatics were boarded by parishes in private madhouses or kept in workhouses.

By the beginning of the nineteenth century there was growing concern about the apparently rapid increase in insanity, which included concern about the numbers of mad poor. In fact the growing population made more mentally ill people inevitable. In addition to general awareness of the madness of George III, two influential philosophies increased interest in the deranged among educated people. Evangelicals, with their humanitarian and paternal concern for the lower orders, wanted to help by religion and physical care the mad poor who did not threaten existing society. The Benthamites, concerned for efficiency and order, appreciated the discipline of the asylum. Expanding county expenditure on prison building and the reform of prisoners suggested a way of handling the insane poor.[1]

A select committee was set up by parliament in 1807 to consider the state of criminal and pauper lunatics, leading to the County Asylums Act passed in 1808. Part of the immediate impetus came from the committee and therefore the act came from the well known Gloucestershire prison reformer Sir G.O. Paul. While she

[1] W.L.
Solitary of
'The Paup
(1996), pp.
County Asy
Gloucestershi

he wrote to the secretary of state about the criminal and pauper insane. The committee recommended that each county should have an asylum, with a committee of governors nominated by local justices and financed by a county rate. The act permitted counties to raise a rate to build an asylum, with the power to mortgage the rate for up to fourteen years. An appeal for voluntary subscriptions was also to be made. The act laid down several criteria for the building of an asylum. A healthy site was to be chosen with a good supply of water; male and female patients should have separate wards, with a further separation of convalescent patients from the incurables; and all the lunatics were to have dry and airy cells.[1]

The progress of the building undertakings was very slow. Few counties decided to build in the following years. The act of 1808 was only permissive and the cost of building and the burden of county expenditure on other matters deterred the majority of county quarter sessions. Conflicting pressures affected the justices in deciding upon the advisability of building an asylum. On the one hand, there was a strong urge to build on humanitarian grounds, for lunatics in workhouses had to be chained to prevent them escaping. Their physical condition deteriorated through lack of exercise and cramped conditions, and there was no chance of treatment leading to possible recovery. The legislation, though only permissive, still provided encouragement to build. Voluntary subscriptions were available, and in some counties private action and money began local interest. Subscription mad houses were a model for voluntary contributions. Capital was often borrowed, as for other county building. On the other hand, building costs were heavy, expenditure on all the other county responsibilities was regarded as high and was unpopular with the ratepayers, while in the rural counties in the 1820s agricultural depression was used up as an additional reason for not raising the rates.

These pressures are visible in connection with the proceedings of at least two quarter sessions concerning the building of an asylum within a few years of the 1808 act. In Norfolk a committee of justices appointed in 1809 reported on 13 July that there were 153 lunatics in the county, but that 'as the said act is not imperative for the providing a lunatic asylum . . . Resolved to defer the consideration of the expediency and necessity of providing such a house'. Nevertheless, in October 1810 the

Parry-Jones, *The Trade in Lunacy* (London, 1972), pp. 7–15; A. Scull, *The Most Solitary of Afflictions* (New Haven and London, 1993), pp. 38–43, 84–87; L.D. Smith, 'The Pauper Lunatic Problem in the West Midlands, 1815–1850', *Midland History*, 21 (1996), pp. 101–2; A. Bailey, 'An Account of the Founding of the First Gloucestershire Asylum, now Horton Road Hospital, Gloucester, 1792–1823', *Bristol and Gloucestershire Archaeological Society Transactions, 1971*, 110 (1972), p. 181.

Table 11.1

The Building of Pauper Lunatic Asylums[2]

Date	County	Number of Patients Planned	Cost
1809–12	Bedfordshire	40	c. £13,000
1810–15	Norfolk		£35,221
1811–12	Nottinghamshire (jointly with borough and voluntary subscribers; (county share one-third)	85	nearly £20,000
1812–19	Staffordshire (including furniture)		at least £35,000
1812–20	Lancashire	290	c. £42,000
1814–24	Gloucestershire (as for Nottinghamshire; (excluding fittings)	120	c. £42,000
1815–19	Yorkshire, West Riding	250	£48,528
1817–21	Cornwall (jointly with subscribers; (county share seven-elevenths)	112	c. £16,000
1817–20	Lincolnshire (jointly with subscribers)	78	c. £15,000
1821–30	Lancashire (improvements)		£23,043
1825–27	Bedfordshire (extension)	26?	£5065
1827–29	Suffolk (including building bought for £8000)	150	c. £27,500
1827–29	Cheshire	90	£25,125
1828–32	Dorset (jointly with subscriber); (£3000 by voluntary subscription, and gift of mansion and £4000 three per cents)	60	c. £13,500
1829–31	Kent	168[?]	£52,337
1829–31	Middlesex	300	£124,440
1830–32	Norfolk (addition)		c. £4700

court considered the act and an unanimous resolution in favour of proceeding by the grand jury at the last assizes, and decided to build, appointing a committee to superintend the building.[3]

In January 1812 these justices reported that they 'deem themselves bound not only to attend to economy, that the burthen on the county

[2] *Sources: Parliamentary Papers*, (1825), vi; LSE, Webb Local Government Collection, vol. 204; *Parliamentary Papers* (1825), vi; S. Lewis, *A Topographical Dictionary of England*, iii (1831), p. 431; Lancashire RO, CTA 2; Gloucestershire RO, HO 22/1/1, p. 237 etc.; *Parliamentary Papers* (1825), vi; C.T. Andrews, *The Dark Awakening: A History of St Lawrence's Hospital, Bodmin* (Bodmin, 1978), p. 44; *Parliamentary Papers* (1825), vi; Staffordshire RO, QS B1 Translation, 1819; Smith, 'The Pauper Lunatic Problem', p. 103; Lancashire RO, CTA 3; Bedfordshire RO, A.D. 4007 and QS M 28 i; East Suffolk RO, 105/2/70; Lewis, *Topographical Dictionary*, i (1840), p. 522; E. Boswell, *The Civil Division of the County of Dorset* (Dorchester, 1833), p. 95; Dorset RO, QS 08; Centre for Kentish Studies, Q/GFa 4; Lewis, *Topographical Dictionary*, ii, p. 352; *Parliamentary Papers* (1833), xxxii.
[3] LSE, Webb Collection, Norfolk, vol. 204, 13 July 1809, 4 October 1810.

may be rendered as light as possible, but most materially to judicious expedition and dispatch, in order that the humane intention of the legislative, may be carried into execution without any delay . . .'[4] In turn, Hampshire decided at Easter sessions of 1814 that it was expedient to build an asylum under the 1808 act; at Michaelmas a committee was appointed and a site in the vicinity of Winchester recommended. A petition was then received from occupiers of land contributing to the county rates asking that the measure be abandoned or its operation suspended; this led to a year's suspension, then a decision at Epiphany sessions in 1816 not to act indefinitely until a fresh order was made.[5]

Conflicting views among the justices are very clearly brought out in a debate at a meeting of a committee of Suffolk justices in April 1826. On the one side, the forwarding of the scheme to build an asylum was urged on humanitarian grounds, to carry out the wishes of the other justices as already expressed and the requirements of the act. Lord Calthorp 'with great energy and feeling', suggested 'that whatever diversity of opinion there might be as to the expediency of erecting an Asylum for the County, he was certain but one feeling pervaded the meeting, viz. that the greatest share of comfort should be extended towards those unfortunate individuals who laboured under aberration of mind . . .' A county lunatic asylum would offer a better chance of cure or at least the amelioration of their living conditions than was available at present. Another leading justice, Sir T.S. Gooch, said that he agreed with the views of his brother justices in the Beccles division: that the recommendations of the act should be carried out, and that an asylum was needed in the county.

On the other side, petitions were read from several hundreds appealing to the justices to abandon the scheme. A.H. Steward spoke of the great financial burden set against the trifling cost and fine treatment available in the London hospitals for lunatics (St Luke's and Bedlam); two other justices agreed. The extent of the conflict of opinion is shown by the fact that the meeting ended by voting eight to five in favour of an adjournment to Midsummer 1827. As an example of the ratepayers' opposition the *Ipswich Journal* had published a letter on 25 March from a S.S. Quilter of Walton to Gooch and Sir William Rowley, both MPs as well as justices, asking them on behalf of the yeomanry and tenantry to oppose an asylum 'the expense of which is to be charged upon the present alarmingly augmented county rates', which had in fact increased more

---

[4] Norfolk RO, C/S4/2 QS minutes, 1812–19, p. 3.
[5] Hampshire RO, QO 30, fos 18, 37, 54, 145.

than poor rates.[6] It is not surprising that counties took separate courses regarding the construction of an asylum. The majority gave the matter no recorded consideration in the years following 1808, or like Hampshire and the North Riding between 1810 and 1815 discussed it and finally dropped the issue. Only nine counties decided to build by 1824, the majority had still taken no action by the early 1830s.

Among the fourteen counties that began building an asylum by 1830, expenditure varied between about £15,000 for the Nottinghamshire and Lincolnshire buildings, designed for eighty-five and seventy-eight patients respectively, to the great Middlesex asylum for 300 patients costing over £100,000 (probably about £130,000 including the furniture). The three biggest, at Lancaster, Wakefield and Hanwell, Middlesex, were serving heavily urbanised, highly populated counties. Despite the differences in outlay and the amount of accommodation for patients, the asylums had basically similar features. Both the site and buildings were extensive because the aim was not merely the custody of the lunatics but their proper care in a comfortable environment and, where possible, their cure. As the 1808 act specified, the site was carefully chosen. In the case of the Gloucestershire asylum a site was selected in the parish of Wooton outside the city of Gloucester. 'The views of the surrounding countryside would be beneficial for the inmates whilst the hospital was conveniently situated for the city. Other factors influencing the decision were the potential water supply and the fact that the site was near enough to the Gloucester to Cheltenham tramroad to permit running a single track to the building site for the carriage of bricks etc.' In October 1814 the West Riding justices decided to choose a suitable place near Wakefield, making a decision next month after turning down nine offers of sites which were all deemed ineligible.[7]

The buildings, generally of two or three stories, consisted of a central block with accommodation for the staff, with the two sides for men and women respectively. Both comprised day rooms and cells. As an example of one of the smaller asylums the Bedfordshire building, erected between 1809 and 1812 for about £13,000 (including the furnishings and the site) and extended in 1825–7 for £5065 5s. 0d. (again including the site), may be described. Built of brick with stone quoins and fascias, it consisted of one main building with a projecting centre, terminating in two wings which formed the extension of the 1820s. Excluding the kitchens,

---

[6] *Ipswich Journal*, 25 March 1826, 1 April 1826.
[7] Bailey, 'Account of the First Gloucestershire County Asylum', p. 183; West Yorkshire RO, minutes of the committee for building a lunatic asylum, Wakefield, 1814–18.

cellars and offices, there were three stories; the middle part of the building was occupied by the superintendant and the staff, with a committee
room for the justices; the accommodation for several classes of male
patients lay on the right and that for the female lunatics on the left, with
a room for each patient. The building of the two wings provided more
accommodation, common sitting rooms, hospitals and nurseries.[8] The
larger West Riding asylum at Wakefield, costing £48,258, was for 250
patients; it was a three-story building surrounded by twelve airing yards
for the twelve classes of inmates (Fig. 11.2).[9]

The most ambitious project of all was the building of the Middlesex
asylum between 1829–1831. The search for the site involved advertisements in the London newspapers, for 'not less than twenty five acres of
land, in an airy and healthy situation, and well supplied with water . . .',
and inquiries by the surveyor, Robert Sibley, to the principal landowners in the county. At one point, in March 1828, Sibley gave the justices
some detailed observations on the choice of the site; the aspect should
be capable 'of exciting agreeable feelings on the approach'; there should
be an ascending approach terminating on a comparatively level site,
exposed to the south and sheltered on the north. So far as the nature
of the soil was concerned, clay was unsuitable as cold and damp and
retentive of moisture; pasture lands were most healthy, while water
meadows and thick weedlands were unhealthy. There was a need for
pure, cheap water; and accessibility to sun and wind and the avoidance
of stagnant air. After five months of careful inspection and inquiries, the
county contracted to buy forty-four acres from the earl of Jersey at Hanwell
at £250 an acre (that is, £11,000). The original scheme (in November
1827) was for an asylum for 600 patients with separate wards for dangerous, incurable, curable and convalescent patients of each sex, nearly
400 separate sleeping cells with rooms for the remaining 200 patients,
and twenty-four day rooms. The committee corresponded with those
responsible for other asylums about architectural plans. The architect's
detailed estimate of the cost on 5 May 1829 was £123,730 13s. 0d. Because
of the high figure the plans had to be altered to accommodate 300; next
month the tender of William Cubitt for £63,200 to build according to
the reduced scheme was accepted. In April 1830 the surveyor reported
that a further £29,380 needed to be spent on more buildings, such as a
brewhouse, bakehouse, store room, drying room etc., boundary walls

[8] J.H. Matthiason, *Bedford and its Environs* (Bedford, 1831), p. 117.
[9] Watson and Pritchett, *Plans, Elevations, Sections and Description of the Pauper Lunatic Asylum* (York, 1819), pp. 26–29; *Parliamentary Papers* (1825), vi.

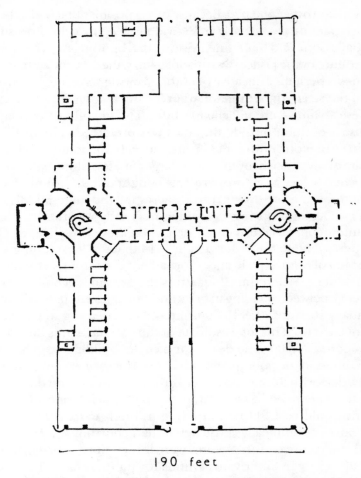

190 feet

Fig. 11.2. West Riding pauper lunatic asylum, built 1815–19. One of the largest of the early county asylums costing nearly £50,000. The ground plan shows
the cells opening onto corridors and most of the ancillary accommodation,
including day rooms, bath rooms and staff rooms, grouped around the two
staircases; the east side was for males, the west side for females; there were
twelve airing yards round the building for the twelve classes of lunatics.

and furnishing and fitments. The final cost was stated at £124,440, including the furniture, a figure almost the same as the original estimate for
the larger building in May 1829.[10]

Altogether the expenditure on the fourteen asylums between 1812 and

[10] Greater London RO, MA/A/J 1,2; S. Lewis, *Topographical Dictionary of England*
(London, 1840), ii, p. 352; Scull, *Afflictions*, p. 89.

1831 totalled over £500,000. Because of the facilities that had to be provided for each patient, particularly an individual sleeping cell, and also the share of a day room and staff supervision, the buildings were expensive. As expenditure by the justices was not obligatory, the total outlay by the fourteen counties is perhaps indicative of both a growing sense of responsibility and also of the strength of humanitarian feeling among county magistrates.

These asylums were still cheaply built. The site often cost relatively little because a position outside the town was preferred. The three-acre field bought by Bedfordshire cost £345 out of a total expenditure of about £13,000. The site of seven acres for the much larger Staffordshire asylum cost £1421. Only when a very large property was bought did the county spend a size-able sum on the site: the forty-four acres for the huge Middlesex asylum cost £11,000. Stone facing was sometimes used, but otherwise bricks were the building material usually chosen when they were cheaper. Ornament was often avoided. It was decided in 1814 that the West Riding asylum was 'to be built of brick as plain and unornamental as is consistent with propriety and neatness'. When the Gloucestershire asylum was built after 1816 the difference between building in brick and stone was estimated by the surveyor in January 1816 at £2058 10s. 0d. and the idea of using stone was given up. It is not clear what his total estimate of the cost was at this time; it may have been about £26,000. The desire for a cheap building was also implied by his readiness to use poor-quality brick. The surveyor recommended a cover-ing of bricks with Roman cement to give a handsome and durable exterior, the extra expense being saved largely by the use of inferior brick: the Roman cement would cost £1157, the saving in brick £575. Altogether asylums were more economically constructed than courthouses.[11]

Only two more county asylums were built before construction became compulsory in 1845. Private asylums for paupers as well as workhouses filled the gap in institutional provision. Highly populated counties such as Surrey did not have a county asylum, and there was only one in the industrialised west midlands. However one-third of the benches ran asylums by 1832. With judges' lodgings, they show the spread of county building work under various social and administrative pressures. Both types of building increased sessions' borrowing, begun in the 1780s for new prisons. Although some asylums were in part privately financed, the largest involved an outlay similar to that of the larger prisons.

[11] Bedfordshire RO, A.D. 4007; Staffordshire RO, Q/AIc box 1 and table 11; Greater London RO, MA/A/J 1, p. 232; West Yorkshire RO, minutes of the committee for build-ing a lunatic asylum, Wakefield, 1814–18; Gloucestershire RO, HO 22/1/1, pp. 24, 29, 86–87.

12

Conclusion

1830 is a watershed in English county building. Shire bridge works fell permanently from the 1830s, English and Welsh annual expenditure being about £85,000 in 1825–34, and about £57,000 in both the next two decades. The new Over and Marlow bridges marked the end of a building age. Prison work declined in the 1830s after the 1823 Prison Act had been generally implemented, causing a lull before over 140 prisons were built or changed from 1842 to 1877 (when county-run prisons ended), partly to provide separate confinement. While at least two county halls were erected in the 1830s, the main age of shire hall building had ended. There was even a relative pause in pauper asylum construction. Although the fall in new shire halls and asylums is partly explained by building in the 1810s and 1820s, which to some extent satisfied existing needs, county rates were arousing growing hostility by the early 1830s. This was both on account of their sharp rise and the feeling that some of the county charges were of national rather than local concern. As it was not mandatory, asylums and shire halls were not built.[1]

Construction in general during the mid and later nineteenth century, with growing cities, larger population and higher living standards, was to be much greater than between the Restoration and the 1820s, which was essentially a period of germination when the various types of building either first appeared or became common. The Victorians erected innumerable schools, churches, libraries, museums, town halls and prisons. Between 1839 and 1859 over a million pounds was spent on building, enlarging, repairing and furnishing elementary schools. The greatest outlay on a building in the nineteenth century was £2,400,000 on the Houses of Parliament between 1834 and 1860. Manchester Town Hall

[1] U.R.Q. Henriques, *Before the Welfare State: Social Administration in Early Industrial Britain* (London, 1979), p. 181; B.R. Mitchell and P. Deane, *Abstract of British Historical Statistics* (Cambridge, 1962), pp. 412–13; J. Redlich and F.W. Hirst (ed. B. Keith-Lucas), *The History of Local Government in England* (1903; reprinted London, 1970), pp. 160–62; S. and B. Webb, *English Local Government: The Parish and the County* (1924; reprinted London, 1963), pp. 595–97.

cost a million pounds in 1867–77, and at least nine other Victorian town halls or buildings cost more than £100,000. By 1860 England was covered by railway lines whose bridges, tunnels and stations involved unprecedented cost: 25,000 railway bridges were built between 1830 and 1860, more than the previous total number of bridges. While the later Georgian age was a golden era in the building of prisons, shire halls and bridges by county quarter sessions, in the Victorian period county work was dwarfed by building paid for in other ways.[2]

As this study has shown, prisons and courthouses are well-documented examples in the history of institutional building, which developed particularly from the 1770s. There is much evidence about county bridge construction, an important accompaniment of the growth of road transport, making possible a detailed survey of their growing cost, the ways they were financed and the men responsible. The sources also make clear the social, cultural administrative and economic context for these almost innumerable works. From the 1760s and 1770s the growth of population and hence of crime, the increase of farming, industry and trade, the consequent greater availability of money among the well-to-do, the desire for social control and rising humanitarianism, greater administrative efficiency, and the wish to improve appearances and material comforts, all led to more and better building.

There were major differences in the history of construction among the counties. The West Riding court worked on bridges ceaselessly with a relatively large outlay throughout the period: in contrast, Lincolnshire only began in a small way during a national boom in bridge construction about 1810. Some counties did not erect a shire hall, and only a third built pauper lunatic asylums between 1810 and 1830; others erected both in this twenty-year period. While about half did not replace a prison before the 1770s, some built four or more between 1770 and 1830. Among the causes of this varied pattern were the inheritance of past buildings, differing rates of demographic and economic change, and the degree of interest among justices.[3]

---

[2] C.G. Powell, *An Economic History of the British Building Industry, 1815–1979* (London, 1980), p. 16; C. Cunningham, *Victorian and Edwardian Town Halls* (London, 1980), pp. 255–87; E. de Mare, *The Bridges of Britain* (London, 1954), p. 185.

[3] *Parliamentary Papers (1831)*, xvi. In addition to these contrasts among English county works, the pattern differed from Wales which also had quarter sessions with similar judicial and administrative powers doing building, not discussed in this book. Sessions and assizes met in town halls and no pauper asylums were erected before 1830. Most counties built gaols between the 1780s and 1820s. They were small because of modest shire populations and also of the relatively low crime level in Wales, an isolated rural

Before 1760 English county building charges were much lower than later. A few courts spent much of their total outlay on bridges, on a regular basis, with the rare big expenditure on a prison or shire hall in some counties. In others almost no work was ever done. Many counties built one or two, frequently small, bridewells, and did a little bridge work. Remembering that total expenditure was about £20,000 in 1700 and about £60,000 in 1760, bridges probably did not take more than £3000 or £4000 a year on average between 1650 and 1760; prisons cost much less at under £500 annually before 1700 and about £800 or £900 afterwards. Soldiers' pensions took much more in the later seventeenth century and most expenditure was on handling prisoners and vagrants between 1700 and 1760, when the charges imposed by these two problem groups rose faster than building costs.

The share spent on construction rose from the mid 1760s. For some sessions it was a major item in total outlay in the 1770s, and almost all courts were spending large sums on building after about 1785. This may be illustrated in the decade 1821–30. County expenditure totalled £6,406,839. Of this bridges absorbed £689,967 on building and maintenance, or about 10.8 per cent, and prisons (including upkeep) 16.8 per cent. Shire halls cost at least another £600,000 and pauper lunatic asylums £470,000 (both with repairs). Altogether over 40 per cent of expenditure was on bridges and buildings.

Considering all public building, counties outside London paid about a quarter of the expenditure during the early nineteenth century. According to Dr Grady's figures, between 1800 and 1839 about £652,000 was spent on public buildings in the West Riding of Yorkshire, to which should be added its contribution to York gaol improvements after 1825. The court's works (including the gaol) cost about £180,000 or £200,000. In London expenditure on county prisons, shire halls and the asylum was dwarfed by the numerous great buildings unique to the capital.[4]

The total expenditure on public building in the 1820s was about a million pounds a year. County prisons, shire halls and asylums cost about

continued
region. County bridge works were extensive, reflecting numerous shire bridges and the need for river crossings in mountainous districts. In the 1820s prisons and bridges cost the twelve Welsh counties an annual average of £11,219, the lowest figure being £8036 in 1821 and the highest £13,910 in 1825. The average per county was only £935. Altogether building was on a smaller scale than in England. *Parliamentary Papers* (1831), xvi; (1839), xliv.

[4] K. Grady, *The Georgian Public Buildings of Leeds and the West Riding*, Thoresby Society Publications, 62 (Leeds, 1989), pp. 47, 67. The data in the previous paragraphs are drawn largely from Chapter 3.

£2,000,000 in the decade, or about £200,000 a year. All public building in the provinces may have cost £800,000 annually. The special buildings of London erected on relatively dear sites may have cost £2,000,000 in the decade or £200,000 a year. There were further charges to the public funds of over £1,000,000 for work on the largely residential Buckingham Palace and Windsor Castle in 1825–30.[5]

As this book has shown, justices, gentry and later clergy initiated county work and oversaw the course of construction. They were advised by leading surveyors, sometimes in the case of the most important buildings by architects of national repute. Well-established local firms were given contracts, supplemented in the Home Counties by London builders.

County building outside the biggest towns boosted employment in a wide area. Sudden demand was met by the temporary migration of carpenters, bricklayers, masons and other craftsmen and labourers from twenty or thirty miles, who were taken on by local contractors. The effect may be imagined of building the gaol and shire hall at Stafford in the later 1780s and 1790s, with a population of 3892 in 1801. Craftsmen from the Black Country and the Potteries had to supplement those from neighbouring rural parishes and Lichfield. Most public building was done in years when house construction was at a high level, so that it largely failed to help in years of poor employment for building workers.

It is also possible to estimate approximately the county proportion of expenditure on all bridges between 1800 and 1830. Shire charges totalled £2,238,434. According to Dr Ginarlis, aggregate bridge construction cost £5,122,105, so that counties paid for between one-third and a half. Much of the rest was spent on four London company bridges. Unlike shire prisons and halls, county bridges gave useful work when other building was at a low ebb, as in the early 1780s and later 1790s.[6]

County construction reached a peak by the 1820s. Sessions works were among the most important public structures, symbolising contemporary social and economic changes. Although the judicial and administrative authority of sessions continued to grow until the 1870s, Victorian non-residential building was mostly financed by other institutions and private sources.

[5] J.M. Crook and M.H. Port, *The History of the King's Works*, vi, *1782–1851* (1973), pp. 664–65.

[6] J.E. Ginarlis, 'Road and Waterway Investment in Britain, 1750–1850' (unpublished Sheffield University Ph.D. thesis, 1970), p. 279.

A Note on Sources

County quarter sessions order or minute books before 1830 used in this study begin at the following dates:

Devon 1592
Yorkshire, North Riding c. 1603
Somerset 1607
Hampshire 1607
Nottinghamshire c. 1607
Hertfordshire 1619
Durham 1620
Staffordshire 1620
Kent (West) 1625
Warwickshire 1625
Wiltshire 1627
Dorset 1663 (earlier 1625–39)
Lancashire 1631
Yorkshire, West Riding 1638
Middlesex 1639
Suffolk 1640 (gap 1652–58)
Sussex 1640
Norfolk 1650
Essex 1652
Kent (East) 1653
Surrey 1659
Cambridgeshire 1660
Cheshire 1660
Herefordshire 1665
Lincolnshire (Lindsey) 1665
Westmorland 1669
Gloucestershire 1672 (gap 1692–1701)
Lincolnshire (Kesteven) 1674 (gap 1704–24)
Buckinghamshire 1678
Leicestershire 1678
Northamptonshire 1679
Northumberland 1680
Derbyshire 1682
Lincolnshire (Holland) 1684

Shropshire 1686
Oxfordshire 1688
Worcestershire 1693
Cumberland 1696
Berkshire 1705
Yorkshire, East Riding 1708 (earlier 1647–51)
Bedfordshire 1711
Cornwall 1737
Rutland 1743
Monmouthshire 1787

These records typically include names of justices, surveyors, contractors and craftsmen, and lenders (if money was borrowed); rates, estimates, contract prices and payments for work are often stated; the building task is seldom described in detail. In general references become more extensive by the early nineteenth century. Throughout the period court orders are not always noted; rates apart from bridge levies are usually not recorded in the seventeenth century, and several counties do not note bridge projects after 1800. Special order books survive for a few important undertakings, such as the erection of the Kent gaol at Maidstone, 1805–23, and of the West Riding lunatic asylum at Wakefield, 1814–18.

Treasurers' accounts from the late seventeenth and early eighteenth centures exist for several counties in an often incomplete form. There are main series of annual accounts beginning between the 1730s and the 1760s for a quarter of English shires; more county series are available from the 1780s and particularly 1792, from which date figures are printed in *Parliamentary Papers* (1825), vi; (1833), xxxii, etc. Detailed bills and accounts exist occasionally for individual projects, particularly in the Lancashire quarter sessions papers. Contracts with specifications and sometimes drawings, mostly after 1780, survive for many bridges in Devon and Leicestershire; a few exist in about half the quarter sessions archives. Correspondence of the justices and county officials about construction is rare. Contemporary local newspapers are also an invaluable source, including advertisements for building tenders and references to the attitudes of the justices.

Appendix 1

County Expenditure, 1748–1831

A. Income and Expenditure of All Counties, 1792–1831*

Year	Total Income	Total Outlay	Bridges	Gaols	Prisoners' Maintenance	Prosecutions	Constables and Vagrants
	£	£	£	£	£	£	£
1792	206,088	214,032	31,318	69,754	33,749	7287	15,705
1793	196,759	204,170	36,351	57,358	33,230	6618	11,171
1794	184,758	199,849	28,671	48,294	31,611	5040	10,854
1795	201,122	213,245	40,348	35,285	31,213	6551	12,707
1796	211,672	224,678	47,482	27,260	39,481	6596	10,710
1797	227,232	260,471	43,264	27,571	32,715	8569	10,044
1798	252,196	229,713	38,170	25,346	38,000	9543	11,003
1799	271,810	253,283	40,984	24,721	42,080	11,088	10,905
1800	277,873	271,100	44,008	30,538	62,278	18,258	16,202
1801	306,575	332,450	50,086	34,985	72,120	22,156	19,875
1802	297,604	283,043	45,201	32,241	59,130	14,743	17,990
1803	266,534	258,852	40,230	31,084	51,879	15,507	14,322
1804	279,748	264,041	40,969	36,163	53,019	14,644	12,982
1805	308,357	312,128	54,865	45,148	51,660	15,073	13,341
1806	318,273	315,885	46,000	64,912	52,743	16,718	13,751
1807	347,267	324,905	49,620	58,480	50,699	15,921	13,812
1808	332,921	347,927	57,403	62,276	55,877	16,941	14,448
1809	374,517	394,787	72,712	66,503	62,498	19,923	14,188
1810	414,398	416,547	84,708	79,613	67,456	20,653	13,363
1811	475,075	455,007	90,923	97,037	67,727	19,192	13,989
1812	477,431	474,036	103,069	96,229	86,321	25,843	17,688
1813	523,004	521,523	112,139	84,035	93,295	30,555	21,341
1814	538,165	497,725	121,466	72,835	100,844	27,852	22,089
1815	514,414	542,059	139,147	86,147	109,892	36,332	28,897
1816	503,510	532,678	107,331	98,114	111,798	42,193	31,187
1817	544,232	564,968	90,066	96,911	140,896	50,854	47,426
1818	616,438	629,606	84,598	126,556	148,899	71,246	51,129
1819	628,185	634,592	79,209	137,710	145,683	84,516	56,298
1820	671,501	649,213	78,721	135,198	143,719	90,217	60,062
1821	644,049	625,939	52,987	114,800	157,494	100,535	57,570
1822	585,075	565,804	59,648	116,415	151,759	79,460	26,586
1823	548,541	551,606	54,208	105,109	150,327	77,458	18,213
1824	534,015	569,469	66,418	95,433	189,758	86,893	15,781

*On account of nil returns by some counties, figures until 1823 are estimates.

1825	633,614	626,193	87,981	101,768	201,841	85,964	17,069
1826	697,535	706,872	84,033	138,088	204,374	102,067	21,185
1827	690,576	722,259	78,138	126,066	207,100	129,049	27,035
1828	679,412	678,498	75,601	106,420	193,495	116,269	26,577
1829	650,477	672,765	65,346	92,785	207,192	128,079	29,832
1830	669,842	687,434	65,607	82,066	221,549	129,083	32,047
1831	712,944	732,325	73,809	82,118	227,590	142,836	41,151

Estimated deficiencies: 1792 44 per cent; 1793–95 45 per cent; 1796 43 per cent; 1797 38 per cent; 1798 33 per cent; 1799–1800 31 per cent; 1801–2 27 per cent; 1803 31 per cent; 1804 2 per cent; 1805–11 25 per cent; 1812–15 20 per cent; 1816–20 12 per cent.
Source: *Parliamentary Papers* (1839), xliv.

B. Expenditure of the West Riding of Yorkshire, 1748–95

Year	Total Outlay	Bridges	Gaols & Prisoners' Maintenance	Prosecutions	Constables and Vagrants
	£	£	£	£	£
1748	1784	420	200	7	714
1749	2672	898	161	92	1057
1750	2881	491	259	40	1056
1751	1990	506	181	60	517
1752	1850	582	237	58	416
1753	2528	965	247	74	547
1754	2653	942	206	249	582
1755	2130	488	265	193	529
1756	2380	565	289	169	755
1757	2079	640	251	101	695
1758	2734	1007	220	172	937
1759	2307	636	282	157	893
1760	4463	2093	256	143	743
1761	5871	1152	224	74	874
1762	3345	561	194	49	737
1763	3591	1041	246	42	882
1764	3231	895	200	70	1727
1765	2960	1544	185	145	740
1766	4598	2699	333	326	643
1767	4644	2580	681	241	761
1768	4458	1703	1552	199	571
1769	6234	3454	1257	355	637
1770	5199	3435	462	291	578
1771	5372	3557	441	240	576
1772	4971	3085	381	275	693
1773	6832	3990	1326	357	655
1774	7947	4486	1385	402	839
1775	7273	4543	417	500	868
1776	7969	4882	577	717	870
1777	8291	4094	1910	424	820
1778	7864	4941	777	571	671
1779	13,707	7857	446	663	1039
1780	7734	3359	473	330	1130
1781	2438	804	481	143	495
1782	6459	2911	782	382	965
1783	5789	1676	923	539	1168
1784	7714	2897	670	935	1781
1785	8257	4296	740	853	1190
1786	7015	3284	951	889	944
1787	7494	2468	1531	1360	735
1788	8603	1952	2682	1530	754
1789	9725	2086	3168	1068	881
1790	9913	2396	2187	1634	873
1791	8822	2187	1650	1233	939
1792	7421	2279	1600	837	841
1793	8062	2420	1857	862	656
1794	9804	2341	2362	1284	793
1795	10,544	1581	1812	1918	1133

Source: Parliamentary Papers (1839), xliv.

Appendix 2

County Expenditure on Bridge Building and Repair, 1729–1830

(From treasurers' accounts beginning before 1780)

Year	Gloucestershire	Hampshire	East Riding	Durham	Middlesex	Dorset	Shropshire	Essex
	£	£	£	£	£	£	£	£
1727	78							
1728	114							
1729	63	101						
1730	63	70						
1731	63	129	205					
1732	63	4	186					
1733	56	48	216					
1734	69	3	0	120				
1735	51	14	21	43				
1736	51	45	15	71				
1737	51	65	16	120				
1738	51	4	56	219				
1739	74	53	0	182				
1740	51	56	94	239	202			
1741	53	11	29	82	746	7	170	
1742	43	16	22	122	890	224	77	
1743	806	6	327	110	1800	104	11	
1744	77	8	0	107	895	31	7	74
1745	114	16	67	132	483	61	80	80
1746	99	14	51	138	23	0	44	195
1747	39	20	71	84	13	116	0	163
1748	55	91	29	107	9	46	100	371
1749	56	370	56	131	9	44	16	163
1750	50	323	14	178	22	92	15	324
1751	108	144	11	82	419	8	102	213
1752	39	23	14	61	18	41	92	267
1753	39	64	18	1005	0	(188)	42	565
1754	39	28	70	619	9	7	147	213
1755	43	287	24	193	9	85	143	145
1756	48	734	16	321	18	168	33	125
1757	49	189	8	81	0	32	22	261
1758	40	534	32	187	16	20	54	147
1759	48	405	37	125	372	84	45	829
1760	39	283	189	120	30	39	8	566
1761	73	63	107		9	22	1	178
1762	14	54	123		9	105	56	521
1763	14	56	51		0	99	46	1139
1764	14	167	72		23	10	63	1539
1765	106	85	158		9	186	43	1033

Year	West Riding £	Wiltshire £	Somerset £	Leices- tershire £	North Riding £	Stafford- shire £	Average Expenditure (Constant prices of 1750s in brackets) £
1727							78
1728							114
1729							82
1730							67
1731							132
1732							84
1733							107
1734							48
1735							32
1736							46
1737							63
1738							83
1739							77
1740							128
1741							157
1742							199
1743							452
1744							150
1745							129
1746							81
1747							72
1748	420						136
1749	898						193
1750	491						168
1751	506						177
1752	582						126
1753	965						321
1754	942	40					211
1755	488	25					134
1756	565	78					211
1757	640	24					134
1758	1007	63					211
1759	636	54	60				244
1760	2093	40	34	0			287
1761	1152	71	73	1			189 (150)
1762	561	46	123	12			148 (150)
1763	1041	51	251	5			250 (236)
1764	895	251	115	4			268 (253)
1765	1544	39	169	0			311 (293)

Year	Glouces-tershire	Hamp-shire	East Riding	Durham	Middle-sex	Dorset	Shrop-shire	Essex
	£	£	£	£	£	£	£	£
1766	62	24	99		25	100	166	699
1767	149	9	84		1018	21	74	450
1768	174	326	84		512	9	650	255
1769	48	338	59		574	37	852	786
1770	45	17	275		2022	373	567	478
1771	14	217	556		560	96	1062	1197
1772	141	237	270		20	115	1641	796
1773	80	226	162		301	59	636	780
1774		270	96		96	24	1402	611
1775		316	199		261	701	725	598
1776		214	73		27	1292	949	577
1777		78	24		6	808	779	103
1778		6	105	c. 718	0	709	1148	1049
1779		47	52	899	37	56	1783	181
1780		175	16	343	448	37	1367	237
1781		413	223	c. 494	1239	264	503	624
1782		1076	77	c. 430	1406	275	1017	230
1783		1715	112	614	2187	699	19	189
1784		1945	169		865	382	60	538
1785	51	823	146		873	340	172	2404
1786	212	635	222		11	126	20	1873
1787	154	79	187		211	60	4	1079
1788	48	159	237	1125	11	191	10	635
1789	53	62	172	c. 825	11	58	293	408
1790	57	181	163	702	11	54	1822	727
1791	66	544	68	935	11	105	2504	21
1792	165	1419	80	407	11	357	1255	271
1793	16	957	118	1818	73	1078	1787	396
1794	16	135	79	2558	11	1590	982	100
1795	147	314	72	c. 1187	11	999	1901	384
1796	159	231	73	694	765	162	3312	1052
1797	107	718	128	668	831	181	4617	542
1798	51	25	182	1477	340	41	1691	324
1799	102	1214	134	2938	160	46	70	16
1800	57	696	211	1314	74	112	1842	166

Year	West Riding	Wiltshire	Somer-set	Leices-tershire	North Riding	Stafford-shire	Average Expenditure (Constant prices in brackets)
	£	£	£	£	£	£	£
1766	2699	73	133	12	1472		464 (438)
1767	2580	41	72	0	1839		528 (498)
1768	1703	76	213	0	1380		449 (424)
1769	3454	182	257	0	860		621 (586)
1770	3435	15	77	0	704		557 (629)
1771	3557	65	235	0	995		705 (629)
1772	3085	55	109	0	2247		731 (653)
1773	3990	25	53	0	4712		919 (821)
1774	4486	205	175	4	1123		772 (690)
1775	4543	283	111	0	861		782 (699)
1776	4882	34	43	6	2287		944 (843)
1777	4094	208	36	2	1296	336	648 (579)
1778	4941	22	101	48	640	236	747 (666)
1779	7857	58	75	165	1018	207	957 (854)
1780	3359	15	411	18	1326	331	622 (556)
1781	804	53	122	0	1902	592	557 (471)
1782	2911	22	148	1	1697	524	755 (639)
1783	1676	21	24	96	705	371	649 (550)
1784	2897	97	251	0	1020	373	716 (607)
1785	4296	6	118	81	1412	712	880 (746)
1786	3284	207	139	115	1554	631	694 (588)
1787	2468	113	224	421	1585	585	552 (468)
1788	1952	19	186	230	1212	881	493 (418)
1789	2086	60	269	20	2162	243	480 (407)
1790	2396	122	301	225	3015	761	753 (638)
1791	2189	52	556	155	2641	664	751 (544)
1792	2279	19	596	260	1275	298	621 (480)
1793	2420	22	343	138	2276	1257	907 (651)
1794	2341	428	1314	0	3339	1126	1001 (725)
1795	1581	33	580	1657	2728	2044	974 (706)
1796	0	80	605	767	3283	2509	1053 (634)
1797	6758	19	544	30	3380	2994	1537 (924)
1798	5510	63	443	51	2831	2420	1104 (665)
1799	6351	34	162	10	3144	2929	1236 (745)
1800	6320	52	406	18	4013	4885	1440 (867)

Year	Glouces-tershire	Hamp-shire	East Riding	Durham	Middle-sex	Dorset	Shropshire	Essex
	£	£	£	£	£	£	£	£
1801	63	654	363	0	0	179	1363	76
1802	116	65	245	588	52	553	513	108
1803	470	511	527	1028	59	316	1423	83
1804	16	51	204	3790	0	315	441	525
1805	43	146	286	6098	349	318	60	1379
1806	160	284	615	1598	3050	95	838	58
1807	41	44	518	1535	448	461	736	0
1808	231	154	205	1898	1032	348	1158	105
1809	56	935	133	3486	160	223	2083	216
1810	191	371	234	2190	2134	3006	2715	0
1811	348	3179	294	1564	270	5488	3206	30
1812	73	654	286	1083	203	4719	3555	274
1813	205	1080	2554	2580	1221	7664	2801	94
1814	133	468	2782	5082	1349	3895	1797	55
1815	4273	438	3108	2740	213	3113	2016	112
1816	5446	1314	1800	839	85	1538	346	913
1817	1083	1328	1465	1593	25	230	576	249
1818	255	1332	1435	765	6	720	1943	455
1819	1303	1721	2870	1028	384	1095	1479	740
1820	452	2002	1982	2015	550	1856	1226	1181
1821	214	1253	102	1954	2014	1640	1280	621
1822	43	1381	172	2812	2522	1476	1113	957
1823	181	1086	233*	1385	1950	1340	2879	800
1824	214	1491	362	2607	4266	2784	650	960
1825	205	1165	594	6652	7725	1543	1912	2664
1826	1740	453	261	1793	5886	2869	2310	2436
1827	13,603	204	304	1184	1956	4000	2487	986
1828	17,175	741	174	1941	1010	1731	1514	1336
1829	10,833	772	304	1088	2208	1516	2590	1572
1830	3121	775	285	912	2513	1134	1179	918

*or 274

Year	West Riding	Wiltshire	Somer-set	Leices-tershire	North Riding	Stafford-shire	Average Expenditure (Constant prices in brackets)
	£	£	£	£	£	£	£
1801	8317	34	318	957	4371	4298	1613 (720)
1802	6853	133	292	159	3586	4309	1255 (560)
1803	5335	540	171	12	1595	3018	1078 (481)
1804	5571	207	301	64	1779	4214	1248 (557)
1805	8472	72	755	35	3087	5087	1871 (835)
1806	8374	141	1296	251	3249	5010	1787 (687)
1807	6824	57	739	48	3077	4680	1372 (528)
1808	5762	121	1025	37	3060	7495	1617 (622)
1809	6398	3301	382	391	4381	7071	2087 (803)
1810	8084	5036	718	994	5161	4305	2510 (965)
1811	9772	1394	889	970	5101	7472	2856 (1058)
1812	10,592	936	860	644	4873	8458	2672 (990)
1813	11,414	2423	990	404	4692	7575	3264 (1209)
1814	10,180	1628	962	779	4930	7904	2996 (1110)
1815	14788	1104	1104	159	5381	5516	3147 (1166)
1816	12,982	192	1540	175	8425	6589	3013 (1205)
1819	11,218	610	1327	499	6441	6313	2354 (942)
1818	8934	489	1279	180	5179	2986	1854 (742)
1819	10,231	283	1449	295	5021	1253	2075 (830)
1820	7138	1720	1084	2135	5142	1514	2134 (854)
1821	6102	1166	1182	974	5766	1990	1876 (802)
1822	5282	864	1861	3289	2331	4145	2018 (862)
1823	6301	666	1243	798	2863	6170	1861 (795)
1824	11,067*	3068	1263	2020	2618	6223	2821 (1206)
1825	12,165	1843	1456	981	3151	5414	3398 (1452)
1826	12,619	825	1431	899	2951	6025	3036 (1368)
1827	8793	647	1017	543	2251	7970	3283 (1479)
1828	6257	1220	1750	605	2076	3939	2962 (1334)
1829	5340	999	2122	620	1551	4782	2593 (1168)
1830	6132	1034	1252	259	1401	7797	2051 (924)

*or 5801

Sources: 1. For sums from 1792 to 1830, *Parliamentary Papers*, 1825, vi; and 1833, xxxiii. For earlier figures: Hampshire RO, QT1, 2, 16; Somerset: Appendix to the Report of the Commissioners on the State of Ilchester Gaol, *Parliamentary Papers*, 1822; xi; Shropshire RO, county treasurers' accounts; Staffordshire RO, Q/FAa1/1–4; North Yorkshire RO, QS treasurers' accounts books A, B; Essex RO, Q/FAa4/1–3; *Parliamentary Papers*, 1839, xliv; Humbershire RO, CT1–2; Durham RO, Q/F1–3; Dorset RO, county treasurers' accounts. Greater London RO, MF1–2; Leicestershire RO, Q5.111/1/2; five series beginning before 1780 not used on account of inadequacies.

Appendix 3

Bridge Building and Major Repairs in Two Counties

A. *Larger Warwickshire Bridge Works, 1625–1830*
1. *Bridge Works Costing More than £100, 1625–1760*

Year	Bridge	Cost	Type of Work
		£	
1649	Barford	125	
1649	Bidford	190	repair
1649	Leamington	183	repair
1649	Fazeley	130	repair
1651–52	Deritend	363	rebuilding
1651	Halford	190	repair or rebuilding
1670	Shuttington	260	repair and widening
1680	Finford	140	repair
1693–94	Barford	140	repair
1703	Shuttington	215	repair
1710	Deritend	100	making causeways
1711–12	Barford	400	repair and widening
1713	Bidford	113	repair
1714	Edmondscote	130	repair and making walls
1716	Coleshill	115	repair
1717	Curdworth	215	repair
1720	Witherley	100	repair
1734	Polesworth	100	repair
1735–37	Oversley	120	repair
1750	Deritend	500	rebuilding
1756	Brownsover	111	repair

2. Bridge Works Costing More than £100 (in Constant Prices of 1750s), 1760–1830

Year	Bridge	Cost: Constant	Prices of 1750s	Type of Work
		£	£	
1762	Barford	120	113	repair
1765	Salford	230	217	widening and repair
1766	Stone	250	236	repair
1771	Ryton	199	177	repair
1774	Fazeley	143	128	repair and widening
1776	Polesworth	365	326	rebuilding
1778	Salford	145	129	lengthening end
1779	Witherley	168	150	repair
1780	Duke	333	300	rebuilding to widen
1783–86	Barford	1274	1080	repair
1783	Wixford	123	104	repair
1786	Ryton	701	594	rebuilding
1786	Wixford	174	147	repair
1787–88	Fielden	765	648	rebuilding
1790	Brownsover	266	225	repair
1792–93	Bidford	151	109	repair
1791–94	Barford	2471	1791	'work'
1793–96	Oversley	921	667	repair
1794–96	Fieldon	255	185	repair
1800–01	Wixford	1621	831	repair
1801	Crackley	267	119	rebuilding
1803	Edgbaston	250	112	rebuilding
1807–11	Leamington	3335	1283	building
1809–10	Safford	3510	1350	
1810–11	Bensford	573	216	
1810	Wixford	334	128	
1811–13	Saltley	363	134	rebuilding
1811–13	Hockley	871	323	rebuilding
1812–13	Aston	2006	743	rebuilding
1815–18	Saltley	2702	1001	rebuilding
1815–17	Bretford	873	374	building and repair
1816–18	Shuttington	1475	590	building and repair
1823–26	Stonebridge	2115	904	rebuilding
1826	Grendon	1200	541	
1826	Preston Bagot	455	205	
1827	Fazeley*	5864	2642	rebuilding
1827	Peats	300	135	
1830	Salford	252	114	

*Warwickshire part.

Source: S.C. Ratcliff and H.C. Johnson, *Warwickshire County Records, 1625–96* (Warwick, 1935–64); Warwickshire RO, QS 39/1–7, 40/1/7–12, 24/61–6.

B. *Larger Dorset Bridge Works, 1663–1825*
(involving expenditure over £100)

Year	Bridge	Type of Work	Cost	Cost (Constant Prices of 1750s)
			£	£
1674	Kingsmill	replacing wooden footbridge with stone cart bridge (probably done)	250 (money voted)	
1675	Canford	repairs	160	
1687	Longham	rebuilding	150	
1716	Frampton	repairs	101	
1720	Crawford	repairs	123	
1726	Blandford	rebuilding and repairs	126	
1725–28	Longham	repairs	c. 270	
1728–39	Longham	rebuilding	2000 (contract)	
1739–40	Blandford	repairs	160	
1742–43	Blandford	repairs	185	
1756	Wareham	repairs	145	
1765	Crawford	repairs	119	113
1770	Wool	repairs	330	311
1775–78	Wareham South	rebuilding	3050	2723
1775	Mohuns	repair and new building	188	168
1781	Longham	repair	172	154
1782	Great Mohuns	repair and widening	224	190
1783–84	Blandford	widening and repair	813	690
1784	Canford	work and materials	128	108
1785	Crawford	repair and gravelling	170	145
1792–93	Five Bridges	widening and repair	699	507
1792	Longham	widening and repairing	899	652
1793	Canford	widening and repairing	700	507
1794–95	Yeovil	rebuilding	1236	896
1800–1	Barnaby	repairs	209	107
1802	Canford	work	255	114
1804	Crickmore	rebuilding and repair	247	110
1809–10	Durnston	rebuilding and repair	c. 380	c. 146
1809–13	Canford	rebuilding and repair	6477	2444
1809–13	Blandford	rebuilding and repairs	4310	at least 1626
1810–15	expenditure on unnamed bridges by Dyson		8685	3217

Year	Bridge	Type of Work	Cost	Cost (Constant Prices of 1750s)
1812–13	Long	repair	at least 400	148
1814	Longham	rebuilding and repair	2300	852
1817–18	Haywards	repair	1140	456
1819	King's Mill	repair	529	212
1819	Crawford	repairs	514	206
1820–21	Sturminster	repairs	315	130
1821–22	Hayward	building	1494	638
1821–22	Hayward	repairs	1825	780
1823	Beckhampston	rebuilding	300	128
1823–24	King's Mill	building and repairs	1089	465
1823–24	Charmouth	building and repairs	816	349
1824	Hayward	building and arches work	[not known]	

Sources: Dorset RO, QS orders, 1663–74, 1686–1744; minutes, 1669–87; county treasurers' accounts, 1739–1825; and bridge contracts. The precise work is often unspecified, and 'repairs' sometimes included substantial rebuilding in the same form.

Index